(Continued)

Young Children Reinvent Arithmetic

IMPLICATIONS OF PIAGET'S THEORY

— **Second Edition** —

Constance Kamii

with *Leslie Baker Housman*

Teachers College, Columbia University
New York and London

All tables in Chapter 3 originally appeared in Perret-Clermont, A.-N. (1980). *Social Interaction and Cognitive Development in Children*. New York: Academic Press. Reprinted by permission of Academic Press Ltd.

The cards in Figure 11.15 are copyright © 1993, 1999 Suntex International Inc. Reprinted by permission.

Published by Teachers College Press, 1234 Amsterdam Avenue, New York, NY 10027

Library of Congress Cataloging-in-Publication Data

Kamii, Constance.
    Young children reinvent arithmetic : implications of Piaget's
theory. — 2nd ed. / Constance Kamii with Leslie Baker Housman.
      p.   cm. — (Early childhood education series)
    Includes bibliographical references and index.
    ISBN 0-8077-3904-9 (pbk. : alk. paper)
    1. Arithmetic—Study and teaching (Elementary) 2. Number concept—
Study and teaching (Elementary)   I. Housman, Leslie Baker, 1969–
II. Title.   III. Series: Early childhood education series
(Teachers College Press)
QA135.5.K186   2000
372.7'2044—dc21   99-40866

ISBN 0-8077-3904-9 (paper)

Printed on acid-free paper
Manufactured in the United States of America

07 06 05   8 7 6 5 4

Contents

Part IV.   Results

Acknowledgments

This book could not have been written without Charlotte Brown, Principal of South Shades Crest Elementary School in Hoover, Alabama. She is one of those rare principals who has studied Piaget's constructivism and who supports with conviction the kind of teaching we advocate.

We also want to express appreciation to the nine teachers with whom we work closely at South Shades Crest Elementary School—Teresa Ballard and Lauri George in kindergarten; Lori St. Clair, who is the other first-grade teacher; Janet Edwards and Meredith Livings in second grade; Kristen Green and Angela Coppins in third grade; and Ann Dominick and Sherry Parrish in fourth grade. Their help and support have been invaluable in carrying out the research reported in this book.

Several people have reacted to earlier drafts, and we are especially grateful to Faye B. Clark, who read the entire manuscript and made many thoughtful suggestions. We are also indebted to the teachers who read the chapters on games and offered valuable comments. Among them are Catherine Essary, Amy Kari, and Judy Rummelsburg, of Rio Vista Elementary School in Bay Point, California; and Lynn Kirkland, who recently joined the faculty of Early Childhood Education at the University of Alabama at Birmingham.

Introduction

The first edition of *Young Children Reinvent Arithmetic* (Kamii, 1985) needed revision for many reasons. First, children in kindergarten and first grade are capable of much more than I thought in the early 1980s. The research of Olivier, Murray, and Human (1991) in South Africa and Carpenter, Fennema, and others at the University of Wisconsin–Madison (Carpenter, Ansell, Franke, Fennema, & Weisbeck, 1993) in particular demonstrated that young children are capable of solving word problems traditionally considered to be multiplication and division problems. The teachers I now work with near Birmingham, Alabama, give these kinds of problems, and kindergartners and first graders use repeated addition to solve "multiplication" and "division" problems.

Second, I recommended only two kinds of activities to stimulate numerical thinking in the first edition—the use of everyday situations and games. It later became obvious that a third kind of activity had to be added, solving word problems.

After studying first-grade arithmetic, I went on to second grade (Kamii, 1989a) and third grade (Kamii, 1994). Some of the ideas I used to have about first grade changed while I focused on second-grade arithmetic, and what I did not notice about second-grade arithmetic became evident when I went on to third grade. For example, I said in the first edition of *Young Children Reinvent Arithmetic* (Kamii, 1985) that "the base-10 system (or any other base system) involves multiplication" (p. 58), and that multiplication is a third-grade topic. This was a statement based on adult common sense that needs to be modified. Second graders can understand place value using additive thinking, and they can do double-column addition with additive thinking. For example, most do 25 + 38 by adding 2 *tens* (10 + 10) and 3 *tens* (10 + 10 + 10) and then adding 5 + 8 to 5 *tens*. They may say "2 *tens*," which *appears* to be multiplicative thinking, but additive thinking is perfectly adequate to add 2 tens and 3 tens.

The importance of knowing all the combinations that make 10 (9 + 1, 8 + 2, 7 + 3, and so on) became evident when I went to second grade. The children who knew these combinations very well tended to go easily from single-digit addition to *tens*. For example, when presented with 9 + 6, they changed the problem to 10 + 5. This is why we include in Chapter 11 of the present volume many games requiring children to find two cards that make a total of 10.

When I wrote the book about second-grade arithmetic, I had no idea that the teaching of conventional algorithms, such as those of "carrying" and "borrowing" as recommended by most textbook series, is harmful to children's development of numerical reasoning. I simply thought that children taught by constructivist teachers did better at the end of second grade than those receiving traditional textbook instruction, and that place value was difficult for the latter group. By the time I wrote about third-grade arithmetic (Kamii, 1994, chap. 3), however, I was convinced that those rules of "carrying" and "borrowing" actually "untaught" place value. As I pointed out in 1994 with extensive evidence, these rules make blindly obedient machines out of children and make them lose their intuition about what makes sense.

For example, the reader will see in Chapters 5 and 14 of the present volume that many first graders who are taught to align columns and to add each column begin to produce answers such as 11 for 22 + 7 written vertically. (They do 2 + 2 + 7 = 11). When I wrote the first edition of *Young Children Reinvent Arithmetic*, I was totally unaware of this kind of problem being created in the name of education.

Empiricism dies hard even after studying Piaget's theory under him for more than a dozen years, and my goal for single-digit addition in the first edition was that "children engage in the mental action of operating on numbers and *remember the results of these actions*" (p. 65, emphasis added). This was still an atomistic, empiricist view suggesting that the goal for children is to remember many sums, each one separately. I corrected this goal in Chapter 5 of the present edition, and it is now to encourage children to construct a *network of numerical relationships* (illustrated in Figure 5.2).

Another remnant of my empiricist upbringing is the mistake I made in the first edition (pp. 143 and 155) of recommending TILE dice and TILE cards. (TILES are similar to base-10 blocks but are two-dimensional and used in Japan. The TILE standing for *one* is a square, and the TILE standing for *ten* is a long rectangle with 10 square segments.) I knew that children do not construct units of more than one by empirical abstraction from objects or pictures, but it took many years for me to overcome my blind spots.

Some first graders develop more slowly than others and are not yet at the point of enjoying addition games. Teachers of these children as well as kindergarten teachers have asked what they can do for those students. Their concern is addressed in this edition, especially in Chapter 10, describing games that do not involve addition or subtraction.

The first edition of this book was written with Georgia DeClark in the early 1980s when we thought that she was the only first-grade teacher in the country not using the textbook and workbook and helping children to invent arithmetic. Times have changed since then, and this revised edition was written with Leslie

Baker Housman, who read *Young Children Reinvent Arithmetic* as a textbook in an undergraduate course.

This example of the use of a recent publication as a textbook makes progress seem quick and natural, but educational institutions live by tradition rather than by scientific truths. As Kuhn (1970) pointed out, even many scientists react to new theories with lifelong resistance, and Taylor (1949) stated that it took 150 years for the heliocentric theory to become universally accepted.

"Math wars" are currently raging in California and elsewhere, and, for a similar but less public disagreement over teaching methods, I had to leave the school where the research reported in 1989 and 1994 was conducted. However, I had the good fortune to find a "school within a public school" at South Shades Crest Elementary School in Hoover, Alabama, a suburb of Birmingham. There are two classes each of kindergarten and grades 1–4 in this school within a school, and I plan to continue my research with fourth graders who have never been taught the conventional rules of "carrying," "borrowing," and cross multiplying. This planned research in the upper grades should indicate to the reader that the results reported in the present volume about first graders can be extrapolated to the fourth and fifth grades. I expect the research to show that there are better ways of "teaching" fractions, decimals, percents, ratios, and proportions than the method recommended by textbooks.

The term *arithmetic* used in the title of this book requires explanation. To many educators, arithmetic has become a pejorative term implying memorization of rules and "number facts" as opposed "mathematics," which involves reasoning. For Piaget, however, mathematics had two major branches—geometry (spatial reasoning) and algebra (numerical reasoning, which begins in arithmetic). In other words, I am using the term *arithmetic* in opposition to "geometry" and not in opposition to "mathematics." Children invent geometry, too (Piaget, Inhelder, & Szeminska, 1948/1960), and I wanted to indicate that this book is not about geometry.

The book is divided into four parts. The first part (Chapters 1–3) deals with Piaget's scientific theory explaining how children acquire number concepts, the nature of representation, and the importance of social interaction. Because his theory is very different from traditional views, it is explained in some detail with evidence from research.

The second part deals with goals and objectives beginning with the overall goal of autonomy (Chapter 4) and objectives for first-grade arithmetic such as addition, subtraction, multiplication, and division (Chapters 5–7). In textbook instruction, goals and objectives are set without any justification or accountability. We believe that educators should be required to justify their goals on the basis of scientific research and theory rather than mere "philosophies," or opinions. We therefore present the evidence on which we base our aims and objectives.

Part III consists of activities and principles of teaching. Chapters 8–11 discuss activities such as the use of situations outside the math hour, word problems, and games. Chapter 8 was written by Leslie Baker Housman, the teacher with whom I worked to write this book. Chapters 12 and 13 present principles of teaching the teacher should keep in mind in all these activities.

The book ends with Part IV, concerning the outcome of the kind of teaching we advocate. We are confident about our approach and present empirical proof for the following statement Piaget (1948/1973) made more than 50 years ago:

> Every normal student is capable of good mathematical reasoning if attention is directed to activities of his interest, and if by this method the emotional inhibitions that too often give him a feeling of inferiority in lessons in this area are removed. (pp. 98–99)

Constance Kamii
February, 1999

Part I

THEORETICAL FOUNDATION

CHAPTER 1

How Do Children Acquire Number Concepts?

During the past 20 years, I (CK) have been asking educators in audiences all over the United States and abroad how they think children acquire number concepts, such as the *idea* (not the word) of "eight." Some of the answers have been: "By counting objects," "by seeing one nose, 2 eyes, 3 cookies, and so on," and "by making one-to-one correspondence." The most common explanation given is that children acquire number concepts through "experience." When I ask "What kind of experience?" the responses remain vague and diffuse.

Physicians base their practice on scientific explanations, and they try to determine and then eliminate the cause of an illness. In the case of cancer, physicians know that the cause of this disease has not been explained scientifically and that all they can do is to deal with symptoms. In education, by contrast, textbook writers and teachers are teaching arithmetic without a scientific explanation of exactly how children acquire number concepts. The absence of a scientific foundation is a characteristic of an art like folk medicine.

Piaget's theory provides the most convincing scientific explanation of how children acquire number concepts. It states, in essence, that logico-mathematical knowledge, including number and arithmetic, is *constructed (created) by each child from within*, in interaction with the environment. In other words, logico-mathematical knowledge is not acquired directly from the environment by *internalization*. Before explaining Piaget's theory, it is necessary to review the epistemological background behind his research.

EMPIRICISM, RATIONALISM, AND PIAGET'S CONSTRUCTIVISM

Piaget is often believed to have been a psychologist, but he was actually an epistemologist. Epistemology is the study of the nature and origins of knowledge, expressed in such questions as "How do we know what we think we know?" and "How do we know that what we think we know is true?" Historically, two main currents have developed in response to these questions—the empiricist and the rationalist currents.

Empiricists (such as Locke, Berkeley, and Hume) argued in essence that knowledge has its source outside the individual and that it is *internalized* through the senses. They further argued that the individual at birth is like a clean slate on which experiences are "written" as he or she grows up. As Locke stated in 1690, "The senses at first let in particular ideas, and furnish the yet empty cabinet, and the mind by degrees growing familiar with some of them, they are lodged in the memory" (1947, p. 22).

Rationalists (such as Descartes, Spinoza, and Kant) did not deny the importance of sensory experience, but they insisted that reason is more powerful than sensory experience because it enables us to know with certainty many truths that sensory observation can never ascertain. For example, we know that every event has a cause, in spite of the fact that we obviously cannot examine every event in the entire past and future of the universe. Rationalists also pointed out that since our senses often deceive us (e.g., perceptual illusions), sensory experience cannot be trusted to give us truth with certitude. The rigor, precision, and certainty of mathematics, a purely deductive discipline, remains the rationalists' prime example in support of the power of reason. When they had to explain the origin of this power, many rationalists ended up saying that certain kinds of knowledge or concepts are innate and that these unfold as a function of maturation.

Piaget saw elements of truth and untruth in both camps. As a scientist trained in biology, he was convinced that the only way to answer epistemological questions was to study them scientifically rather than by continuing to argue on the basis of speculation. With this conviction, he wanted to study humanity's construction of mathematics from its prehistoric beginning, because to understand human knowledge he believed that it was necessary to study its development rather than only the end product. However, the prehistoric and historical evidence was no longer available to him, and this is why he decided that a good way to study the evolution of empirical knowledge and reason was to study their development in children. His study of children was thus a means to answer epistemological questions scientifically.

While Piaget saw the importance of both sensory information and reason, his sympathy lay on the rationalist side of the fence. His 60 years of research with children was motivated to a large extent by a desire to prove the inadequacy of empiricism. The three kinds of knowledge and the nature of logico-mathematical knowledge, which are discussed next, should be understood in light of this background.

THE NATURE OF LOGICO-MATHEMATICAL KNOWLEDGE

Three Kinds of Knowledge

Piaget (1967/1971, 1945/1951) distinguished three kinds of knowledge according to their ultimate sources and modes of structuring: physical knowledge, social (conventional) knowledge, and logico-mathematical knowledge.

Physical knowledge is knowledge of objects in external reality. The color and weight of counters or any other object are examples of physical knowledge. The fact that counters do not roll away like marbles is also an example of physical knowledge. The ultimate source of physical knowledge is thus partly *in* objects, and physical knowledge can be acquired empirically through observation. (Our reason for saying "partly" will be explained shortly.)

Examples of *social knowledge* are languages such as English and Spanish, which were created by convention among people. Other examples of social knowledge are holidays such as the Fourth of July, the rule of extending our right hand to shake hands, and rules about when to say "Good morning." The ultimate source of social knowledge is thus partly in conventions made by people. (Our reason for saying "partly" will also be clarified shortly.)

Logico-mathematical knowledge consists of mental relationships, and the ultimate source of these relationships is in each individual. For instance, when we are presented with a red counter and a blue one, we can think about them as being *different* or *similar*. It is just as true to say that the counters are different (because one is red and one is blue) as it is to say that they are similar (because they are both round and made of plastic). The similarity and difference exist neither *in* the red counter nor *in* the blue one, and if a person did not put the objects into a relationship, these relationships would not exist for him or her.

Other examples of relationships the individual can create between the two counters are *the same in weight* and *two*. From the point of view of weight, the two counters are the same. If the individual wants to think about the same counters numerically, the counters become "two." The counters are observable, but the "twoness" is not. Number is a relationship created mentally by each individual.

We hasten to say that "two" is not a good number to choose to illustrate the logico-mathematical nature of number concepts because two is a *perceptual number*. Small numbers up to four or five are perceptual numbers, as will be explained shortly. However, two can also be a *logico-mathematical number* for an adult, who has constructed logico-mathematical numbers. We chose the number two because, with two counters, we could illustrate other relationships such as "similar," "different," and "the same in weight."

Children go on to construct logico-mathematical knowledge by putting previously made relationships into relationships. For example, by coordinating the relationships of "same" and "different," children become able to deduce that there are more animals in the world than dogs. Likewise, by putting four twos into relationships, they become able to deduce that $2 + 2 + 2 + 2 = 8$, that $4 \times 2 = 8$, and that if $4x = 8$, x must be 2.

Piaget thus recognized external and internal sources of knowledge. The source of physical and social knowledge is partly external to the individual. The source of logico-mathematical knowledge, by contrast, is internal. This statement will be clarified shortly when we discuss the two kinds of abstraction distinguished by Piaget. Let us first review the conservation-of-number task, which will clarify the differences among the three kinds of knowledge.

The Conservation-of-Number Task

Conservation of number refers to our ability to deduce, through logical reasoning, that the quantity of a collection remains the same when its spatial arrangement and empirical appearance are changed. The procedure described below (Inhelder, Sinclair, & Bovet, 1974) may appear rather standardized. However, each interview must be adapted to the particular child, especially with regard to the latter's understanding of the terms used in quantification.

Materials: About 40 counters, 20 red ones and 20 blue ones

Procedure

A.   Equality
The interviewer makes a row of 8 blue counters and asks the child to put out the same amount of red ones ("as many as," "the same much," etc.).
The interviewer records the child's response. If necessary, the red and blue counters are put in one-to-one correspondence, and the child is asked whether the two rows have the same amount.
Note: At least 7 counters must be used because small numbers up to 4 or 5 are *perceptual numbers*. Small collections such as "oo" and "ooo" are called perceptual numbers because they can be distinguished at a glance. When 7 objects are presented, however, it is impossible to distinguish "ooooooo" from "ooooooo" with certainty by merely looking at them. Small numbers greater than 4 or 5 are called "elementary numbers."

B.   Conservation
The interviewer says, "Watch carefully what I'm going to do" and modifies the spatial arrangement in front of the child's watchful eyes by spacing out the counters in one row and/or pushing them close together in the other row (see Figure 1.1). The following questions are then asked: "Are there as many blue ones as red ones [running his or her finger along each row], or are there more here [indicating one row] or more here [indicating the other row]?" and "How do you know?"

C.   Countersuggestion
If the child has given a correct conservation answer with a logical explanation, the interviewer says, "But another boy [or girl] said there

Figure 1.1. The arrangement of the counters when the question is asked about conservation.

O   O   O   O   O   O   O   O

OOOOOOOO

are more in this row [indicating the longer row] because this row is longer. What do you think? Are you right, or is the other child right?"

If, on the other hand, the child gave an answer of nonconservation, the interviewer reminds him or her of the initial equality: "But remember how you put a red counter in front of each blue one before? Another child said there are just as many red ones as blue ones now because all I did was move them. Who do you think is right, you or the other child?"

The Three Levels Found

Level 1. At Level 1, the child cannot make a set that has the same number. Some children put out all the red counters as shown in Figure 1.2a. They stop putting counters out only because there are no more left. Figure 1.2b shows a more advanced response within Level 1. The children who do this do not put out the same number of red counters as blue ones but carefully use the spatial frontiers of the rows as the criterion for deciding the "sameness" of the two quantities. (When children have not yet built the logic of number, they use the best criterion they can think of to judge the quantitative "sameness." In this case, the criterion is the spatial frontiers, which they can *see*.)

Level 2. At Level 2 children can make a set that has the same number by using one-to-one correspondence, but they cannot conserve this equality. When asked the conservation question, they reply, for example, "There are more red ones because the red line is longer."

Level 3. At Level 3 children are conservers. They give correct answers to all the questions, are not swayed by countersuggestions, and give one of the following three arguments to explain why they think the two rows have the same quantity:

- "There's just as many blue ones as red ones because you didn't add anything or take anything away" (the *identity* argument).
- "We could put all the red ones back to the way they were before, and you'll see that there's the same number" (the *reversibility* argument).

Figure 1.2. Two sublevels within Level 1.

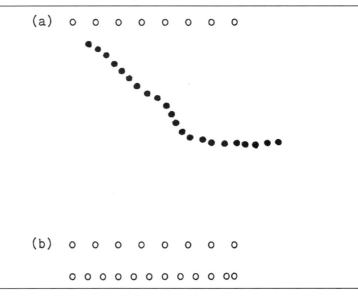

- "The red row is longer, but there's more space in between. So the number is still the same" (the *compensation* argument).

Intermediate level. Conservation is not achieved overnight, and there is an intermediate level between Levels 2 and 3. Intermediate-level children hesitate and/or keep changing their minds ("There are more blue ones . . . , no, red ones . . . , no, they're the same. . . ."). When children give the correct answer but cannot justify it, they are also categorized at the intermediate level.

The conservation task is a test of children's logico-mathematical knowledge. Counters are cultural objects (social knowledge), and knowing that counters stay on the table without melting like ice cubes is physical knowledge. However, physical knowledge is not enough to deduce that the quantity in the two rows stays the same when their empirical appearance changes. Only when children can make numerical relationships among the chips can they deduce, with the force of logical necessity, that the two rows have the same number. This statement will be clarified by the following discussion of two kinds of abstraction Piaget distinguished.

Empirical and Constructive Abstraction

In *empirical abstraction*, we focus on a certain property of the object and ignore the others. For example, when we abstract the color of an object, we simply ignore the other properties such as weight and the material with which the object is made (plastic or glass, for instance).

Constructive abstraction involves making mental relationships between and among objects, such as "the same," "similar," "different," and "two." As stated earlier, these relationships do not have an existence in external reality. The similarity or difference between one counter and another is constructed, or mentally made, by each individual by constructive abstraction.

Constructive abstraction is also known as "reflective" or "reflecting" abstraction. The French term Piaget usually used was *abstraction réfléchissante*, which has been translated as "reflective" or "reflecting" abstraction. Piaget also occasionally used the term *constructive* abstraction, which seems easier to understand.

Having made the theoretical distinction between empirical and constructive abstraction, Piaget went on to say that, in the psychological reality of the child, one cannot take place without the other. For example, we could not construct the relationship "different" if all the objects in the world were identical. Similarly, the relationship "two" would be impossible to construct if children thought that objects behave like drops of water (which can combine to become one drop).

Conversely, we could not construct physical knowledge, such as the knowledge of "red," if we did not have the category "color" (as opposed to every other property such as weight) and the category "red" (as opposed to every other color). A logico-mathematical framework (built by constructive abstraction) is thus necessary for empirical abstraction because children could not "read" facts from external reality if each fact were an isolated bit of knowledge, with no relationship to the knowledge already built and organized. This is why we said earlier that the source of physical knowledge is only *partly* in objects and that the source of social knowledge is only *partly* in conventions made by people.

While constructive abstraction cannot take place independently of empirical abstraction up to about 6 years of age, it becomes possible later. For example, once the child has constructed number (by constructive abstraction), he or she can operate on numbers and do 5 + 5 + 5 + 5 and 4 x 5 without empirical abstraction from objects.

The distinction between the two kinds of abstraction may seem unimportant while children are dealing with small numbers up to 10 or 20. When large numbers such as 999 and 1,000 are involved, however, it becomes clear that numbers cannot be learned by empirical abstraction from sets of objects. Numbers are learned by constructive abstraction as the child constructs relationships. Because these relationships are created by the mind, it is possible for us to understand numbers such as 1,000,001 even if we have never seen or counted 1,000,001 objects.

The Synthesis of Hierarchical Inclusion and Order

Piaget went on to explain that the development of number concepts results from the synthesis of two kinds of relationships: hierarchical inclusion and order. These are explained below.

Hierarchical Inclusion. If we ask 4-year-olds to count 8 objects arranged in a row, they often count them correctly and announce that there are "eight." If we then ask them to "show me eight," they often point to the eighth object, saying "That one" (see Figure 1.3a). This behavior indicates that, for this child, the words *one, two, three,* and so on, are names for individual elements in a series, like "Monday, Tuesday, Wednesday," and so forth. For this child, the word *eight* stands for the last object in the series and not for the entire group.

To quantify a collection of objects numerically, the child has to put them into a relationship of hierarchical inclusion. This relationship, shown in Figure 1.3b, means that the child mentally includes "one" in "two," "two" in "three," "three" in "four," and so on. When presented with 8 objects, the child can quantify the collection numerically only if he or she can put them mentally into this hierarchical relationship.

Figure 1.3. (a) The absence and (b) the presence of hierarchical inclusion in a child's mind.

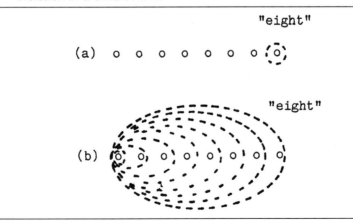

Four-year-olds' reaction to the class-inclusion task helps us understand how difficult it is for young children to make a hierarchical structure (Inhelder & Piaget, 1959/1964). In the class-inclusion task, the child is presented with 6 miniature dogs and 2 cats of the same size, for example. He or she is first asked, "What do you see?" so that the interviewer can use words from the child's vocabulary. The child is then asked to show "*all* the animals," "*all* the dogs," and "*all* the cats" using the words from his or her vocabulary (e.g., "doggy"). Only after ascertaining the child's understanding of these words does the adult ask the following question: "Are there more dogs or more animals?"

Four-year-olds typically answer "More dogs," whereupon the adult asks, "Than what?" The 4-year-old's answer is "Than cats." In other words, the question the interviewer asks is "Are there more dogs or more animals?" but what young children "hear" is "Are there more dogs or more cats?" Young children hear a question that is different from the one the adult asks because once they mentally cut the whole (animals) into two parts (dogs and cats), the only thing they can think about is the two parts. For them at that moment, the whole does not exist any more. They can think about the whole, but not when they are thinking about the parts. In order to compare the whole with a part, the child has to perform two opposite mental actions *at the same time*—cut the whole into two parts and put the parts back together into a whole. In other words, they must be able to think about the whole and the parts at the same time. This is precisely what 4-year-olds cannot do.

By 7 to 8 years of age, most children's thought becomes mobile enough to be reversible. Reversibility refers to the ability to mentally perform two opposite actions *simultaneously*—in this case, cutting the whole into two parts and reuniting the parts into a whole. In physical, material action, it is impossible to do two opposite things simultaneously. In our minds, however, this is possible when thought has become mobile enough to be reversible. Only when the parts can be reunited in the mind can a child "see" that there are more animals than dogs.

The class-inclusion task clearly illustrates the inadequacy of empiricism. All the animals remain in front of the 4-year-old's eyes throughout the task. However, 4-year-olds cannot *see* the "animals" when they cannot *think about* them. They can see the "animals," "dogs," and "cats," one group at a time, but they cannot "see" the "animals" simultaneously with the "dogs" because they cannot think about the whole and the parts at the same time.

Class inclusion is similar to the hierarchical structure of number but different. Class inclusion deals with qualities such as those that characterize dogs, cats, and animals. In number, on the other hand, all qualities are irrelevant, and a dog and a cat are both treated as "ones." Another difference between number and class inclusion is that in a class, there is usually more than one object. In number, by contrast, there is only one element at each hierarchical level.

Order.   All teachers of young children have seen the common tendency among 4-year-olds to count objects by skipping some and counting others more than once. When given 8 objects arranged as shown in Figure 1.4a, a child who can recite "One, two, three, four . . ." up to 30 may claim that there are 30. This behavior shows that the child does not feel the *logical necessity* of putting the objects in a relationship of order to make sure not to skip any or count the same object more than once. The only way we can be sure of not overlooking any or counting the same object more than once is by putting them into a relationship of order as illustrated in Figure 1.4b. The child does not have to put the objects literally in a spatial order to put them into an ordered relationship. What is important is that he or she order them *mentally*.

Why Nonconservers Do Not Conserve and Conservers Do.   The various levels found in the conservation task can now be explained by the mental structure of number that children gradually construct. This structure, as discussed above, results from the synthesis of hierarchical inclusion and order by constructive abstraction.

The Level-1 arrangement shown in Figure 1.2b indicates that the child's logic has become strong enough to make an arrangement superior to the one in Figure 1.2a. Children who use the spatial frontiers of the rows do so because they are now thinking about quantities. Because Level-1 children's logic is still weak, they use their eyes and make a quantity that *looks* the same. They thus think of the space occupied by the counters and use the frontiers of the two rows as the criterion of "same quantity."

My (CK) studies of children from middle-income families indicate that the logic of most has advanced to the point of thinking about one-to-one correspondence by about 4 years of age. However, this logic is not yet strong enough to overcome the perceptual "trap" set by destroying the visible one-to-one correspondence. Like the advanced Level-1 children who use space to judge the equality of the two rows, Level-2 children use space to make the one-to-one

Figure 1.4. (a) The arrangement of eight objects and (b) the mental relationship of order made by a child.

(a)   (b)

correspondence. When this observable correspondence is destroyed, the logic of the Level-2 child is not strong enough to overcome the perceptual trap.

Most children from middle-income families begin to conserve number between the ages of 5 and 6, thereby attaining Level 3. (Those in lower socio-economic groups attain Level 3 later.) Level-3 children say that there are as many counters in the longer row as in the shorter one and justify this answer with one of the three logical arguments given earlier. Level-3 children conserve because they have constructed the logic synthesizing hierarchical inclusion and order (Figures 1.3b and 1.4b).

Note that to "conserve" is a verb. Children conserve or do not conserve by doing their own reasoning. However, most authors of books about Piaget's theory misinterpret conservation because they do not know the difference between physical and logico-mathematical knowledge. For example, Ginsburg and Opper (1988) say, "If quantity is seen to change whenever mere physical arrangement is altered, then the child fails to appreciate certain basic constancies or invariants in the environment" (p. 141). Conservation is not an *appreciation* of an empirical fact. The constancy of quantity is a logical deduction and not an appreciation of something that exists in the environment.

Many other authors tell us that, at Level 3, children come to "understand" or "recognize" that the quantity does not change when counters are moved. Many authors also tell us that children "discover" conservation. These terms all reflect an empiricist assumption that conservation is "out there" to be "discovered," "understood," or "recognized." America was already "out there" when it was discovered. But conservation is not out there in the external world waiting to be discovered by children. The ability to conserve results from children's logic, which they construct from within.

The synthesis of hierarchical inclusion and order can be seen in another task in which one-to-one correspondence is made empirically. The difference between empirical knowledge and logico-mathematical knowledge can again be seen in this task that teachers can use.

A Task Involving the Dropping of Beads

This task, originally devised by Inhelder and Piaget (1963), uses two identical glasses and 30 to 50 counters. The child is given one of the glasses, and the interviewer takes the other glass. The interviewer then asks the child to "drop a counter into your glass each time I drop one into *my* glass." When about 5 counters have thus been dropped into each glass with one-to-one correspondence, the adult says, "Let's stop now, and you watch what I am going to do." The interviewer then drops one counter into his or her glass and says to the child, "Let's get going again." The adult and the child drop about 5 more counters into each glass with one-to-one correspondence, until the adult says, "Let's stop."

The following is what has happened so far:

Adult: $1 + 1 + 1 + 1 + 1 + 1 + 1 + 1 + 1 + 1 + 1$

Child: $1 + 1 + 1 + 1 + 1 \quad\quad + 1 + 1 + 1 + 1 + 1$

The interviewer now asks, "Do you and I have the same amount, or do *you* have more, or do *I* have more?"

Four-year-olds usually reply that the two glasses have the same amount. When asked, "How do you know that we have the same amount?" 4-year-olds explain, "Because I can see that we both have the same amount." (Some 4-year-olds reply that *they* have more, and when asked how they know that they have more, their usual answer is "Because.")

The interviewer goes on to ask, "Do you remember how we dropped the counters?" and 4-year-olds usually give all the empirical facts correctly, including the fact that only the adult put an extra counter into his or her glass at one point. In other words, 4-year-olds remember all the empirical facts correctly and base their judgment of equality on the empirical appearance of the two quantities.

By age 5 or 6, however, most middle-class children deduce logically that the adult has one more. When asked, "How do you know that I have one more?" the children invoke exactly the same empirical facts as the 4-year-olds.

One-to-one correspondence is made empirically in this task, but children who have not constructed number concepts (logico-mathematical knowledge) can get only empirical knowledge from this correspondence. When they have synthesized hierarchical inclusion and order, on the other hand, it becomes obvious to them that there is one more counter in the adult's glass.

If the child says that the adult's glass has one more counter, the interviewer goes on to ask the next question: "Suppose we continued to drop counters in the same way (with one-to-one correspondence) until supper time. Would you and I have the same number, or would you have more, or would I have more?" The 5- and 6-year-olds divide themselves into two groups at this point. The more-advanced children say, "You would always have one more, no matter how long we went on." By contrast, the less-advanced children give more concrete answers, such as "You don't have enough counters to keep going until supper time," or "I can't tell because we haven't done it yet."

These responses indicate that the 5- and 6-year-olds may have constructed small numbers, but not large ones. As Piaget (Piaget & Szeminska, 1964) pointed out, number concepts seem to be constructed progressively, up to about 7 first, then to about 15, and later to about 30.

The Universality of Logico-Mathematical Knowledge

Cross-cultural research has documented that children all over the world become able to conserve number (discontinuous quantities) as well as continuous quantities such as amounts of water and clay. The conservation of continuous quantities is discussed in some detail in Chapter 3. Studies in Aden (Hyde, 1959), Algeria (Bovet, 1974), Iran (Mohseni, 1966), Martinique (Piaget, 1966), Nigeria (Price-Williams, 1961), Montreal and Rwanda (Laurendeau-Bendavid, 1977), Scotland and Ghana (Adjei, 1977), and Thailand (Opper, 1977) are among the investigations giving unequivocal support to the statement that children all over the world become able to conserve continuous and discontinuous quantities. Children of indigenous peoples such as the Aborigines in Australia (Dasen, 1974; De Lemos, 1969) and the Atayal in Taiwan (Kohlberg, 1968) have also been found to conserve without any instruction.

The ages of attainment vary from one group to another, but the fact of this attainment remains certain. Researchers who have studied deaf children (Furth, 1966), blind children (Hatwell, 1966), and children and adolescents with severe mental retardation (Inhelder, 1943/1968) have also reported that these children attain the conservation of continuous and discontinuous quantities. Logico-mathematical knowledge is thus universal because there is nothing arbitrary in it: 2 and 2 make 4 in every country. The words "one, two, three . . ." are different from "uno, dos, tres . . . ," but the numerical ideas underlying these words are universal. There are likewise more animals than dogs in every culture. If B is larger than A, and C is larger than B, adults and older children in every part of the world can also deduce that C is larger than A.

On the basis of Piaget's research and theory, and its cross-cultural verification, I hypothesized in 1980 (Kamii, 1985) that if children construct their own number concepts, they should be able to construct numerical relationships out of these numbers that are in their heads. They should be able to invent arithmetic for themselves because all numbers are created by the repeated addition of "one." The *idea* of 5, for example, is $(1 + 1 + 1 + 1 + 1)$, and $5 + 3$ is therefore $(1 + 1 + 1 + 1 + 1) + (1 + 1 + 1)$.

This hypothesis was amply verified in 1980–81 and 1981–82 by Georgia DeClark's first graders (Kamii, 1985). It continues to be verified every year in many other classrooms in the United States and abroad.

THE IMPORTANCE OF A SCIENTIFIC EXPLANATORY THEORY

For centuries, education has been an art based on opinions called "philosophies." While education is still an art, it entered a scientific era when it embraced behaviorism, associationism, and psychometric tests. Associationism is less rigorous than behaviorism, but both grew out of empiricism, according to which knowledge is acquired by internalization from the environment. Both scientifically proved the importance of reinforcement, and both have been verified all over the world. These scientific theories grew out of empiricist common sense and reinforced the commonsense belief that drill and reinforcement enhance the internalization of knowledge.

Behaviorism and Piaget's constructivism are both scientific theories that have been verified all over the world. The question that must be answered is: How can two scientific theories be so contradictory and both be true?

The answer to this question is that behaviorism and Piaget's constructivism are related in the way illustrated in Figure 1.5a. This figure shows that Piaget's theory can explain everything behaviorism can explain, but that the converse is not true. As a biologist, Piaget (1967/1971) pointed out that all animals adapt to reward and punishment, and that higher animals like dogs can anticipate the appearance of meat when they hear a bell, for example. Piaget also explained what behaviorists call "extinction" by saying that when the meat stops appearing, the dog stops anticipating its appearance.

While Piaget's theory can thus explain everything behaviorism can explain, behaviorism cannot explain children's acquisition of knowledge in a broader, deeper sense. Only Piaget's theory can explain scientifically why children all over the world become able to conserve quantities without a single lesson in conservation. Once children become able to conserve quantities solidly, no amount of reinforcement can extinguish their logic.

Behaviorism can explain changes in animals' surface behaviors, and associationism can explain children's learning of bits of knowledge (such as nonsense syllables and sums). However, the deep and general logic underlying children's construction of number concepts can be explained only by Piaget's constructivism. It is true that human beings can be conditioned, but there is much more to human knowledge than what animals and young children can learn.

As can be seen in Figure 1.5b, the relationship between behaviorism and Piaget's constructivism is analogous to the one between the geocentric and heliocentric theories of the universe. The geocentric theory existed first and was based on common sense. The heliocentric theory went beyond the primitive theory by encompassing the old one.

An interesting phenomenon in a scientific revolution is that while the new theory makes the old one obsolete, the old theory remains true within a limited scope. The geocentric theory became untrue when people stopped believing that the sun went around the earth. However, from the limited perspective of earth, it is still true today that the sun rises and sets. This "truth" is reported daily in the news. It is likewise still true, from the limited perspective of surface behavior, that drill and reinforcement "work." From a deeper and longer-range perspective, however, we no longer think that human beings acquire knowledge by internalization, reinforcement, and conditioning.

Figure 1.5c shows a similar relationship between Euclidean and non-Euclidean geometry. When non-Euclidean geometry was accepted, it became un-

Figure 1.5. The relationships between (a) behaviorism and Piaget's constructivism, (b) the geocentric and heliocentric theories, and (c) Euclidean and non-Euclidean geometry.

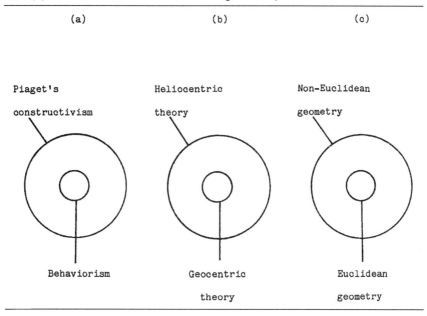

true that the shortest distance between two points is a straight line. Within the limited perspective of Euclidean geometry, however, it is still true that the shortest distance between two points is a straight line. Many other examples of scientific revolutions can be given to show that a more adequate, later theory goes beyond a primitive theory by encompassing it. The relationship between Newtonian physics and quantum physics is another example of a scientific revolution.

All that a scientific theory does is to *describe* and *explain* phenomena, and the practical application of an explanatory theory to an applied field like medicine, architecture, or education is not the business of science itself. However, a scientific theory can be enormously useful in an applied field because it enables us to *change the focus of the debate* from "this method of teaching versus that method of teaching" to *how children acquire number concepts* (or any other kind of knowledge).

As stated at the beginning of this chapter, there is no disagreement in medicine about the fact that the cause of cancer has not been explained scientifically. Disagreement about how to treat cancer always begins with agreement about what is known and unknown scientifically about the cause(s) of cancer.

In education, by contrast, debates about how to teach arithmetic rage on without even asking how children acquire number concepts. Debates in education are often based on unproven assumptions, just as people in medicine used to argue in favor of bloodletting and the use of leeches, citrus fruit, and herbs.

Once we agree, scientifically, on how children acquire number concepts, we can debate at a higher level how best to foster children's process of learning. A growing minority of educators have recognized the superiority of Piaget's constructivism and have drastically changed their way of teaching. Just as conservers cannot go back to nonconservation, and humanity cannot go back to the geocentric theory after accepting the heliocentric theory, teachers who know how children acquire number concepts cannot go back to empiricist teaching.

It took 150 years for the heliocentric theory to become universally accepted (Taylor, 1949). We hope it will not take 150 years for Piaget's constructivism to be accepted by educators.

CHAPTER 2

Representation

In Chapter 1, we explained how children construct number concepts. The representation of these concepts will be discussed in this chapter. Piaget's theory about representation is different from the traditional, empiricist assumptions on which mathematics education has been based. These differences give rise to classroom practices that diverge from traditional instruction.

Workbooks for kindergarten and first-grade math have many pictures. These pictures are there on the assumption that young children go from the "concrete" (objects) to the "semiconcrete" (pictures), and then to the "abstract" (written numerals). We will argue in the first part of this chapter in light of Piaget's theory that this assumption is erroneous and that children do not need any of those pictures.

Teachers often ask, "Why do you give playing cards to kindergartners? I thought young children needed concrete objects to manipulate." The issue of "manipulatives" and representation will be discussed in the second section of this chapter. The third section will deal with equations. More specifically, problems such as 4 + _____ = 6 and "equations" such as "5 + 5 = 10 + 5 = 15" will be discussed.

PICTURES IN WORKBOOKS

Authors of workbooks assume that numerals and mathematical symbols (e.g., "+") are too abstract for first graders at the beginning of the school year and that pictures are halfway between concrete objects and mathematical symbols. According to Piaget (1945/1951), pictures and mathematical symbols have different sources, and working with pictures is not necessarily a step toward becoming able to deal with mathematical symbols.

Symbols and Signs

Piaget (1945/1951) distinguished between *symbols*, such as pictures and tally marks (the left-hand side of Figure 2.1), and *signs*, such as words and written numerals (the right-hand side). His terminology is confusing at first because he used the term *symbol* differently from common parlance.

Figure 2.1. The representation of "eight" in Piaget's theory.

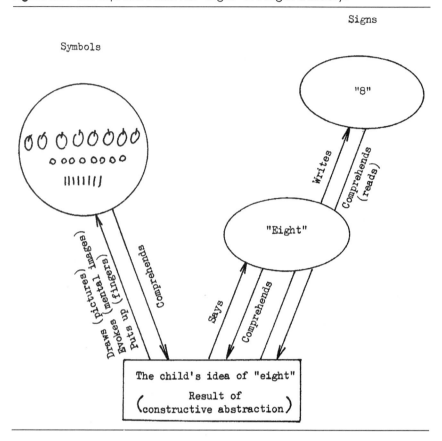

In Piaget's theory, symbols such as pictures bear a resemblance to the objects represented and *can be invented* by each child. In other words, the source of symbols is children's thinking. For example, children can think about "eight" (the rectangle in Figure 2.1 labeled "The child's idea of 'eight'") and draw 8 apples or 8 people without any instruction. Likewise, they can use 8 fingers, 8 counters, or 8 tally marks as symbols for 8 apples. Because children can invent their own symbols, the pictures they get in workbooks are unnecessary. If they need a picture to solve a problem, they will draw their own pictures, as we will see later in this chapter and in Chapter 9.

Examples of signs (the right-hand side of Figure 2.1) are the spoken words "apple" and "eight" and the written numeral "8." Signs do not resemble the objects represented, and their source is conventions, which are made by people. In other words, signs belong to social (conventional) knowledge and, unlike pictures and tally marks, signs cannot be invented by children. Signs are parts of systems, and other examples of such systems are mathematical signs (such as "+"), musical notations, and the Morse code, which require social transmission.

Symbols and signs thus have different sources, and signs (such as written numerals) do not develop out of symbols (such as pictures). Furthermore, there is no such thing as a "concrete number." The distinction Piaget made between *abstraction* and *representation* clarifies this point. Let us return to the conservation-of-number task, which was discussed in Chapter 1, to show what Piaget meant by *abstraction*.

Abstraction and Representation

When the conservation question is asked, both conservers and nonconservers have concrete objects in front of them. Conservers conserve because they are at a higher level of abstraction (constructive abstraction). Those who do not conserve do not do so because they do not have number concepts in their heads. Counters are concrete and observable (physical knowledge), but the number *eight* (logico-mathematical knowledge) is not concrete and not observable. Numbers are always abstract because, as explained in Chapter 1, each child constructs them through constructive abstraction. There is thus no such thing as a "concrete number," and if concrete numbers do not exist, "semiconcrete numbers" do not exist either.

The following study clarifies how young children *represent* different ideas at different levels of *abstraction*. The children were asked to represent on paper groups of objects that were in front of them.

Sinclair, Siegrist, and Sinclair (1983) individually interviewed 4-, 5-, and 6-year-olds in a kindergarten and day-care center in Geneva, Switzerland, where no formal academic instruction had been given. There were 15 children in each age group, making a total of 45. The interviewers used up to 8 identical objects such as pencils, small rubber balls, and toy cars.

Presenting the child with 3 small rubber balls, for example, as well as a pencil and paper, the interviewer asked, "Could you put down what is on the table?" This request was carefully worded to avoid using terms such as "how many" and "number" that would have suggested quantification. After giving several similar items (2 balls and 5 houses, for example), the researchers asked the child, "Could you write 'three' [then 'four,' 'four houses,' and so on]?" The purpose of this request was to find out if the children could write numerals when explicitly asked to do so in the absence of objects.

The following six types of notations were found (see Figure 2.2):

1. *Global representation of quantity*. An example of this type is "////" for 3 balls and "/////" for 2 balls. Children also invented other symbols such

Figure 2.2. Examples of notation types.

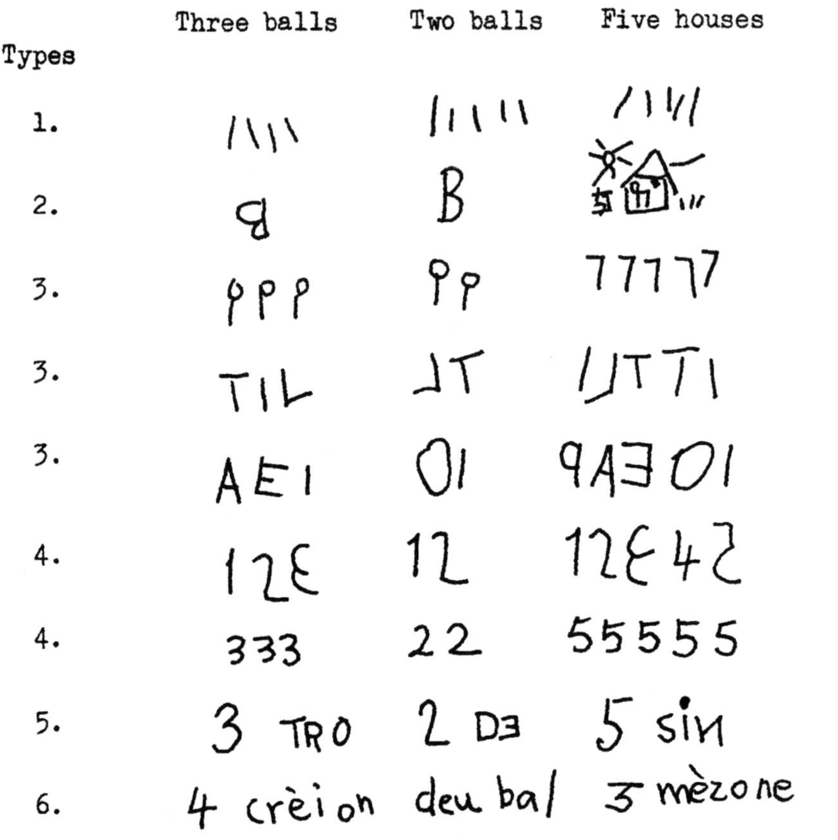

Types	Three balls	Two balls	Five houses
1.	/\\\	|\ \ \\	/\\/\/
2.	ꝺ	B	
3.	ppp	pp	7777ʔ
3.	TIᒪ	ꓕT	ᑌTTl
3.	AEl	Ol	ꝯAⱻOl
4.	12ε	1ᒪ	12ε42
4.	333	22	55555
5.	3 TRO	2 Dꓱ	5 siɯ
6.	4 crèion	deu bal	ꝫ mèzone

Source: Sinclair, A., Siegrist, F., & Sinclair, H. (1983). Young children's ideas about the written number system. In D. Rogers & J. A. Sloboda (Eds.), *The acquisition of symbolic skills* (pp. 535–542). New York: Plenum. Used by permission.

as hooks. These children can be said to be representing the vague quantitative idea of "many," "a bunch," or "more than one."

2. *Representation of the object-kind.* These notations show a focus on the qualitative rather than the quantitative aspect of each set. The examples in Figure 2.2 show a "B" for 3 balls and 2 balls, and the drawing of a house for 5 houses.

3. *One-to-one correspondence with symbols* ("symbols" in the Piagetian sense). Some children invented symbols to represent the correct number, and others used 3 conventional letters as symbols to represent

3 balls (such as "TIL" and "AEl," which are not words). This is the first type in which precise numerical ideas made an appearance.

4. *One-to-one correspondence with numerals.* One of the examples for 3 balls is "123," and another example is "333." It can be said that the children who wrote these numerals felt the need to represent each object or their action of counting.

5. *Cardinal value alone.* We finally see "3" for 3 balls and "5" for 5 houses (along with "invented" spelling in French for the spoken numerals *trois*, *deux*, and *cinq*).

6. *Cardinal value and object-kind.* Examples of this type are "4 pencils" and "5 houses." ("*Crèion*" and "*mèzone*" are invented spellings for *crayons* and *maisons*.) These representations show a simultaneous focus on the quantitative and qualitative aspects of each set.

Type-1 representation was found mainly among the 4-year-olds, and Types 5 and 6 were found mostly among those older than 5 and a half. Types 3 and 4 (one-to-one correspondence) were most frequently found in the middle of the age range, at about the time children become conservers. It must be noted that there are no clear-cut levels in this development, as half of the children used more than one type of representation.

A significant finding is that many children who used only Types 1, 2, or 3 were perfectly able to write "3," "4," and so on, when asked "Can you write 'three' [then 'four' and so on]?" The question that arises is: Why did they not write the numerals they knew?

Our answer to this question is that children represent *their ideas* about reality and not reality itself (Piaget, 1977). When they saw 3 balls, for example, some children thought about them as "a bunch" or "more than one" and made a Type-1 representation. Others thought "balls" and made a Type-2 representation. These 4-year-olds thought about the objects either from a vaguely quantitative or from a qualitative point of view and not both.

At age 5, when children construct number, they tend to make Type-3 and Type-4 representations. These children think about 3 objects, for example, with numerical precision but still think about each object. Type 4 is especially significant because it shows that even when they have acquired the social knowledge of written numerals, children use this knowledge at their respective levels of abstraction. No one teaches children to write "123" or "333" to represent 3 objects, and no one teaches them to write "TIL" for 3 objects either. But Types 3 and 4 reveal children's attention to *each object* rather than to the *total quantity*.

Type-5 representation was made mostly by the oldest children, reflecting their thinking about the *total quantity* of objects. At this point, it seems best to write one numeral and not 3 symbols or signs. Type 6 further reflects children's ability to think simultaneously about numerical quantity and object-type.

The arrows in Figure 2.1 labeled "Draw, etc." and "Writes" going out from the child's idea indicate that when children represent their ideas on paper, they externalize *their* ideas at *their* respective levels of abstraction. Those who think "a whole bunch" represent this idea. Those who can think "eight" represent this idea, first by still paying attention to individual objects and later by thinking about the totality.

"MANIPULATIVES"

A new trend appeared in the 1990s called "manipulatives." The rationale for manipulatives remains vague, in my opinion, but it seems to be rooted in the belief that children go from the "concrete" to the "semiconcrete" and then to the "abstract." Manipulatives are concrete and therefore believed to give a better foundation for understanding mathematical signs.

Counters are generally thought to be manipulatives, but it is theoretically more correct to think about them as symbols (see Figure 2.1). Like every other symbol and sign, counters can be used at a high or low level of abstraction. Playing cards can be manipulated, too, but they involve symbols (such as 3 hearts) and signs (such as the numeral "3"). Base-10 blocks are believed to represent "ones," "tens," and so on, but this belief is based on the erroneous assumption that objects can represent ones, tens, and so on. The use of counters, playing cards, and base-10 blocks will now be discussed.

Counters versus Fingers and Children's Own Drawings

First graders can be given counters to solve the following problem: *I have 4 little candles but need 7 for a birthday cake. How many more candles do I need to get?* Many children put out 4 counters, then 7, count some or all of them, and give the answer of 7 or 11.

These are examples of the use of counters as symbols at a low level of abstraction. If children can make a part-whole relationship in their minds, through constructive abstraction, they answer "Three." If they cannot, they make two wholes, namely "four" and "seven," and answer "Seven" or "Eleven." Each child thus uses symbols at his or her level of abstraction.

The following example also illustrates children's use of counters as symbols at various levels of abstraction. The problem was: *I got out 4 bowls to serve soup to 4 people. I want to put 3 crackers in each bowl. How many crackers do I need?* Many first graders align 4 counters to represent 4 bowls (or 4 people). They then put 3 counters in front of each "bowl." Many then count all the counters and give the answer of 16, but others count only those they meant to stand for crackers and answer "Twelve."

All 16 of the counters look identical and are often arranged in 4 columns, each of 4. However, when children can make higher-level relationships (through constructive abstraction), they unmistakably know which ones stand for "bowls" and which ones were meant to be "crackers." When they can make only vague and fleeting relationships, they forget that some counters were meant to represent bowls. Manipulatives are thus not useful or useless in themselves. Their utility depends on the relationships children can make, through constructive abstraction.

Children's Preference for Drawing.   Olivier, Murray, and Human (1991) made the following statement about children in a constructivist math program they developed in South Africa:

> Although informal writing materials as well as counters are always available, it seems that students seldom use counters to model a problem. Rather, the problem context is *drawn* in greater or lesser detail, and then solved by further drawing in the actions needed. For example, Leana (grade 1) divides 18 cookies among three children one at a time [see Figure 2.3], and Conrad (also grade 1) two at a time. (p. 17)

I (CK) have asked many kindergarten and first-grade teachers in many parts of the United States and Japan to conduct research in their classrooms to test the validity of Olivier et al.'s statement. I asked them to remind their students frequently that they (the students) were free to use the counters, paper, pencil, or anything else in the classroom to solve word problems.

Figure 2.3. Two first graders' ways of finding out how many cookies each child would get if three children divided 18 cookies.

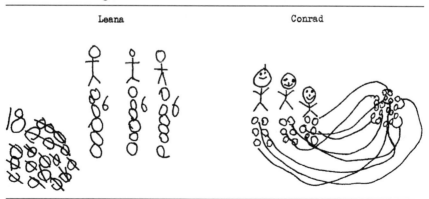

Leana   Conrad

Source: Olivier, Murray, & Human (1991, p. 17).

The teachers reported that, most of the time, children prefer to draw rather than to use the counters that were equally accessible. The only exception, they said, was at the beginning of the school year, when the students were unfamiliar with word problems. The other observation the teachers made was that many children prefer to use their fingers. When the numbers got bigger than 10, however, these students switched to tally marks.

Figures 2.4–2.7 are examples of first graders' graphic representations made to answer the question in *One Gorilla* (Morozumi, 1990). This book begins with the picture of a gorilla accompanied by the words "Here is a list of things I love. One gorilla." Each time we turn a page, there is one more animal than before: 2 butterflies, 3 budgerigars, 4 squirrels, 5 pandas, 6 rabbits, 7 frogs, 8 fish, 9 birds, and 10 cats. The question is: How many animals does the author love? Figures 2.4–2.7 show the various ways in which the children made graphic representations to do 1 + 2 + 3 + 4 + 5 + 6 + 7 + 8 + 9 + 10.

These first graders were slightly older than the oldest children interviewed by Sinclair et al. (1983), but the levels they manifested were very similar. Figures 2.4 and 2.5 have elements of Sinclair et al.'s Types 2 and 3. Precise one-to-one correspondence can be seen in these drawings, but the qualitative characteristics of the animals were also very important to these children.

The difference between Figures 2.4 and 2.5 is that the latter is much better organized in rows going from "1" to "10." We can see here another disadvantage of worksheets and workbooks. When children fill out worksheets, they do not have to organize their thoughts on paper. When they are given a blank sheet of paper with only the problem written at the top, they have a chance to organize their thoughts and decide how to externalize them on paper.

Figure 2.6 is clearly an example of Type-3 representation, except that the child added qualitative characteristics such as "G" for "gorilla" and "B" for "butterflies." (This picture book probably emphasizes the different kinds of animals, and young children are intensely interested in the differences among them.) Figure 2.7 is a Type-5 representation, and the child drew circles and crossed them out as he added the numbers.

The great variety of graphic representations suggests why children prefer to draw rather than to use counters. When they are presented with a word problem and a sheet of paper, they evoke mental images or imageless numerical ideas and externalize them on paper. For those who made Figures 2.4 and 2.5, the characteristics of the animals were very important. For those who drew Figures 2.6 and 2.7, these characteristics were irrelevant. When children use paper and pencil, they can externalize their own ideas and use these representations as tools. By contrast, counters have their own physical properties that interfere with children's ideas. This is probably why young children do not choose to use counters to solve word problems.

Figure 2.4. A drawing made to find out how many animals the author loved.

Figure 2.5. A well-organized drawing made to find out how many animals the author loved.

We will see in Chapter 9 that our first graders generally made drawings like Figure 2.4 at the beginning of the year and gradually shifted to tally marks and then to numerals. However, they often used more than one type of representation each day and also went back and forth from one type of notation to another.

Figure 2.6. Symbols used to find out how many animals the author loved.

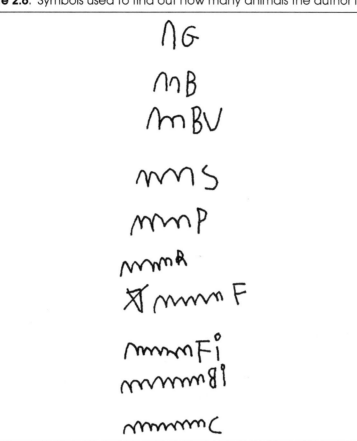

Children's Use of Fingers.   As stated earlier, kindergartners and first graders use their fingers much more than counters. Fingers are symbols used in the service of thinking.

Just as children use counters at different levels of abstraction, they use fingers at many different levels. The two most obvious levels are those of "counting-all" and "counting-on." Counting-all refers to children's doing 4 + 3, for example, by counting 4 fingers, then 3, and counting all 7 of them all over beginning with "one." In counting-on, by contrast, children count up from 4 and say "five-six-seven."

It will be explained further in Chapter 5 why counting-on is so difficult for many kindergartners and some first graders. Essentially, this difficulty stems from the difficulty of making a part-whole relationship. In adding two numbers, chil-

Figure 2.7. Signs and symbols used to find out how many animals the
author loved.

dren start with two wholes (4 and 3 in this example) and combine them into a
higher-order whole (7) in which the previous wholes become two parts. As explained in Chapter 1, children make part-whole relationships through constructive abstraction. If they can make this relationship, they use their fingers (symbols) at a higher level than those who cannot.

   Independently of counting-all or counting-on, some children count on fingers methodically while others do not. Some always start with the index, count
the other 3 fingers in sequence, and then the thumb. Others always start with
the thumb and proceed in sequence to the little finger. Whichever method they
invent, these children consistently use the same sequence. Others are inconsistent in their use of fingers and get incorrect answers. Children's inconsistent
and organized methods are both manifestations of the relationships they make
or do not make in their heads, through constructive abstraction.

Playing Cards

   As stated earlier, teachers often ask why we use playing cards in kindergarten when Piaget said to give concrete objects to young children. Piaget would
say that children use objects as well as pictures of objects at their respective levels
of abstraction. In playing Double War (see Chapter 11), for example, some

children deal the cards with an organized sequence, but others do not follow a consistent pattern and are surprised toward the end of the game that one player has more cards than the other. (In Double War, children compare 2 cards showing 3 and 3, for example, with 2 cards showing 3 and 2. The one who has the larger total takes all 4 cards.) Those who count the symbols on the cards by counting-all would also count-all if the same quantities were presented with counters.

Playing cards in Double War serve only to communicate questions, and cards make it possible for addends to come up by chance. If objects were used in Double War, the game would be unacceptably cumbersome. Whether the question is presented with symbols, signs, or objects, the arithmetic of the game takes place in children's heads, through constructive abstraction.

Base-10 Blocks

Base-10 blocks and Unifix cubes are used on the assumption that *they* represent or embody "ones," "tens," "hundreds," and so on. According to Piaget, however, objects, pictures, and words do not represent (Furth, 1981). Representing is an action, and people can represent objects and ideas, but objects, pictures, and words cannot. As indicated in Figure 2.1 with three arrows labeled "Comprehends," children understand symbols and signs by assimilating them to *their* idea at their respective levels of abstraction. In other words, children represent meanings *to themselves* when they see or hear a symbol or sign. An example was seen in Chapter 1 in connection with the class-inclusion question, "Are there more dogs or more animals?" Children at a low level of abstraction "hear" a very different question from that which the adult meant.

When adults look at a long base-10 block, for example, they can represent "one ten" and "ten ones" *simultaneously* to themselves. Adults can do this representing because they are already at a high level of abstraction. Young children, who can think only *successively* about "one ten" and "ten ones," cannot put the same meaning adults can into a long base-10 block.

There is a world of difference between being able to think only *successively* about "one ten" and "ten ones" and being able to think about both *simultaneously*. Figure 2.8a shows that when kindergartners and most first graders count 34 toothpicks, they think about 34 *ones*. They constructed these ones through constructive abstraction. Figure 2.8b shows the mental partitioning of these ones into segments of 10. This is the structure of base-10 blocks, as well as of Unifix cubes and toothpicks bundled together in groups of 10.

The difference between being able to think *simultaneously* and only *successively* about "tens" and "ones" can be seen when we give 34 toothpicks grouped into three groups of 10 and 4 loose ones to first graders and ask them to count them by tens. Many say "Ten, twenty, thirty" as they count the groups of 10, and "forty, fifty, sixty, seventy" as they count the ungrouped toothpicks.

Figure 2.8. The difference between (a) counting by *ones*, (b) the partitioning of *ones* into segments of 10 and, (c) the construction of *tens* out of the *ones*.

(a) Thirty-four ones

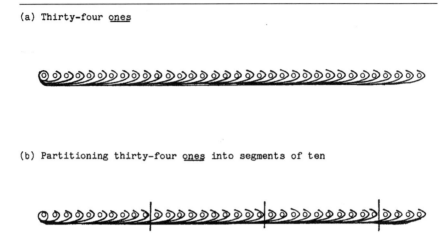

(b) Partitioning thirty-four ones into segments of ten

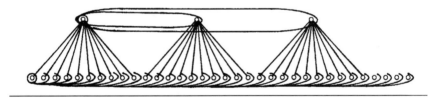

(c) Three tens and four ones

They count in this way because they cannot yet think simultaneously about *tens* and *ones* as shown in Figure 2.8c.

Figure 2.8c illustrates the system of tens the child has constructed out of the system of ones, through constructive abstraction. When the child has constructed the system of tens out of the system of ones, he or she has both systems, which can function *simultaneously*. If children can think about the ones at the same time that they think "ten, twenty, thirty," they know when they must shift to counting by ones. If they can think only about the tens while counting by tens, they cannot shift to the ones because they are not thinking about the ones.

Figure 2.8c further illustrates the relationships of order and hierarchical inclusion that were discussed in Chapter 1. When adults count by tens, they put both the ones and the tens into relationships of order and hierarchical inclusion. Just as they include "one" in "two," "two" in "three," and so on, adults can include "one ten" in "twenty," "twenty" in "thirty," and so on. All these relationships are much too complicated for most first graders to make *simultaneously*.

"Ones" and "tens" are discussed further in Chapter 5 in connection with place value. If children cannot think simultaneously about tens and ones, they cannot possibly represent these ideas simultaneously with a writing system involving place value. Children's understanding of the "1" in "16" is discussed in detail in Chapter 5.

In conclusion, base-10 blocks are not "concrete numbers" or an "embodiment" or a "representation" of the base-10 system. Children cannot construct the system of *ones* by empirical abstraction from objects, and they cannot construct the system of *tens* by empirical abstraction from objects either. When they see a long block, children who can make higher-level relationships (through constructive abstraction) can represent higher-level meanings to themselves and think "one ten" and "ten ones" *simultaneously*. Those who can make only lower-level relationships make lower-level representations and think "one ten" and "ten ones" *separately*.

EQUATIONS IN FIRST GRADE

So far, this chapter has focused on numbers and numerals. We now discuss equations, which involve the representation of operations. First-grade math books include missing-addend problems such as 4 + ____ = 6, and it will be argued that becoming able to fill in such blanks on paper is not a valid objective for first graders. We will also discuss why we do not correct "equations" such as 5 + 5 = 10 + 5 = 15.

Missing Addends

In card games such as Piggy Bank (see Chapter 11), most first graders who turn over a 2 become able to say that they need a 3 to make 5. In other games described in Chapter 11, first graders likewise have no difficulty with missing-addend problems.

When presented with a written problem such as 2 + ____ = 5, however, many of these children write "7" or a random number. The difficulty of written missing-addend problems is one of *reading*, or *representation*.

As can be seen in Figure 2.9, 2 + 3 = ____ presented in writing requires thinking in only one direction. By contrast, 2 + ____ = 5 requires thinking from

Figure 2.9. Thought that must go in two directions to understand a written missing-addend problem.

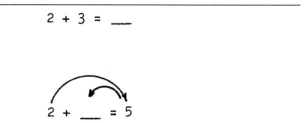

the first addend to the sum, and back to the second addend, *simultaneously*. This thinking involves reversibility of thought, which was discussed in Chapter 1 in connection with class inclusion. Since many first graders' thought is not yet reversible, written missing-addend problems are too hard for many of them to understand. In other words, many first graders cannot answer the question because they do not understand the question in written form. In Piggy Bank, by contrast, the numeral 2 has to be read, but the 5 is in the child's head. This is why missing-addend problems are easier in a card game.

It was hypothesized in the following study that when children's thinking becomes reversible (constructive abstraction), they become able to read the question (representation) correctly without any instruction.

Kamii, Lewis, and Booker's Study (1998).   The children who participated in the study were 110 students in five classes of first graders attending two public schools in a suburb of Birmingham. None of the first-grade teachers involved taught children to write answers to problems such as 2 + _____ = 5, but all of them played math games with children every day.

In May, toward the end of the school year, the five teachers were asked to give to their first-grade classes the group test shown in Figure 2.10. As I (CK) watched, each teacher distributed the test to the children in her class and asked, "What number do you think should go in the first box?" The class reacted with such expressions as "These are too easy!" The teacher called on one of the volunteers, who explained why "3" was the answer. The teacher went on to say, "Let's work one more problem together to make sure you know what to do with the rest of the sheet." A volunteer quickly explained why a 4 had to go in the next box, and the five classes took 4 to 7 minutes for the entire test.

Ninety-two percent of the first graders handed in papers that had either no errors (85%) or only one error (7%). The five classes produced similar percentages, and the first graders thus demonstrated their ability to solve written missing-addend problems without any formal instruction.

Eight of the 110 children (7%) demonstrated their difficulty either by leaving the boxes empty or by writing in what appeared to be sums or random numbers. I hypothesized that in second grade if these children did not receive any instruction in missing addends, their thinking would still advance to a level of being able to answer these questions.

In second grade in September, I attempted to find the 8 children who had demonstrated difficulty, but 4 had moved away. The second-grade teachers of the remaining 4 children were asked if, and when, they planned to teach missing addends. The same 6 problems were given to the 4 children in February and March, before their teachers formally discussed missing addends, and all 4 produced perfect papers. The hypothesis that children become able to read missing-addend problems without specific instruction was thus confirmed.

This study exemplifies the arrow in Figure 2.1 labeled "Comprehends (reads)." Those at a high level of abstraction can get higher-level meaning from an equation than children at a low level of abstraction. When we read, we represent meaning to ourselves. Written signs do not represent by themselves. The following study further explains many first graders' difficulty in reading equations.

Kamii and Ozaki's Study (1999).   In a study involving 204 first graders in six public schools in the United States and Japan, I (CK) wrote "4 + 2 =" in front of the child in individual interviews. Almost none of them had trouble writing the correct answer, as the interviews took place during the second half of the school year. I then stood a doll in front of the child and provided him or her with about

Figure 2.10. The group test with missing-addend problems.

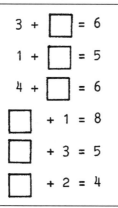

40 chips. "Could you give to the doll what's written here?" I said, running a finger over the entire equation, 4 + 2 = 6. If necessary, I elaborated by saying, "The doll is reading this [indicating the equation], and he wants this many counters [again indicating the equation]."

About two-thirds of the first graders gave 6 counters to the doll, but approximately one-third gave 12. This happened because a third of the first graders read the equation as "4 2 6" or "4 + 2 6." The study was conducted in six rather different schools in the United States and Japan, but the percentages were surprisingly similar in all locations. Two schools were in an affluent suburb of Birmingham, Alabama. One was in a small town in Alabama, and one was on the south side of Chicago. The Japanese sample was interviewed in two schools in Sapporo, the largest city in Hokkaido.

These first graders could read and define each of the signs in the equation. They could also write the correct answer to "4 + 2 = ____." However, when they read the finished equation, those who could make only low-level relationships (abstraction) put low-level meanings into what they read (representation).

In the same study, the children were asked to write numerals to represent a mathematical event. This writing part of the interview (the arrow in Figure 2.1 labeled "Writes") was actually given before the reading part just described (the arrow labeled "Comprehends [reads]"). The child's writing was requested first to avoid suggesting that they write an equation.

I showed a doll to the child and told him or her, "I'm going to turn him around [turning the doll's back toward the child] so that he won't be able to see what I'm going to do. I'm going to do something here [pointing to about 40 chips and a small, transparent, plastic container], and when I am finished, I want you to write with numbers what I will have done, so that the doll will be able to read your writing and know what happened." I then dropped 3 chips simultaneously into the container saying, "First, I am putting 3 in." I went on to drop 2 more chips into the container saying, "And I am *adding* two." My request to the child was: "Could you write with numbers what I just did so that the doll will be able to read your writing and know what happened?"

Many children wrote "5." When this happened, I said, "Yes, that's how many there are now. But I first put 3 in." I emptied the container, dropped 3 chips into it, and asked, "Could you first write '3' on your paper to say that I first put 3 in?" After the child wrote "3," I demonstrated with chips again, saying, "I am *adding* 2," emphasizing the word *adding*.

The findings are summarized in Table 2.1. The first observation that can be made from this table is that not many first graders wrote "3 + 2 = 5" or "3 + 2." Only 68%, 18%, 22%, and 62% of the four groups, respectively, wrote these conventional expressions. We say "only 68%" because we expected almost all the children to write a conventional expression, as they had been completing worksheets for months, since kindergarten in many cases.

Table 2.1 Percentage of First Graders in Four Locations Representing the Addition of Three to Two

	United States			Japan
	Suburb $n = 62$	Small town $n = 49$	Chicago $n = 29$	$n = 64$
3 + 2 = 5	60	18	11	48
3 + 2	8	0	11	14
3 + 2 =	2	0	0	5
32 or 3 2	8	24	35	17
35 or 3 5	6	29	11	9
Others	18	28	33	6

Examples from U.S. (The Japanese sample had only 6% in this category.)

3 + 2 5	+ 3 2 - 5	3 + 5 = 5
3 2 5	$\frac{3}{+2 = 5}$	3 4 5
5 3 2		12345
2 3 5	$\frac{3}{5}$	5322

Note: When a child conventionally represented the addition vertically, he or she was asked to write "the same thing" horizontally.

A surprising number of first graders wrote only two numerals—"3 + 2," "3 + 2 =," "3 2," or "3 5." Eighteen, 24, 46, and 36%, respectively, of the four groups wrote only a 3 and a 2, representing the two original wholes. Those who wrote a 3 and a 5 can be said to have represented the original whole and the whole at the end (first there were 3, and then there were 5).

The variety of the other representations was surprising, and the rarer ones are grouped under the heading of "Others." The most instructive writing not presented in this category came from a child who refused to write anything but "5" and explained, "I can't write '3' because the 3 are already in the 5." This statement explained why so many children wrote either "3" and "2" ("You put in 3 and then 2 more") or "3" and "5" ("First, there were 3, and then there were 5"). The writing of three numerals in this task required thinking hierarchically about a part-whole relationship, which was too hard for many first graders.

An important point to be made about Table 2.1 concerns the infrequency of the "+" and "=" signs. Furthermore, there were children who wrote "+" without writing "=," but no one wrote "=" without writing a "+." The infrequent use of the "+" and "=" signs among first graders was also observed by Allardice (1977).

She further noted that only three of the seven first graders who wrote the "+" sign wrote the "=" sign. The "+" sign appears earlier than the "=" sign in both studies because the relationship between the 3 and the 2 is at one level of abstraction, whereas the relationship among the 3, the 2, and the 5 involves a part-whole relationship at two hierarchical levels.

The last three examples in Table 2.1 are versions of Type-4 representation in Sinclair et al. (1983). One-to-one correspondence can be seen in "3 4 5" and "12345." The child who wrote "5322" represented "five" and "three" with Type-5 notation, and "two" with Type-4 notation (22).

When adults write equations such as "3 + 2 = 5," we represent each original whole twice—once in the "3" and again in the "5" as part of the higher-order whole, and once in the "2" and again in the "5" as part of the higher-order whole. Children who cannot make this kind of part-whole relationship often leave out the "5" and/or the "=" sign. Their ways of writing thus help us understand why so many first graders read "4 + 2 = 6" as "4 2 6" or "4 + 2 6."

"Equations" such as "5 + 5 = 10 + 5 = 15"

Many teachers vehemently object to nonconventional "equations" such as "5 + 5 = 10 + 5 = 15 + 5 = 20 + 5 = 25" (which are incorrect because the two sides of all the "=" signs are unequal). Our first graders often write this kind of equation, but we do not correct them in first grade. There is no point in correcting first graders because their thought is not mobile enough to remember the beginning of such an equation by the time they reach its end. Moreover, children in our classes use writing for two purposes: to facilitate their own *thinking* and to facilitate *communication*.

In solving a problem such as the one in *One Gorilla* cited earlier, our children often write "1 + 2 = 3 + 3 = 6 + 4 = 10 + 5 = 15. . . ." This is an example of an equation used to facilitate one's own thinking. Children keep track of their work in this way and can use their writing to decide what to do next. They can also go over their work when they think they may have made an error. Correcting this kind of equation would interfere with children's thinking.

During a whole-class discussion, children volunteer to explain how they got the answer in a variety of ways. When one child says, for example, "First, I added 1 and 2," the teacher writes "1 + 2" on the board for two purposes related to communication: to let the speaker know what she has understood, and to enable the other members of the class to follow what the speaker is saying. The teacher writes also to teach the social (conventional) knowledge of equations by modeling their use in a meaningful context.

When the speaker continues by saying, "That was 3," the teacher writes "= 3" after "1 + 2." If the child says, "Then I added 3 to it," the teacher writes "+ 3" leaving the following equation on the board: 1 + 2 = 3 + 3. Every child in the class can follow this writing, and it would take more time unnecessarily for the teacher to write, "1 + 2 = 3," "3 + 3 = 6," "6 + 4 = 10," and so on.

There is plenty of time for first graders to learn conventions. The important thing for young children is to *think* and to *exchange ideas with other children*. For children who can think, conventions will be easy to learn later.

CONCLUSION

In this chapter, we tried to explain that children do not go from the "concrete" to the "semiconcrete" and then to the "abstract." By understanding the distinction Piaget made between *abstraction* and *representation*, it becomes possible for teachers to focus on children's thinking, or the relationships they make, namely, abstraction. Children use objects (such as counters) at a high or low level of abstraction. When they can make higher-level relationships, they draw higher-level pictures and put higher-level meanings into mathematical signs such as "=." When they can make only low-level relationships, they use objects as well as pictures, words, and written signs at a low level.

CHAPTER 3

The Importance
of Social Interaction

Piaget is often said to have overlooked the importance of social factors in children's development. However, this view is completely false as Lourenço and Machado (1996) and DeVries (1997) pointed out with many references such as Piaget (1967/1995). According to Piaget, the exchange of points of view with others is indispensable for children's development of logic (Piaget, 1947/1963) and for scientists' construction of science (Piaget & Garcia, 1983/1989). It can also be seen in *The Moral Judgment of the Child* (Piaget, 1932/1965) that the exchange of viewpoints is essential for children's moral development.

In this chapter, we limit ourselves to children's intellectual development and deal with sociomoral development in Chapter 4. We first discuss Piaget's theory about the importance of social interaction with reference to the conservation of continuous quantity. We then present Perret-Clermont (1980) and Doise and Mugny's (1981/1984) empirical studies that support Piaget's theory. In the third part of the chapter, we deal with the necessity of discussion for scientists' construction of science and conclude by comparing Piaget's idea of cooperation with the arguments presented by advocates of "cooperative learning."

THE ROLE OF SOCIAL INTERACTION
IN CHILDREN'S DEVELOPMENT OF LOGIC

All young children begin by being egocentric and prelogical. Egocentricity means being able to think only from one point of view, usually one's own. Nonconservation is an example of young children's egocentricity as well as their prelogical thinking. When they think that there are more chips in the longer row, they are centering on the space occupied by the chips because their logic does not yet permit them to think numerically. When other children express other viewpoints, children are obliged to *decenter*, or coordinate their own perspective with that of others. In other words, when children exchange points of view with others, they cannot remain egocentric and illogical because they are obliged to put the relationships they are making into relationship with those that others are making.

Let us review what Piaget (Piaget & Szeminska, 1941/1952) said about the conservation of liquid to give an example of the coordination of relationships. It will be recalled that conservation of number is generally attained by 5 to 6 years of age among children from middle-income families. Conservation of liquid becomes possible a little later, between the ages of 7 and 8 on average.

Conservation of Liquid and Logico-mathematical Knowledge

In this task, the interviewer first pours colored water ("fruit juice") into glass A (see Figure 3.1) and asks the child to pour the same amount into A'. When the child is certain that the two glasses contain the same amount, the interviewer asks him or her to "watch what I'm going to do" and pours the contents of A' into another glass of different dimensions, such as D. The child is then asked, "Do A and D have the same amount of 'fruit juice,' or does A have more, or does D have more?" The three cognitive levels found in this task are similar to those described in Chapter 1 with respect to conservation of number.

Conservers are convinced that A and D have the same amount and are not swayed by countersuggestions. When asked, "How do you know?" they give one of the following three justifications:

- "You did not add or take away anything" (the *identity* argument).
- "I could put the juice back in A', and you'll see that it's still the same amount" (the *reversibility* argument).
- "The level is higher in D, but D is skinnier than A (the *compensation* argument).

Nonconservers are convinced that there is more in D than in A. When asked how they know this, they explain that the water level is higher in D.

Figure 3.1. The glasses used in the conservation-of-liquid task.

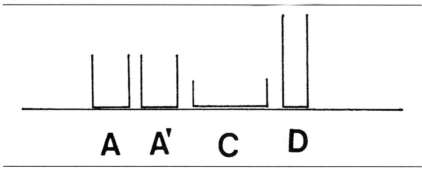

The *intermediate* group consists of children who vacillate between "the same" and "different" or answer correctly without conviction or a logical justification.

The fact that liquids settle in a glass with a horizontal surface is physical, empirical knowledge. However, the quantification of liquid belongs to logico-mathematical knowledge. "Same amount," "more," and "less" are relationships created by the mind. The conserver who says "It's the same amount because you didn't add or take away anything" is basing this judgment on reasoning. The nonconserver, who does not yet have this logic, can depend only on his or her eyes. This is why nonconservers base their judgment on the water level, which is visible and empirically knowable.

Piaget (1947/1963) explained the difference between the nonconserver's empirical knowledge and the conserver's logical deduction in the following way:

> [If we ask a conserver for a justification,] he replies that nothing has been removed or added; but the younger children also are well aware of this, and yet they do not infer identity. . . . Or else he [the conserver] replies that the height makes up for the width lost by the new glass, etc., but [the nonconserver's] articulated intuition has already led to these decentrings. . . . Or else, and this especially, he [the conserver] replies that a transfer from A to B may be corrected by a transfer from B to A . . . , but the younger children [nonconservers] have already on occasion admitted the possibility of a return to the starting point. (pp. 140–141)

In other words, nonconservers have all the empirical knowledge that conservers invoke to justify their answer. Piaget went on to explain the conservers' logic in the following way, in terms of their "grouping," or coordination, of all three logical operations—identity, compensation, and reversibility. Note the difference between bits of empirical knowledge and the logical reasoning made possible by the grouping of logical operations.

> [When operations are "grouped," or coordinated,] the various transformations involved—reversibility, combination of compensated relations, identity, etc.—in fact depend on each other and, because they amalgamate into an organised whole, each is really new despite its affinity with the corresponding intuitive relation that was already formed at the previous [preoperational] level. (p. 141)

In other words, when the child groups the three relationships of reversibility, compensation, and identity into one interrelated whole, through constructive abstraction, this grouping enables him or her to deduce conservation with the force of logical necessity. Conservers all over the world may justify their answers with only one argument, but the argument they give is rooted in the grouping of the three logical operations into an interrelated whole.

Social Interaction and
the Development of Logic

In a chapter entitled "Social Factors in Intellectual Development" in the same book, Piaget (1947/1963) went on to argue that social interaction is essential for children's development of logic. He explained that all human beings begin by being egocentric and able to make relationships only from their own limited perspective. The exchange of points of view is essential for the development of logic because these exchanges necessitate efforts to decenter, to see things from the other person's perspective, and to be coherent and consistent in communicating with each other.

Social interaction stimulates decentering and logical coordination because

> the child first seeks to avoid contradicting himself when he is in the presence of others. In the same way, objectively, the need for verification, the need for words and ideas to keep their meaning constant, etc. are as much social obligations as conditions of operational [logical] thought. (Piaget, 1947/1963, p. 163)

In short, Piaget summarized the importance of social interaction by saying, "Without interchange of thought and co-operation with others the individual would never come to group his [logical] operations into a coherent whole" (p. 163).

Piaget used the term *co-operation* differently from common parlance. When we say, "Your cooperation will be appreciated," what we usually mean is: "We want you to *comply* with our request." By contrast, Piaget used the term to mean "co-operation," with a hyphen, or "operating together." Operating together for Piaget meant to work together, by exchanging points of view, and negotiating solutions in case of disagreement. According to him, cooperation suppresses the spontaneous convictions, such as nonconservation, that characterize egocentrism. Discussion and critical thinking stimulate the construction of logic because people cannot communicate with each other if their thinking is incoherent and inconsistent.

Piaget thus stressed the importance of social interaction but never conducted empirical research to prove his social theory. This research was carried out by a group of social psychologists in Geneva, including Perret-Clermont (1980) and Doise and Mugny (1981/1984). Highlights from their studies are sketched below.

EXPERIMENTS ABOUT THE EFFECTS
OF SOCIOCOGNITIVE CONFLICT

Two experiments by Perret-Clermont and one by Doise and Mugny are presented in this section. These researchers studied the effects of "sociocognitive conflict," which means an intellectual disagreement between or among people.

Perret-Clermont's Experiment I

Perret-Clermont pretested about 100 kindergartners and first graders (ranging in age from 5 years 6 months to 7 years 5 months). Using glasses A, A', and C (refer to Figure 3.1) in the conservation-of-liquid task, she categorized the children as conserving (C), intermediate (I), or nonconserving (NC) and randomly assigned them to experimental and control groups.

The control group did not have any contact with the interviewer between pretest and posttest. The experimental groups consisted of trios. Two members of each trio were conservers, and one was either a nonconserver or an intermediate child. The trios were put in a situation where they were encouraged to deal with disagreements. Two posttests were then given to assess the short- and long-term effects of sociocognitive conflict.

Each trio sat at a small table, and glass A was given to one of the conservers and glass D to the other conserver. The third child, a nonconserver or intermediate child, was given an opaque bottle containing colored water ("fruit juice") and asked to pour it into the glasses of the other two children so that they would have the same amount to drink. The experimenter stipulated that only when the group agreed that everybody had the same amount could they drink the juice. The adult then casually placed glass A' in front of the third child saying that it might be useful.

The interaction lasted about 10 minutes. In most cases, the nonconserver immediately poured juice into glasses A and D. (No child began by pouring juice into A and A'.) Below is an edited example of what happened in an interaction:

Ama (NC): Pours juice up to the same level in A and D.

Pat (C): "There isn't the same to drink."

Bru (C): "No, Pat will have less."

Pat (C): "You should pour it like this" (pours D into A' and equalizes the levels in A and A').

Ama (NC): (pours A' back into D) "There is more in here (D)."

Pat (C): "They are the same."

Bru (C): "They are the same."

Ama (NC): "No." (Takes some juice out of D, pouring it back into the bottle. The level in D is now lower than in A.)

Exp: (To Ama) "The game is that they both have to have the same to drink, but Pat drinks out of this glass (D) and Bru drinks out of this one (A)."

Ama (NC): Puts some more juice in D to equalize the levels in D and A.

Pat (C): "That's not right."

Bru (C): "She's doing it all wrong. You should take A'."

Ama (NC): Follows Bru's instruction and pours from the bottle to A', equalizing the levels in A and A'.
Bru (C): "Now pour (A' into D)."
Ama (NC): Empties D and pours A' into D.
Pat (C): "There, now they are both the same!"
Exp: "Is there the same everywhere?"
Bru (C): "Yes."
Pat (C): "Yes."
Ama (NC): "No, this one (D) has less," . . . "Yes, the same." (p. 49)

Posttest 1. The conservation-of-liquid task was given again a week after the group session, but with glasses A, A', C, and D this time. These glasses allowed the experimenter to ask questions after pouring liquid from A to C, and from A' to D. Table 3.1 shows the relationship between the children's levels on the pretest and the first posttest. It can be observed that 24 of the 37 children in the experimental group progressed either from nonconservation (NC) to conservation (C) or to the intermediate level (I), or from the intermediate level to conservation. By contrast, only 2 of the 12 children in the control group made progress.

To determine the stability of the experimental group's progress, Perret-Clermont gave the same test a second time, a month after the first posttest.

Posttest 2. Table 3.2 presents the relationship between the levels found on the two posttests. It can be observed that:

16 children maintained the progress they had made.
8 children made further progress after the first posttest.
4 children regressed to their pretest level.

The progress found on the first posttest can thus be said to have been maintained. Eight children continued to make progress after the first posttest—a phenomenon that had already been observed by Inhelder et al. (1974). If chil-

Table 3.1 Development Between the Pretest and Posttest 1 in Experiment I

		Experimental		Control	
		NC on pretest	I on pretest	NC on pretest	I on pretest
	NC	11	0	9	0
Level on posttest 1	I	9	2	1	1
	C	8	7	0	1
	(Total)	(28)	(9)	(10)	(2)

Table 3.2 Experimental Subjects' Levels on Posttests 1 and 2 in
Experiment I

		Level on posttest 1			
		NC	I	C	(Total)
	NC	9	2	0	(11)
Level on posttest 2	I	0	3	2	(5)
	C	2	6	13	(21)
	(Total)	(11)	(11)	(15)	(37)

dren's logic had advanced by *internalization* from the conservers, they would
not have shown such striking progress a month after the first posttest.

To clarify the process of construction more precisely and deeply, Perret-
Clermont analyzed the relationship between the arguments conservers gave
in the posttests and the explanations they had heard during the interaction
session.

Analysis of Children's Arguments.   Perret-Clermont reasoned that if children who
became conservers on a posttest gave arguments that they had not heard during the interaction session, their progress could not be attributed to imitation of
a model. Therefore, if a child became a conserver and justified his or her answer with a compensation argument, for example, she examined the interaction
session looking for a compensation argument the child might have heard.

In well over half of the justifications given by those who became conservers on posttest 1, the argument was not one they had heard during the interaction session. This absence of imitation was a sign of the "grouping," or coordination, of identity, reversibility, and compensation. If conservation had not come
out of this grouping, it would not have been possible for the children to think of
an explanation they had not heard.

Experiment I thus supported the hypothesis that sociocognitive conflict
stimulates the development of logic. However, the findings left several questions unanswered. First, the control group did not have any contact with the
materials or other children between the pretest and the first posttest. What would
have happened if this group had spent the same amount of time interacting with
the materials and other children *without* any sociocognitive conflict? Second,
the conservers were always in the majority in Experiment I. Was the progress
made by the nonconservers at least partly due to pressure exerted by the majority? Third, was the children's progress limited to the conservation of liquid, or
did progress occur in any other area of cognition? To answer these questions,
Perret-Clermont conducted Experiment II.

Perret-Clermont's Experiment II

Experiment II was similar to Experiment I, but the following four kinds of groups were compared (a fifth group, Experimental Group IV, was not large enough to include in this summary):

Experimental Group I: 2C + 1 NC
Experimental Group II: 1C + 2 NC
Experimental Group III: 3 NC
Control Group: 3 NC

The nonconservers were thus in the minority in Experimental Group I, and in the majority in Group II. Experimental Group III and the control group consisted only of nonconservers. There were 5 trios in Group I, 6 trios in Group II, and 3 trios each in Group III and the control group.

In Experiment II, there were no intermediate cases because Perret-Clermont reasoned that the intermediate category by definition consisted of children who were already beginning to "group" logical operations. She thought that the results of the experiment would be more convincing if she eliminated the intermediate cases, who were already well on the way to conservation.

To understand the effects of sociocognitive conflict more broadly and deeply, Perret-Clermont included the following tasks in the pre- and posttests: the conservation of number, matter (clay balls), and length.

Posttests 1 and 2 in Conservation of Liquid.   As can be seen in Table 3.3, progress was made by Experimental Groups I and II, but not by Experimental Group III and the control group. It can therefore be said that children's logic did not

Table 3.3 Progress from Nonconservation on the Pretest to Posttest 1 in Experiment II

		Pretest				
		Experimental				
		Gr. I (1 NC)	Gr. II (2 NC)	Gr. III (3 NC)	Control	(Total)
	NC	1	7	9	7	(24)
Level on posttest 1	I	3	0	0	1	(4)
	C	1	5	0	1	(7)
	(Total)	(5)	(12)	(9)	(9)	(35)

Note: All the subjects in this table were nonconservers on the pretest.

progress if nonconservers interacted only with other nonconservers or if they did not have any experience of sociocognitive conflict.

Was this progress stable? The answer is yes, and one child each in Experimental Groups I and II showed further progress on posttest 2. Regression was not found in Experimental Group I, but it did occur in 2 cases in Experimental Group II.

Experimental Group III is very informative. While this group did not show any progress on posttest 1, 7 of the 9 children progressed between the two posttests. This advance is in sharp contrast with what happened in the control group. Of the 2 children in the control group who showed progress on posttest 1, one later regressed. Only one child who did not show any progress on posttest 1 progressed by the time of posttest 2. It can therefore be said that sociocognitive conflict is beneficial even if the participants are all nonconservers. It can also be said that the nonconservers' progress cannot be attributed to majority pressure exerted by conservers.

Relationship Between Conservation of Number and of Liquid.   The general conclusion reached so far is that if nonconservers experience sociocognitive conflict about amounts of liquid, they are likely to make progress in conservation of liquid. If the effects of sociocognitive conflict were domain-specific, such findings would not be educationally very significant. If, on the other hand, advance in one domain is related to advance in other domains, sociocognitive conflict can be said to contribute to children's development of logic in a general way. To examine the generality of progress in children's logic, Perret-Clermont analyzed the relationship between children's conservation of number on the pretest and the progress they showed on the conservation-of-liquid task. It will be recalled that conservation of number is children's first conservation, showing the first sign of logical "grouping."

At the time of the pretest, Perret-Clermont had 37 children who were nonconservers on the liquid task. (There were 2 who were assigned to Experimental Group IV, which was too small to include in this chapter, as stated before.) The conservation-of-number task was given to the 37 children at the time of the pretest, and 9 of them were found to be conservers, 4 were intermediate, and 24 were nonconservers. The question she posed was: Were the conservers in the number task in the pretest those who made progress on the conservation-of-liquid task?

The answer can be seen in Table 3.4. It shows that not all the children in the intermediate or conserving category on the number task showed progress in posttest 1, but that these children made more progress than nonconservers (8 out of 13 compared with 4 out of 24).

A similar analysis can be seen in Table 3.5 with respect to posttest 2. It can be seen again that although some who did not conserve number made progress

Table 3.4 Relationship Between Initial Level on the Conservation-of-Number Task and Progress in Conservation of Liquid, Posttest 1

		Liquid, posttest 1		
		Progress	No progress	(Total)
Number pretest	NC	4	20	(24)
	I or C	8	5	(13)
	(Total)	(12)	(25)	(37)

by the time of posttest 2 (9 out of 24), it was the intermediate and conservers of number who made the most progress (9 out of 13). These results indicate that, while the relationship between the two is not strong, there is a tendency for those at a certain level of logic to progress in conservation of liquid. In other words, the progress seen on the conservation-of-liquid task appears to show more than specific learning about quantities of liquid.

Relationship Between Conservation of Matter (Clay Balls) and of Liquid. Conservation of matter (clay balls) is generally attained at about the same time as conservation of liquid, beginning at about 7 years of age. Perret-Clermont reasoned that if children show progress on the clay-ball task, this would also be evidence of their development of logic in a general sense because clay does not behave like a liquid. As can be seen in Table 3.6 showing the progress of children in Experimental Groups I and II in posttest 1, the 6 who advanced in the liquid task also advanced in the clay-ball task. Likewise, the 8 who did not progress in one task did not advance in the other task either. Only 3 of the 17 children advanced in the liquid task without advancing in the clay-ball task.

Relationship Between Conservation of Length and of Liquid. Conservation of length (which is described shortly) is generally observed later than conservation of quantity of liquid or clay. Perret-Clermont reasoned that if any progress is observed in conservation of length, this would be highly significant because length was not considered at all in the sociocognitive conflict situation.

Table 3.5 Relationship Between Initial Level on the Conservation-of-Number Task and Progress in Conservation of Liquid, Posttest 2

		Liquid, posttest 2		
		Progress	No progress	(Total)
Number pretest	NC	9	15	(24)
	I or C	9	4	(13)
	(Total)	(18)	(19)	(37)

Table 3.6   Progress Made by Experimental Groups I and II by Posttest 1 in Conservation of Matter (Clay) and Liquid

		Liquid		
		Progress	No progress	(Total)
	Progress	6	0	(6)
Matter	No progress	3	8	(11)
	(Total)	(9)	(8)	(17)

As can be seen in Table 3.7, of the 12 children in all 5 groups who progressed in the conservation-of-liquid task by posttest 1, 6 were either intermediate or conserving in the length task. This finding again confirmed that the sociocognitive conflict the children experienced was not limited to progress on the liquid task.

These experiments were conducted with small samples, and each session took only 10 minutes on average. The outcome, however, is sufficient to suggest that if children engaged in similar debates during 10 years of schooling, their level of logic would be much higher at the end of high school.

Doise and Mugny's Experiment

The most convincing study of the effects of sociocognitive conflict may be that of Doise and Mugny (1981/1984) involving the conservation of length. Since this study was described in detail in Kamii (1989a), only the highlights will be summarized here. This experiment is convincing because the two people who disagreed during the experiment were equally wrong at the same cognitive level. After a session in which they experienced sociocognitive conflict, the children nevertheless demonstrated progress on the posttests.

In the conservation-of-length task, the child is shown two identical sticks approximately 10 cm long and is asked if the two sticks are equally long. The interviewer then places the sticks in visual correspondence as shown in Figure

Table 3.7   Relationship Between Conservation of Length and of Liquid in Posttest 1

		Liquid			
		NC	I	C	(Total)
	NC	23	4	2	(29)
Length	I	1	0	1	(2)
	C	0	1	4	(5)
	(Total)	(24)	(5)	(7)	(36)

3.2a and ascertains the child's belief that the sticks still have the same length. The interviewer then pushes one of the sticks to the right (see Figure 3.2b) and asks the child if one stick is as long as the other, or if one is longer than the other.

Conservers deduce immediately that the two sticks have the same length and explain, "All you did was move this stick, and we can put it back to the way it was before," or "This one sticks out on this side, but the other one sticks out on the other side." Nonconservers, on the other hand, usually focus on the stick that has been pushed and say that that stick is longer because it sticks out. These nonconservers are comparing the two ends on the right-hand side and overlooking the left-hand side. The intermediate cases are in between. They vacillate between conservation and nonconservation or give an answer they cannot justify.

Doise and Mugny's interaction session involved a nonconserver and an adult stooge. In the experiment, two rails were placed in visual correspondence (as in Figure 3.2a), and one of them was pushed to the right (as in Figure 3.2b). When the experimenter asked the child if the two rails had the same length, the nonconserver predictably replied that the top rail was longer. The experimenter then turned to the stooge and asked, "What do you think?" The stooge always gave an answer that contradicted the child's.

The stooge responded differently to the different statements the child made. If the child agreed with the stooge, which was often the case, the stooge shifted to the child's response: "But I changed my mind. I think *you* were right when you said this one [at the top] is longer because it sticks out." If, on the other hand, the child gave the correct answer of equal length, the stooge repeated his wrong answer. At the appropriate time, the experimenter pointed out that there seemed to be a disagreement and asked if the two individuals could "talk this over" and come to an agreement.

The nonconservers who were contradicted by the stooge and argued vigorously with him showed impressive progress on the posttests. Since the posttests consisted at least in part of the conservation-of-*un*equal-length task, the posttests could not be said to reflect the internalization of the correct answer.

This experiment is significant because the arguments of both participants were incorrect. The correct answer had to be constructed out of two lower-level

Figure 3.2. The arrangement of sticks in the conservation-of-length task.

(a)   (b)

relationships, by encompassing the lower-level relationships at a higher level. Sociocognitive conflict is thus useful in stimulating the resolution of a disagreement through the coordination of egocentrically made relationships. In other words, Piaget's constructivism states that logic is *constructed* by constructive abstraction *inside the child*, in interaction with other people, rather than being acquired *from* other people by *internalization*.

In all the experiments described in this chapter, as stated before, the children experienced sociocognitive conflict for only 10 minutes on average. If 10 minutes of interaction can produce such progress in logic, 10 years of compulsory education should accomplish much more than it is today.

SOCIAL INTERACTION IN THE CONSTRUCTION OF SCIENCE

Piaget (Piaget & Garcia, 1983/1989) saw parallels between children's construction of logic and humanity's construction of science. Just as children develop by going through one level after another of being "wrong," science has developed through one level after another of being "wrong." For example, as stated in Chapter 1, scientists constructed the geocentric theory before the heliocentric theory. Newtonian physics was likewise a necessary step toward the invention of quantum physics.

As Piaget (Piaget & Garcia, 1983/1989) pointed out, science is a social enterprise. When a scientist makes a new discovery or invents a new theory, he or she presents it to the scientific community for verification. In the construction of science, there is no authority like a teacher who can judge the truth or falsity of an assertion. In science, truth can be verified only by empirical proof and rigorous logic, and verification can come only from fellow scientists. Debate and sociocognitive conflict among peers are therefore a necessary part of advances in science.

If scientists construct science through debate and sociocognitive conflict, this is an argument for saying that children, too, should be able to construct mathematics through debate and sociocognitive conflict. The experiments reported by Perret-Clermont (1980) and Doise and Mugny (1981/1984) amply support this argument.

A significant point to remember about the construction of science is that science never goes back to an earlier theory. Once humanity accepted the heliocentric theory, it could not go back to the geocentric theory. Likewise, once children become solid conservers, they cannot go back to nonconservation. There are regressions when children are in process of constructing their logic, but once logical operations are "grouped" solidly, conservers do not go back to nonconservation. In mathematics education, if children construct their own knowledge solidly through debate and critical thinking, the need for repeated review no longer arises at the beginning of every school year.

CONCLUSION

Many educators now believe that children should interact in "cooperative groups," and many believe in "cooperative learning." However, when we ask them exactly how "cooperation" facilitates the learning of mathematics, they do not have a precise rationale. Johnson, Johnson, Holubec, and Roy (1994), for example, made the following statement:

> Class members are split into small groups after receiving instruction from the teacher. They then work through the assignment until all group members have successfully understood and completed it. Cooperative efforts result in students striving for mutual benefit so that all group members benefit from each other's efforts. (p. 3)

This view states that students *receive* instruction *from* the teacher, and that cooperative efforts result in *mutual benefit*. In Piaget's constructivism, by contrast, children *construct* their logico-mathematical knowledge rather than receiving it. Cooperation is not just for *mutual benefit*, but for mutual criticism and control because other people oblige decentering and the construction of higher-level logic, by constructive abstraction.

Agreeing and disagreeing with others are indispensable not only for children's cognitive development but also for their sociomoral development according to Piaget (1932/1965). Sociomoral autonomy is the topic to which we turn in the next chapter.

Part II

GOALS AND OBJECTIVES

CHAPTER 4

Autonomy: The Aim of Education for Piaget

A long time ago, I (CK) tried to introduce card games such as Double War (see Chapter 11) in a first-grade classroom in Chicago. The teacher of this class assumed that it was her responsibility to control, direct, and police her pupils. To play games, she divided the class into small groups, but the groups quickly dissolved as fights broke out among the children. I concluded that the kind of teaching I advocated was not possible unless the teacher understood the importance of autonomy as the broad aim of education.

The preceding anecdote provides a practical reason for endorsing autonomy in a Piagetian sense. However, autonomy, which was the aim of education for Piaget, has much broader, deeper, and longer-range implications. Those will be discussed later in this chapter and in Chapters 8, 12, and 13, and we begin by discussing what Piaget meant by autonomy.

WHAT IS AUTONOMY?

In common parlance, autonomy means the *right* of an individual or group to be self-governing. For example, when we speak of Palestinian autonomy, we are referring to their political right to make decisions for themselves. In Piaget's theory, however, autonomy means not the right but the *ability* to be self-governing, in the moral as well as the intellectual realm. In a Piagetian sense, autonomy means the ability to decide for oneself between right and wrong in the moral realm, and between truth and untruth in the intellectual realm, by taking relevant factors into account, independently of reward and punishment. Autonomy is the opposite of heteronomy. Heteronomous people are governed by someone else, as they are unable to make judgments for themselves.

Moral Autonomy

An unusual example of moral autonomy is the struggle of Martin Luther King, Jr. for civil rights. King was autonomous enough to take relevant factors into account and to conclude that the laws discriminating against African Americans were unjust and immoral. Convinced of the need to make justice a reality, he worked to end the discriminatory laws, in spite of the police, jails, dogs, water hoses, and threats of assasination used to stop him. Morally autonomous people cannot be manipulated with reward and punishment.

An extreme example of moral heteronomy is the men who served former president Richard Nixon. Nixon's White House aides were governed by Richard Nixon and went along with the Watergate cover-up, expecting to be rewarded by the president for their cover-up efforts.

In *The Moral Judgment of the Child*, Piaget (1932/1965) gave more commonplace examples of autonomy and heteronomy. He interviewed children between the ages of 6 and 14 and asked them whether it was worse to tell a lie to an adult or to another child. Young, heteronomous children consistently replied that it was worse to lie to an adult. When asked why, they explained that adults can tell when a statement is not true. Older children, by contrast, tended to answer that one has to lie to adults sometimes, but it is rotten to do it to other children. When asked for an explanation, the more autonomous children said that breaking the bond of mutual trust is worse than being punished. For autonomous people, lies are bad independently of the reward system, adult authority, and the possibility of being caught.

Piaget (1932/1965) made up many pairs of stories and asked which one of two children was the worse. The following is an example of such a pair:

> A little boy (or a little girl) goes for a walk in the street and meets a big dog who frightens him very much. So then he goes home and tells his mother he has seen a dog that was as big as a cow.

> A child comes home from school and tells his mother that the teacher had given him good marks, but it was not true; the teacher had given him no marks at all, either good or bad. Then his mother was very pleased and rewarded him. (p. 148)

Young children systematically manifested the morality of heteronomy by saying that it was worse to say "I saw a dog as big as a cow." Why was it worse? Because dogs are never as big as cows and adults do not believe such stories. Older, more autonomous children, on the other hand, tended to say that it was worse to say "The teacher gave me good marks," *because* this lie is more believable.

Figure 4.1 shows the developmental relationship between autonomy and heteronomy. In this figure, time is represented along the horizontal axis from birth to adulthood. The vertical axis represents the proportion of autonomy in relation to heteronomy, from 0% to 100% autonomy. The dotted line shows the ideal development of an individual. All young children begin by being heteronomous and unable to judge between right and wrong. Ideally, they become increasingly autonomous, and correspondingly less heteronomous, as they grow

Figure 4.1. Developmental relationship between autonomy and heteronomy.

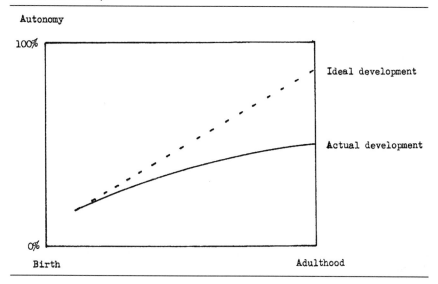

Autonomy

100%

Ideal development

Actual development

0%

Birth   Adulthood

older. To the extent that children become able to govern themselves, they are governed less by other people.

In reality, most adults did not develop in this ideal way. The great majority stopped developing at a low level (see the solid line in Figure 4.1). Piaget (1948/ 1973) noted that it is a rare adult who has developed the morality of autonomy. This observation can easily be confirmed in our daily life. Newspapers are full of stories about corruption in government and about theft, assault, drug trafficking, and murder.

What Makes Some Adults Morally More Autonomous?   The important question for educators and parents is what causes some children to become morally more autonomous adults. Piaget's answer to this question was that adults reinforce children's natural heteronomy when they use reward and punishment, and they stimulate the development of autonomy when they exchange points of view with children.

When a child tells a lie, for example, the adult might deprive him or her of dessert or make the child write 50 times, "I will not lie." The adult can also refrain from punishing the child and, instead, look him or her straight in the eye with skepticism and affection and say, "I really can't believe what you are saying because . . . [and give the reason]. And when you tell me something next time, I am not sure I'll be able to believe you. I want you to go to your room [or your seat] and think about what you might do next time to be believed." Children want to be believed, and when they are confronted with this kind of statement, they are likely, over time, to construct from within the conviction that it is best in the long run for people to deal honestly with each other.

In general, punishment leads to three possible outcomes. The first outcome is calculation of risks. Children who are punished may learn to calculate their chances of getting caught the next time and the price they might have to pay if they are caught. The second possible outcome is, interestingly, the opposite of the first one, namely, blind obedience. Sensitive children will do anything to avoid being punished. Their compliance gives the impression that punishment works. The third outcome of punishment is a derivative of the second, namely, revolt. Many "good," model children surprise us eventually by beginning to cut classes, take drugs, and engage in other acts that characterize delinquency. Their reason for switching to these behaviors is that they are tired of living for their parents and teachers and think the time has come for them to start living for themselves.

Piaget was realistic enough to say that it is sometimes necessary to impose restrictions on children. However, he made an important distinction between *punishments* and *sanctions by reciprocity*. Depriving the child of dessert for telling a lie is an example of a punishment, as the relationship between a lie and dessert is completely arbitrary. Telling the child that we cannot believe what he or she said and sending the child to his or her room to think about it is an example of a sanction by reciprocity. Sanctions by reciprocity are directly related to the act we want to change and to the adult's point of view. They have the effect of motivating the child to construct rules of conduct from within, through the coordination of viewpoints.

In *The Moral Judgment of the Child*, Piaget gave several examples of sanctions by reciprocity. Four of them are discussed below.

1. *Exclusion from the group.* When a group is listening to a story and a child disrupts the group, teachers often say, "You can either stay here without bothering the rest of us, or I must ask you to go to the book corner and read by yourself." Whenever possible, the child must be given the possibility of deciding when he or she can behave well enough to return to the group. Mechanical "time out" serves only as punishment, and children who have served the required time often feel perfectly free to commit the same misdeed again.

2. *Appeal to the direct and material consequence of the act.* An example of this type of sanction has already been given in connection with children's lies. Another example is to say to a child, "If you play in the hall when I think you're running an errand, I won't be able to trust you to run an errand next time."

3. *Depriving the child of the thing he or she has misused.* When children fail to mop up the water under the water table, for example, teachers sometimes say that the water table cannot be used by those children. The teacher then negotiates with each child the right to play with water when the child knows that this right has to be earned.

4. *Restitution.* For example, if a young child spills paint on the floor, an appropriate reaction may be to say, "Would you like me to help you clean it up?" Later in the year, it may be enough just to ask, "What do you need to do?"

One day, in a kindergarten class, a child came up to the teacher crying because his art project had been damaged. The teacher turned to the class and said that she wanted the person who broke the object to stay with her during recess so that she could help him or her repair it. The child responsible for the breakage could see the victim's point of view and was encouraged to construct for himself the rule of restitution and of being careful. When children are not afraid of being punished, they are perfectly willing to come forward and make restitution. The teacher helped the child repair the broken object and told him that next time something similar happened, she wanted him to tell her so that she could help him fix the object.

Piaget pointed out that all the preceding sanctions by reciprocity can quickly degenerate into punishments if a relationship of mutual respect and affection does not exist between the adult and the child. Mutual respect is, in fact, essential for the child's development of autonomy. The child who feels respected for the way he or she thinks and feels is more likely to be respectful of the way other people think and feel.

Piaget's theory about how children learn moral values is fundamentally different from empiricist and commonsense views. The commonsense view is that children acquire moral values by *internalizing* them from the environment. According to Piaget, children acquire moral values not by internalizing them from the environment but by *constructing* them from the inside, through interaction with other people. For example, no child is taught that it is worse to tell a lie to an adult than to another child. Yet young children construct this belief out of what they have been told. Likewise, no child is taught that it is worse to say "I saw a dog as big as a cow" than to say "The teacher gave me good marks." But young children make such judgments by putting into relationships the things they have been told. Fortunately, most of them go on to construct more complex relationships and end up believing that it is worse to say "The teacher gave me good marks."

Most of us have been brought up heteronomously with punishments. To the extent that we also had the possibility of coordinating viewpoints with others, we had the possibility of becoming more autonomous and independent of the clutches of the reward system.

Intellectual Autonomy

In the intellectual realm, too, autonomy means the ability to govern one-self by being able to take relevant factors into account, and heteronomy means being governed by someone else. An outstanding example of intellectual autonomy is Copernicus, or the inventor of any other revolutionary theory in the history of science. Copernicus developed the heliocentric theory when everyone else believed that the sun revolved around the earth. He was even ridiculed off the stage but was autonomous enough to remain convinced of the truth of his own idea. An intellectually heteronomous person, by contrast, unquestioningly believes what he or she is told, including illogical conclusions, slogans, and propaganda.

A more common example of intellectual autonomy is a child who used to believe in Santa Claus. When she was about 6 years old, she surprised her mother one day by asking, "How come Santa Claus uses the same wrapping paper as we do?" Her mother's "explanation" satisfied her for a few minutes, but she soon came up with another question: "How come Santa Claus has the same handwriting as Daddy?" This child had her own way of putting things into relationships, which was different from what she had been taught.

Children may accept and internalize specific, surface bits of information for a while, but they are not passive vessels that merely hold what is poured into their heads. They construct a more general and deeper framework of knowledge by creating and coordinating relationships. When the girl put Santa Claus into relationship with everything else she knew, she began to think that something was wrong somewhere. When children are not convinced by what they are told, they rack their brains to make sense of "facts."

Unfortunately, children are not encouraged to think autonomously in school. Teachers use reward and punishment in the intellectual realm, too, to get children to give "correct" responses. An example of this process is the use of worksheets. In first-grade arithmetic, if a child writes "4 + 4 = _7_ ," most teachers mark this answer wrong. The result of this kind of teaching is that when we walk around a first-grade classroom while children are working on worksheets, and stop to ask individual children how they got particular answers, they typically react by grabbing their erasers, even if their answers are perfectly correct! Already in first grade, many children have learned to distrust their own thinking. Children who are thus discouraged from thinking critically and autonomously will construct less knowledge in the long run than those who are confident and do their own thinking.

If a child says that 4 + 4 = 7, a better reaction is to ask, "How did you get 7?" Children often correct themselves as they try to explain their reasoning to someone else. The child who tries to explain his or her reasoning has to decenter and consider the other person's perspective in order to make sense. This coordination of points of view often leads to a higher level of logic, as we showed in Chapter 3 with experimental evidence. In the next section on autonomy as the aim of education, we argue further that we must replace the memorization of correct bits of knowledge with an education that emphasizes the honest, critical exchange of viewpoints to arrive at truth.

AUTONOMY AS THE AIM OF EDUCATION

Figure 4.2 is our interpretation of Piaget's (1948/1973) aim of education, autonomy, in relation to the goals of most educators and the public today. In the shaded part of the circle labeled "the goals of most educators and the public," we include the unintended goals that resulted in our memorizing words in school just to pass one test after another. All of us who succeeded in school achieved that success by memorizing an enormous number of words without understanding or caring about them. The shaded part also includes the moral heteronomy that schools typically reinforce with rewards, punishments, and ready-made rules.

In the intersection with the circle labeled "autonomy," we put things we did not forget after each test. Our ability to read and write, to do some arithmetic, to read maps and charts, and to situate events in history are examples of what we learned in school that we did not forget after cramming for tests. When

Figure 4.2. The relationship between autonomy as the aim of education and the goals of most educators and the public.

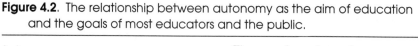

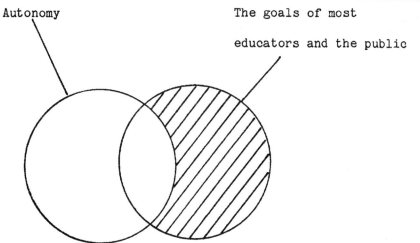

moral and intellectual autonomy is our aim, educators work hard to increase the area of overlap between the two circles.

EDUCATIONAL IMPLICATIONS

On the first day of school, children are often greeted with a list of ready-made rules such as "No talking when the teacher is talking." Some teachers even post rules specifying what the punishment will be for each offense. For the development of children's autonomy, however, it is much better to let problems emerge. The teacher can then say, "It bothers me when somebody talks while I am trying to talk to the group. Was anybody else bothered that you couldn't hear what I was trying to say?"

Once everybody realizes that talking bothers many people including the speaker, the teacher can ask, "Is there anything we can do to solve this problem?" Children are likely to think and suggest a variety of solutions, such as sending culprits to the principal's office. The teacher can then say, as a member of the community like every other member, that he or she would not vote to send people to the principal because the principal has nothing to do with the problem under discussion.

Class meetings to discuss common problems are much better than the imposition of ready-made rules. The reason is that, in class meetings, children have a chance to think about each problem, its cause(s), and who is affected by it. If the teacher does not suggest a solution, the responsibility of solving the problem falls on the children. A rule that is suggested by children and accepted by majority vote is much more likely to be respected by the group than the same rule imposed by the teacher.

Class meetings are good not only for children's sociomoral development but also for their development of logic. For example, when children think about possible solutions to a problem, they think about what is relevant and what is not. The principal and parents, for instance, are irrelevant to the problem of who talks in class. Children also have to think about the conditions under which talking is OK and not OK. This judgment can be made by putting all the parties' perspectives into relationships. Children thus learn to decenter their egocentric point of view and try to coordinate it logically with the perspectives of others.

Today's enormous social problems such as the drug problem, killings in schools, teenage pregnancies, and the spread of AIDS are caused largely by people's inability to take relevant factors into account in making decisions. When they take drugs, people are *deciding* to take drugs. When they shoot others, people are likewise *deciding* to shoot others. When they have unsafe sex or smoke cigarettes, people are also *deciding* to engage in these activities. People who can take relevant factors into account in making decisions are likely to make wiser decisions than those who are blind to relevant factors.

Schools are now dealing with these problems from outside the child, each as a separate problem. For example, schools are using metal detectors to prevent the use of guns. For the prevention of drug abuse, there are locker searches and programs like D.A.R.E., and separate programs exist for the prevention of AIDS. Schools also institute punitive measures that motivate children to sneak better. The morality of autonomy can develop only from inside the child. This takes time, and it can develop only through discussions and decentering in the context of mutual respect.

Moral education goes on every minute of the school day, whether or not we are aware of this fact. When we threaten children with punishment, we reinforce their heteronomy. When we manipulate them with bribes, we likewise reinforce their heteronomy. Principles of teaching flowing from autonomy as the aim of education are discussed more fully in Chapters 8, 12, and 13. We hope to show there that when educators embrace autonomy as the aim of education, everything we do from moment to moment all day long is affected by this goal. The most important principle is to ask children to make decisions for themselves by taking relevant factors into account. Children learn to make decisions by making decisions. They sometimes make bad decisions but learn to make better ones by living through the consequences of the bad decisions they make.

It may seem more efficient to give ready-made rules and truths for children to internalize. To most educators and the public, education reform means working much harder at putting knowledge into children's minds. For us, however, reform necessitates a fundamental change in the way educators think about how children acquire knowledge and moral values.

CHAPTER 5

Addition as an Objective

Adding single-digit numbers is natural for young children. When they construct number concepts, addition is part of this construction because all numbers are created by the repeated addition of *one*. For example, *seven* is made by doing 1+1+1+1+1+1+1, and adding *one* to it makes *eight*, and so on.

Already in the late 1970s and early 1980s, researchers such as Carpenter and Moser (Carpenter & Moser, 1979, 1982) and Ibarra and Lindvall (1982) were publishing data demonstrating that most kindergartners and first graders who had not received any math instruction in school could produce correct answers to questions such as the following:

> Wally had 3 pennies. His father gave him 8 more pennies. How many pennies does Wally have altogether? (Carpenter & Moser, 1979, p. 18)

Neither Carpenter and Moser nor Ibarra and Lindvall explained why 5- and 6-year-olds can solve these kinds of problems without any instruction. From a Piagetian perspective, however, it is clear that since the source of logico-mathematical knowledge is inside the child, children can be expected to construct number concepts and invent arithmetic, through constructive abstraction. Historically, our ancestors invented arithmetic to solve practical problems, such as keeping track of sheep and figuring out when to plant seeds. Therefore, young children, too, can be expected to invent arithmetic out of everyday living. They spontaneously count and add cookies as well as people, chairs, spoons, forks, and so on.

This chapter discusses addition as an objective rooted in children's development. In the first part, we discuss problems with addends up to 10 and go on to the second part dealing with addends above 10. The former begins with a general discussion that applies to all four arithmetical operations—the desirability of starting with word problems; the view that sums, differences, products, and quotients are not *facts*; and the nature of memory. The second part dealing with addends greater than 10 emphasizes the harmfulness of teaching the algorithm of aligning the columns and adding each one.

ADDITION WITH ADDENDS UP TO 10

Authors of textbooks usually introduce computational problems first and later present word problems for children to *apply* their knowledge of computation. In a Piagetian approach, the sequence is the opposite.

Starting with Contents

As stated earlier, mathematics historically developed when our ancestors wanted to solve practical problems. The best place for today's children to invent arithmetic is likewise in dealing with situations in daily living, since arithmetic is the logico-arithmetization of reality. For example, if young children already have some cookies and get some more, they know that they will have more cookies. They have the logic of addition but need to make it more precise by modifying "some cookies and some more" into "3 cookies and 5 more," for example. The addition of contentless numbers such as 3 and 5 develops out of children's thinking about contents (e.g., cookies, pennies, cups, and so on).

Counting-all and Counting-on

Addition is the mental action (constructive abstraction) of combining two wholes to create a higher-order whole in which the previous wholes become two parts. The two wholes we start with may be 3 and 5, for example (see Figure 5.1a). The sum of 8 is a higher-order whole in which the 3 and the 5 become two parts.

As explained in Chapter 1 in connection with class inclusion, part-whole relationships are very hard for young children to make. It is, therefore, not surprising to observe two phenomena when kindergartners and first graders add numbers.

The first one is the behavior of counting-all as opposed to counting-on. In counting-on, children add 3 and 5, for example, by counting on fingers from 3 saying, "Four-five-six-seven-eight." In counting-all, by contrast, they count 3 fingers, then 5 other fingers, and count all of them all over, starting from "one" ("One-two-three-four-five-six-seven-eight").

Children who count-all *need to* count from one for the following reason. When they count 3 fingers, "three" constitutes a whole. When they subsequently count 5 other fingers, "five" constitutes another whole. Because it is hard for them to think simultaneously about the two wholes they have made and a higher-order whole, they "homogenize" the "three" and the "five" by changing both to "$1 + 1 + 1 + 1 + 1 + 1 + 1 + 1$." By thus eliminating the original wholes, they obviate the difficulty of thinking hierarchically.

Figure 5.1. The addition (a) of two mutually exclusive wholes and (b) of two wholes that are not mutually exclusive.

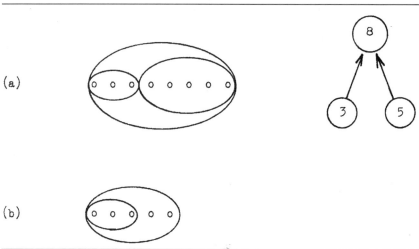

(a)

(b)

For educators who think that addition is only a skill (like penmanship, typing, and swimming), counting-on is merely a skill and, therefore, a legitimate objective. For us, however, counting-on is not a valid objective because addition is a *mental* action (constructive abstraction) rather than a motor skill. The behavioral objective of counting-on goes against the way many young children think. When they outgrow the need to count-all, they *will* start counting-on independently of external pressure.

The second phenomenon related to part-whole relationships can sometimes be observed when young children have been taught the technique of using counters to produce correct answers. Some children get the answer of 5 for "3 + 5" by counting out 3 counters for the first addend and 5 counters for the second addend including the 3 already counted, and counting all the objects. As shown in Figure 5.1b, these children have not constructed the logic of addition and do not know that the 3 and the 5 are *mutually exclusive*. When they construct the logic of addition, through constructive abstraction, they stop making this kind of error.

Addition "Facts" versus the Goal of Building a Network of Numerical Relationships

Most math educators speak of 3 + 5 = 8 as an "addition fact." From a Piagetian point of view, however, there is no such thing as an "addition fact." A fact is empirically observable, and numbers are not observable, as explained in

Chapter 1. Three counters are observable, but the number "three" is not. The counters are an example of physical knowledge, but three is a relationship, made by constructive abstraction, and is logico-mathematical knowledge. If three is not observable, $3 + 5 = 8$ is not observable either.

Sums up to $9 + 9 = 18$ or $10 + 10 = 20$ are often referred to as "addition facts." If $9 + 9 = 18$ were a fact, $19 + 999,999 = 1,000,018$ should also be a fact. However, the latter is apparently not a fact according to most math educators.

If a first grader writes "5" as the answer to $3 + 5$ as we saw earlier, this child usually does not think that this answer is a logical impossibility. Later, however, when the child's logic advances, his or her answer may be incorrect, but it will not be the same as, or smaller than, one of the addends. Addition grows out of children's own logic and is not a "fact" that exists in the external world. The objective of "knowing addition facts," which is often advocated by educators, is therefore not a valid objective.

In the first edition of *Young Children Reinvent Arithmetic*, the objective given for single-digit addition was that children "engage in the mental action of operating on numbers and remember the results of these actions" (Kamii, 1985, p. 65). This objective was too narrow and still too much like knowing "addition facts." We now prefer to conceptualize our objective as children's construction of a network of numerical relationships such as the example in Figure 5.2.

As can be seen in Figure 5.2, there are many ways to think about "seven," for example. Seven is half of 14, 2 more than 5, and 3 less than 10, which in turn is the same as $5 + 5$. Seven is also 1 more than 6, and 6 can be made with $3 + 3$, $4 + 2$, and $5 + 1$. Of all these relationships, most first graders know only $5 + 5 = 10$ and $5 + 1 = 6$ at the beginning of the school year. *Our goal in single-digit addition is that children become able to think flexibly about numbers and construct a network of numerical relationships.* Note that this network includes not only addition but also subtraction and the beginning of multiplication and division.

The Nature of Memory

Many math educators think that children are like computers that store and retrieve information. According to Piaget's theory of memory (Piaget & Inhelder, 1968/1973), however, children "read" "facts" differently at different levels of development. For example, a car is not the same object at ages 5, 10, 15, and 20. If they read facts differently at different levels of development, it follows that they remember different facts at different levels of development.

Children "read" different "facts" off reality because each child interprets what is observable by assimilating it to the knowledge he or she brings to each situation. In other words, a fact is always a construction of an individual at his or her level of development. Memory is therefore a reconstruction of an earlier construction.

Figure 5.2. An example of a network of numerical relationships.

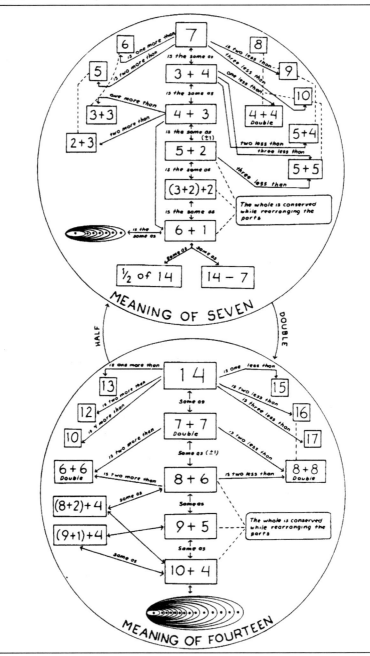

Source: From *Learning from Children*, by Ed Labinowicz; Copyright © 1985 by Dale Seymour Publications. Reprinted by permission.

The following study illustrates this point (Piaget & Inhelder, 1968/1973). The children were shown the model that can be seen in Figure 5.3 and were asked to recreate it from memory by arranging counters or drawing them. Four levels of immediate recall were found.

Materials.   A model (shown in Figure 5.3) consisting of three rows of blue chips glued onto cardboard (3 and 3 in row A; 1, 2, and 3 in row B; and 1 and 5 in row C); 6 red chips; a large number of chips of a third color (at least 80); paper and pencil.

Figure 5.3. The materials used in the memory task.

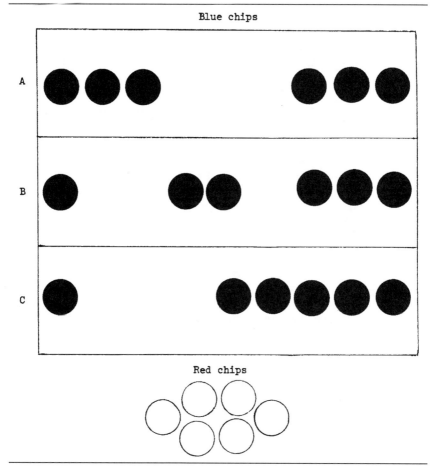

Procedure

A. Comparing the quantity in the three rows (This part can be omitted to simplify the task, and the interviewer can go directly to Part B below.)
    1. The child was first asked to cover up all the blue chips in row B by putting a red one on each blue chip of the model.
    2. He or she was then asked whether it was possible to cover up all the blue chips in row A with the same red ones. After giving an answer, the child was asked to verify it.
    3. The same procedure as "2" above was repeated for row C.
    4. The child was asked:
        If R (the number of red chips) = B (the number in row B).
        If R (the number of red chips) = A (the number in row A).
        If R (the number of red chips) = C (the number in row C).
        If A = B = C.
B. Recall of the model from memory
    The child was asked to "take a good look" at the model because "when you say you are ready, I'm going to take this [model] away and ask you to make one just like this [model]." The model was then removed, and the child was asked for (a) a verbal description and a drawing of the model and/or (b) a reproduction with chips. The model was never shown again after this exposure, and the child was asked to do (a) and/or (b) two more times: a week later and after several months.
C. The conservation-of-number task
    During the second session (a week after exposure to the model) the child was given the conservation-of-number task with 8–10 eggs and egg-cups.

Findings

The 29 children interviewed, who ranged in age from 4-0 (4 years 0 months) to 6-6, were grouped into the following four categories according to three criteria—the numerical equality of the three rows, the coincidence of the extremities, and the subdivision of the rows into subgroups.

Level 1. When children were about age 4, the rows differed greatly in number (12, 8, and 9, for example, or 4, 13, and 15), and their extremities were uneven. Most of the rows were divided into subsets, but the space between chips varied from one subset to another.

Level 2. The characteristics of this level were the opposite of the previous level's. The children became concerned with the equality of the rows, but they judged equality globally by the spatial frontiers of the extremities. They did not make subsets and made long rows of 15, 13, and 13; or even of 21, 26, and 23; or short ones of 7, 5, and 6.

Level 3. The children showed progress toward numerical equality by making two of the three rows the same in number (4, 4, and 8, for example, or 5, 5, and 8). They made the extremities of the rows even, like the Level-2 children, but, unlike Level-2 children, made subgroups. However, neither the sets nor the subsets were numerically the same as the model. The children divided a row of 5 into 1 and 4, for example, or a row of 4 into 1 and 3, remembering the general idea of subsets, and not the exact numbers.

Level 4. The criterion for this level was the numerical equality of all three rows. Only one child, the oldest, reproduced the model exactly. The other seven at Level 4 gave 3 + 3, 2 + 4, and 1 + 5; or 3 + 3, 1 + 4 + 1, and 1 + 5, for example.

The preceding levels of immediate recall were closely related to levels of development in logico-mathematical knowledge as evidenced by the conservation task. Five of the 6 children at the lowest level on the memory task were also at the lowest level on the conservation task. The 14 solid conservers divided themselves into Levels 3 and 4 in immediate recall. They remembered either that all three rows had 6 chips or that two of the three rows had the same number.

The relationship between level of numerical thinking and level of recall can also be seen in children's ability to notice and/or deduce that A = B = C. The percentages of children who said that the numbers in the three rows were the same were 0, 50, 88, and 100, respectively, at Levels 1, 2, 3, and 4 of the memory task.

The levels found in the memory task again support Piaget's (1967/1971) statement that we never see empirical "facts" or "stimuli" as they are "out there" in external reality. A fact is always an assimilation (interpretation). It follows that even in immediate recall, children often remember empirical facts that are different from what has been shown. An "input" is therefore not a simple recording of facts.

An especially interesting phenomenon emerged in long-term memory. Two patterns that did not exist in the model appeared among 45% of the children several months later, namely, *seriation* (6, 5, 4, 3, 2, and 1 [in six rows]; or 8, 7, and 6 [in three rows]) and *symmetry* (4, 1, 4; 2, 1, 2; and 3, 1, 3). The appearance of these patterns is highly significant and attests to the human mind's tendency to organize knowledge by putting bits of information into relationships. Knowledge is indeed not a collection of bits of specific information, and memory is not the mere retrieval of facts that have been stored.

The educational implication of Piaget's theory of memory is that it is important for children to construct sums through their own mental actions. Sums can be memorized in the same way that nonsense syllables can be memorized. However, nonsense syllables do not become part of our long-term memory, and memorized numbers do not become part of our number sense or network of numerical relationships (illustrated in Figure 5.2). Relationships such as 3 + 3 = 1 + 2 + 3 = 1 + 5 are remembered easily when they are rooted deeply in children's logic and remembered through their intrinsic motivation. Our view is that children construct a network of numerical relationships that supports their memory of specific sums.

The Sequence of Objectives

In most first-grade textbooks, objectives in addition are defined by the magnitude of the sum. The first objective may be sums up to 10, and the next objective may be sums up to 18. Objectives continue to be sequenced in this way in spite of the research that showed a quarter of a century ago that difficulty depends on the size of the *addends* (Suydam & Weaver, 1975). For example, 5 + 1 = 6 is easier to remember than 3 + 2 = 5 (a smaller sum). Likewise, 5 + 5 = 10 and 10 + 10 = 20 are easier to remember than 3 + 4 = 7 (a smaller sum).

Our sequence of objectives is based on the addends and findings from research that have been repeatedly confirmed since the publication of *Young Children Reinvent Arithmetic* (Kamii, 1985). As can be seen in the first edition of this book, Georgia DeClark's first graders played math games for about 50 minutes every day during the 1980–81 school year and were never told that they had to work fast or remember sums. They were never given any timed tests.

I (CK) interviewed the first graders individually in October, January, April, and June of the 1980–81 school year, giving them problems with addends up to 6. Table 5.1 gives the percentages of students who gave the correct sum within two seconds of seeing the addends. Table 5.2 gives the findings with addends up to 10 presented only in June.

In Table 5.1, the combinations of addends are arranged in order of difficulty at the time the test was first given in October. At the top are the easiest combinations (known by 96% of the children), and the combination at the bottom is the hardest. It can be observed from this table that progress was made on all the items throughout the year, demonstrating that children can learn sums without worksheets, timed tests, or pressure. It can also be observed that the combinations that were relatively easy at the beginning of the year remained relatively easy throughout the year. Others such as 4 + 3, 3 + 4, 5 + 6, and 6 + 5 were difficult at the beginning and remained relatively difficult at the end of the year.

Table 5.1 Percentage of First Graders Giving the Correct Answer Immediately: Addends 1 to 6

			Oct. $n = 25$	Jan. $n = 26$	April $n = 24$	June, 1981 $n = 24$
(2 + 2)			96%	100%	100%	100%
(5 + 5)			96	100	96	100
(3 + 3)			88	96	96	100
6 + 1	+ 1		80	96	86	100
4 + 1	+ 1		76	88	86	100
(4 + 4)			72	81	96	96
1 + 4	1 +		72	85	71	100
1 + 5	1 +		56	88	83	96
(6 + 6)			28	58	75	88
2 + 3	2 +		28	58	79	100
4 + 2	+ 2		28	50	75	88
3 + 2	+ 2		28	58	71	88
2 + 6	2 +		28	50	63	88
2 + 4	2 +		24	42	67	75
5 + 3			24	35	54	63
6 + 2	+ 2		20	62	63	88
2 + 5	2 +		16	50	67	88
4 + 5			12	31	54	75
5 + 2	+ 2		8	58	75	100
5 + 4			8	46	58	71
5 + 6			8	35	50	50
3 + 4			8	39	46	71
3 + 6			8	35	42	63
6 + 3			4	35	58	79
6 + 5			4	12	50	54
3 + 5			4	35	46	63
4 + 6			4	23	42	67
4 + 3			0	31	42	71

Table 5.2 Percentage of First Graders Giving the Correct Answer
Immediately: Addends 7 to 10

Problem	June, 1981 $n = 24$
9 + 1	100%
7 + 2	100
1 + 10	100
10 + 10	100
2 + 8	88
7 + 3	83
9 + 2	79
9 + 9	63
8 + 5	54
8 + 8	54
7 + 7	50
5 + 7	50
7 + 8	38

The following combinations can be said to be the easiest, confirm-
ing Suydam and Weaver's (1975) review of the research published a long time
ago:

1. The doubles (indicated with ovals in the first column of Table 5.1). Interestingly, 2 + 2 and 5 + 5 were equally easy, and the sequence was
   then 3 + 3, 4 + 4, and 6 + 6. It can be observed in Table 5.2 that 10 + 10
   was much easier than 9 + 9 or 6 + 6, and that 8 + 8 and 7 + 7 were equally
   difficult. Some numbers like 5 and 10 are "friendlier" than others, and
   the sequence of the doubles does not depend entirely on the magnitude of the sum or addends.
2. The combinations in which 1 is added to any number. This is not surprising because any number +1 is simply the next number. Note that
   the sum of 6 and 1 is greater than the sum of 2 and 3, but 6 + 1 is much
   easier than 2 + 3.
3. The combinations in which 2 is added to any number. The ease of this
   combination can be seen in Table 5.1 as well as in Table 5.2. The percentages for 7 + 2, 2 + 8, and 9 + 2 were 79% or higher in June.

A final point that must be made from Table 5.1 concerns children's invention of *commutativity*. For example, 5 + 3 was easier than 3 + 5 in October (24% and 4%, respectively), but their percentages increased to the same level (63%) by the end of the year. This observation confirms Gréco's (1962) finding that children figure out the commutativity of addition around 7 to 8 years of age, as their thought becomes reversible.

The following sequence of objectives is given especially to guide teachers in selecting and modifying the games they present to children. *These objectives are not intended to get children to master one before going on to the next one.*

1. *Adding addends up to 4.* Four seems to be the minimum number necessary to make games such as Double War and Piggy Bank (see Chapter 11) interesting.
2. *Adding addends up to 6.* The basis for this objective is simply that first graders like dice games, and dice go up to 6. If 6 is too big a jump from 4, the teacher may want to change the 6 on a die to another number.
3. *Adding doubles (2 + 2, 3 + 3, etc.) up to 10 + 10.* We define this objective not only because doubles are relatively easy to remember but also because they become anchor points for children to use to solve problems such as 2 + 3, 5 + 6, and so on.
4. *Making 10 with two numbers.* Ten can be made with 9 and 1, 8 and 2, 7 and 3, and so forth. This objective is very important because it facilitates the addition of larger numbers above 5. For example, children can do 8 + 6 more easily if they know 8 + 2 = 10 very well and can change the problem to (8 + 2) + 4.
5. *Partitioning numbers (up to 6, and so on).* Partitioning refers to making two or more parts out of a whole in a variety of ways. For example, 6 can be partitioned into 5 and 1; 2, 3, and 1; 2, 2, and 2; 3 and 3; and so on. In partitioning numbers, children think about numbers in a new way that contributes to their construction of the kind of network illustrated in Figure 5.2.
6. *Adding addends larger than 6.* Many first graders begin to deal with problems such as 7 + 8 by changing it to (8 + 2) + 5, (7 + 3) + 5, or (7 + 7) + 1. However, others know 5 + 5 = 10 but cannot use this knowledge to do 5 + 6. For them 5 + 5 = 10 is an isolated bit of knowledge that has nothing to do with 5 + 6. It is therefore necessary to evaluate children's reasoning before introducing large addends.

Representation with Mathematical Signs

For authors of most textbooks, it seems that the goal of addition is to get children to produce correct written answers to problems such as the following:

$$4 + 2 = \underline{\hspace{1.5cm}}$$

$$\begin{array}{r} 4 \\ \underline{+2} \end{array}$$

$$4 + \underline{\hspace{1cm}} = 6$$

$$\underline{\hspace{1.5cm}} + 2 = 6$$

This emphasis on writing is probably due to authors' belief that children go from the "concrete" to the "semiconcrete" and then to the "abstract" as discussed in Chapter 2. These authors are not aware of the difference between abstraction and representation. To them, children's mastery of mathematical signs is the same thing as the attainment of an abstract level.

For us, by contrast, the heart of mathematics is children's *reasoning* (abstraction), and mathematical signs are only the surface, conventional aspect of arithmetic. Whether the sum is written above, below, or to the right of the addends is only a convention. As explained in Chapter 2, children who are at a high level of abstraction can easily read and write equations (representation).

Georgia DeClark's experience during the 1980–81 school year (Kamii, 1985) illustrates the ease with which children can handle mathematical signs when they are at a high level of abstraction. As a teacher embarking on an experiment believing that she was the only first-grade teacher in the country not using worksheets, Georgia felt insecure about giving only math games to her students. She gave a total of four worksheets to her students during the 1980–81 school year to make sure that they could complete worksheets.

She told her class, for example, that the "4" and the "2" written vertically above the line (or horizontally with a "+" between them) were like 4 dots and 2 dots on two dice. She explained that the students were to write the total of 6 under the line (or after the "="). Each time she gave worksheets, she was reassured that almost all the students could easily complete them. The children who could not complete worksheets were those who could not play games either. She thus became convinced, gradually, that if children's logico-mathematical knowledge is solid, the conventional representation of this knowledge is easy for them.

As explained in Chapter 2, the fact that children can write "6" after "4 + 2 =" does not guarantee that they will be able to read "4 + 2 = 6" correctly understanding the part-whole relationship. The reason for this difficulty was discussed in Chapter 2.

Children who add 4 and 2 in a game are free to think about such combinations as "4, 2, and 6." By contrast, worksheets interfere with children's freedom to think about and remember such combinations. Some have to think hard to know how to write "6." Children who are taught with worksheets do learn sums, but this learning takes place *in spite of* the worksheets.

Children who are not required to write answers are also free to exchange remarks such as "I got 6, too, but with a 3 and a 3." When they roll a 2 and a 4, they are likewise free to invent commutativity and say that 2 + 4 becomes easier when they change the problem to 4 + 2.

Finally, for authors of most textbooks and achievement tests, missing addends are one of the objectives of first-grade arithmetic. For reasons given in Chapter 2, we believe that missing addends are not a valid objective for first graders.

ADDITION WITH ADDENDS ABOVE 10

Authors of most textbooks recommend that place value be taught in first grade with bundles of 10 toothpicks or straws and/or base-10 blocks or Unifix cubes. Once place value has been taught, according to these authors, first graders can learn to add numbers above 10 as long as "regrouping" ("carrying") is not required. This instruction specifies that the columns be aligned and that the ones be added before the tens.

In Chapter 2, we explained why traditionally instructed first graders rarely construct the idea of *one ten*. If children have not constructed the idea of *one ten* (through constructive abstraction), they cannot possibly represent this idea that they do not have. This is why most first graders cannot understand place value.

Research on Place Value

Our research on place value began with a simplification of the procedure developed by Mieko Kamii (1980, 1981, 1982). With samples of children 4 to 9 years of age, M. Kamii found in the Boston area that the proportion of children who thought the "1" in "16" meant *ten* was 13% at age 7, 18% at age 8, and 42% at age 9.

My (CK) first interview with a simplified procedure took place in a Chicago public school. The class was the highest-level group of first graders divided into three ability groups. The procedure was the following:

1. I put 16 chips out and asked the child to count them and to make a drawing of "all these." The children made drawings either in a line or in a bunch as shown in Figure 5.4a.
2. The child was asked to write "sixteen with numbers" on the same sheet to show that there were 16 chips.

3. The child was asked what "this part" meant as I circled the "6" in "16" as shown in Figure 5.4b. The answer was to be indicated by circling some of the chips drawn on the paper.
4. The child was asked what "this part" meant as I circled the "1" in "16" as shown in Figure 5.4c. The answer was again to be indicated by circling some of the chips drawn on the paper.
5. Finally, the child was asked what "the whole thing" meant as I circled the "16" and probed into the relationships among "16," "6," and "1." For example, when a child circled the chips as shown in Figure 5.4c, I asked why "these" (the six chips circled) and "this" (the one circled) were circled but not "these" (the 9 leftover chips).

In spite of all the hours spent with bundles of straws and words such as "2 tens and 3 ones," none of the children in the entire class in Chicago said that the "1" in "16" stood for 10. Details of the findings can be found in Kamii (1985).

One evening at the University of Illinois at Chicago, I talked about Mieko Kamii's research and mine in a graduate class. Georgia DeClark, with whom I later wrote *Young Children Reinvent Arithmetic* (1985), was in this class and reacted with the following remarks: (a) I am not really convinced by your findings because I have been teaching place value successfully for 5 years, and (b) I have to teach place value anyway because it is part of the curriculum I am expected to cover.

This was an ideal situation for an experiment because the teacher believed that she could teach place value. I suggested to Georgia that she teach place value to her group of first graders and allow me to give a posttest when she was sure the children had learned it. Georgia agreed and invited me to come and observe the lessons she gave.

Figure 5.4. Children's understanding of the "1" and the "6" in "16."

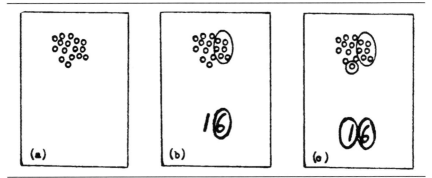

I had observed many first graders in similar lessons, but Georgia's class was superior. Her children hardly ever made an error. They came up to the board, drew circles around groups of ten objects, wrote the correct numerals, and correctly interpreted two-digit numerals.

When Georgia was confident that the children had mastered place value, she invited me to give the posttest. I sat in a corner of her classroom and asked one child after another to come, so that Georgia could watch individual children if she wanted to. The number of children who said that the "1" in "16" stood for 10 was zero!

I became curious about older children in the same school and the junior high school they went to afterward and decided to test students in grades 4, 6, and 8. The proportion of children who circled 10 chips to show what the "1" in "16" meant was 51% in grade 4 (n = 35), 60% in grade 6 (n = 48), and 78% in grade 8 (n = 41). These schools were in an affluent Chicago suburb. When I discussed the findings with two math teachers in the junior high school, they were not surprised. Some children never seem to get place value, they said.

I later changed the task and began to ask children to show chips rather than to circle chips in their drawings. The percentages found in the Chicago suburb were confirmed again and again in suburbs of Birmingham, Alabama. Similar findings have also been reported by other researchers in many other parts of the United States.

How Algorithms "Unteach" Place Value

When I wrote my books on first- and second-grade arithmetic (Kamii, 1985, 1989a), I did not know that algorithms such as those of "carrying" and "borrowing" "untaught" place value. By the time I wrote about third-grade arithmetic (Kamii, 1994), however, it became clear that these rules are harmful to children's numerical reasoning. Chapter 3 of this 1994 book is entitled "The Harmful Effects of Algorithms" and gives many data supporting this conclusion. Only one example is presented below to explain how algorithms "unteach" place value.

Findings from Interviews of Second Graders.   In individual interviews, I asked children in three classes of second graders to solve the following problem without pencil and paper: 7 + 52 + 186. All the classes were heterogeneous and comparable, and the interviews were conducted at the end of the school year. One of the teachers had taught algorithms, but not the other two. However, only the last column of Table 5.3 is labeled "No algorithms" because only one of the two teachers called parents when an algorithm had been taught at home. The middle column, labeled "Some algorithms taught at home," indicates that some parents in this class taught these rules.

Table 5.3 Answers to 7 + 52 + 186 Given by Three Classes of Second
Graders in May 1990

Algorithms $n = 17$	Some algorithms taught at home $n = 19$	No algorithms $n = 20$
9308		
1000		
989		
986		
938	989	
906	938	
838	810	
295	356	617
		255
		246
245 (12%)	245 (26%)	245 (45%)
		243
		236
		235
200	213	138
198	213	—
30	199	—
29	133	—
29	125	—
—	114	
—	—	
	—	
	—	
	—	

Note: Dashes indicate that the child declined to try to work the problem.

It can be seen in Table 5.3 that the "no-algorithms" class produced the greatest percentage of correct answers (45%) at the end of second grade, and that the "algorithms" class produced the smallest percentage (12%). The class in between came out in between (26%). These findings about the proportion of children giving the correct answer demonstrated only that those who had been taught algorithms did not do very well. By analyzing the *in*correct answers the children gave, I began to understand the harmful effects of algorithms.

All the incorrect answers given in each class are listed in Table 5.3, with two dotted lines in the middle to indicate a range that can be considered reasonable. For example, the incorrect answer of 255 is not outlandish, but 295 is (in relation to the addends). Likewise, the incorrect answer of 235 is not unreasonable, but 138 is unreasonable because it is smaller than one of the addends. It can be seen in Table 5.3 that the algorithms class produced the greatest num-

ber of unreasonable answers. The answers in the 900s were produced by adding 7 to the 1 of 186 and carrying 1 from another column. The answer of 29 was
given by adding all the digits as ones—7 + 5 + 2 + 1 + 8 + 6.

By contrast, the wrong answers produced by the no-algorithms class were
more reasonable. The children in this class usually began by adding 180 and 50,
thereby getting 230, and then added the ones. The some-algorithms class came
out in between.

Algorithms are harmful for two reasons: (a) They encourage children to give
up their own thinking, and (b) they "unteach" place value, thereby preventing
children from developing number sense.

When second graders do their own thinking, they add the tens first and
then the ones. Because there is no compromise possible between starting with
the tens and starting with the ones as the algorithm requires, children have to
give up their own thinking to use the algorithm.

When we listen to children using the algorithm to do

$$\begin{array}{r} 29 \\ +16 \\ \hline \end{array}$$

for example, we can hear them say, "Nine and six is fifteen. Put down the five;
carry the one. One and two is three, and one more is four. . . ." The algorithm is
convenient for adults, who already know that the 2 of 29 stands for 20. However, for primary-school children, who have a tendency to think that the "2"
means two, and so on, the algorithm serves to reinforce this error. The incorrect answers given by the algorithms class in Table 5.3 demonstrate that the
algorithms "untaught" what little they understood of place value. The children
in the algorithms class did not notice that their answers of 29, in the 900s, and
so on, were unreasonable for 7 + 52 + 186.

Findings from Interviews of First Graders.   The algorithm for double-digit addition without "regrouping" ("carrying") is likewise damaging to first graders.
The result of this teaching was captured by chance when I tested two classes
of traditionally taught first graders. The testing was done in early May, and
only one of the teachers had taught the algorithm for two-digit addition without regrouping.

As can be seen in Table 5.4, the class that had not been taught the algorithm produced more correct answers to

$$\begin{array}{r} 22 \\ + \ 7 \\ \hline \end{array}$$

than the class who had been taught to add each column. Sixty-seven percent of
the no-algorithm class produced the correct answer by counting-on from 22.
By contrast, only 37% of the algorithm class gave the correct answer.

Table 5.4 Answers to 22 + 7 Given by Two Classes of First Graders in the Same School

Answers given	Algorithm taught $n = 19$	Algorithm not taught $n = 18$
29	7 (37%)	12 (67%)
24, 25, 27, or 28	1 (5%)	4 (22%)
11	6 (32%)	0 (0%)
10 or 12	2 (11%)	0 (0%)
"9 and 2, 92"	1 (5%)	0 (0%)
"a 2 and a 9"	1 (5%)	0 (0%)
9	1 (5%)	0 (0%)
Stuck after 2 + 2 = 4	0 (0%)	1 (6%)
Sits silently and ends up agreeing to skip problem		1 (6%)

Half (48%) of the algorithm class produced the answer of 10, 11, or 12 by adding all the digits as ones (2 + 2 + 7), but none of the no-algorithm class produced such answers. Children who do their own thinking know that the sum *has to be* larger than either addend. If they made errors, their wrong answers were greater than 22, namely, 24, 25, 27, or 28. When children are taught rules they do not understand, they lose the intuition they had and start to read all the digits as ones. Answers such as "9 and 2, 92," "a 2 and a 9," and "9," were found only in the class that had been taught to add columns of ones. These rules are conventional and belong to social knowledge, but addition is logico-mathematical knowledge, which cannot be transmitted to children as if it were social knowledge.

How First Graders Approach Double-Digit Addition When They Are Not Taught the Conventional Algorithm

The great majority of first graders in constructivist classes count-on to solve problems such as 29 + 16. However, a few every year invent *tens* and procedures such as "29 + 1 = 30, 30 + 15 = 30 + 10 + 5 = 45." Another common procedure is "20 + 10 = 30, and since 9 + 1 = another 10, that's 40 + 5, and the answer is 45." Some of these advanced children also invent ways to add even larger numbers such as 27 and 82. Their procedure is usually: 20 + 80 = 100, 7 + 2 = 9, and 100 + 9 = 109. When they are free to do their own thinking, children thus invariably add the tens first and then the ones.

How we encourage second graders to invent double-digit addition can be seen in a videotape (Kamii, 1989b) and *Young Children Continue to Reinvent Arithmetic, 2nd Grade* (Kamii, 1989a). This is a topic beyond the scope of this book, and we conclude by pointing out that when we introduce double-digit addition, we introduce the "regrouping" kind at about the same time we introduce the "no-regrouping" kind.

CONCLUSION

Authors of most textbooks and workbooks base their goals and objectives on empiricist common sense. According to common sense, it seems reasonable to teach sums up to 10 and then up to 18. It also seems reasonable to assume that children are like computers that can store and retrieve information. However, children do not learn arithmetic in these ways. For them, $5 + 5 = 10$ is easier to remember than $3 + 2 = 5$, and $10 + 10 = 20$ is easier to remember than $4 + 3 = 7$. Sums are not "information" or "facts" to internalize from the environment, and children are different from computers that can store information.

It is important to study how children learn with encouragement but no pressure. When objectives are based on how children learn, arithmetic becomes easy for them and a source of pleasure and satisfaction.

CHAPTER 6

Subtraction as an Objective

In first-grade textbooks, subtraction is presented soon after addition. For example, when first graders can do 3 + 2 = _____, problems such as 5 – 2 = _____ appear shortly afterward. Authors of textbooks follow this sequence because, for them, subtraction is merely the inverse of addition. From the perspective of Piaget's theory, however, subtraction is much harder than addition. This statement is explained below. It will be argued that, in first grade, subtraction seems appropriate in word problems but must be deemphasized in games.

WHY SUBTRACTION IS HARDER THAN ADDITION

As can be seen in Figure 6.1a, addition is easy because it involves only "ascending" from two wholes (from 5 and 4, for example) to a higher-order whole (9). During the late preoperational period, this ascending is relatively easy (Inhelder & Piaget, 1959/1964). Subtraction, however, involves two hierarchical levels (see Figure 6.1b) and requires "descending" from the whole (9) to a part (5), and simultaneously "ascending" back to the whole (9) and "descending" to the other part (the unknown number).

Part-whole relationships are very difficult for young children, as we saw in the class-inclusion task in Chapter 1 and in the phenomenon of counting-all in Chapter 5. Thinking in two opposite directions *simultaneously* is so hard in subtraction that it is reflected in the language we often hear in second-grade classrooms such as the following:

I took away the 5 and the 9.
I subtracted the 5 and the 9.
I subtracted the 5 with the 9.

Children also make statements indicating their focus on the number they must act on most directly. Examples are:

Five minus 9 is 4.
Five take away 9 equals 4.

Figure 6.1. The difference in thinking between (a) addition and
      (b) subtraction.

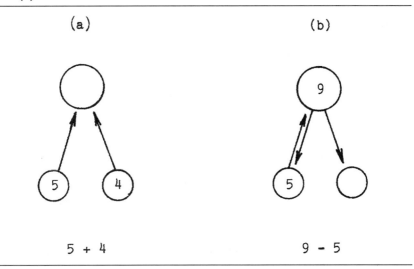

(a)   (b)

5 + 4   9 − 5

Another phenomenon often observed in first- and second-grade classrooms reveals how unnatural subtraction is for young children: When presented with a pageful of addition and subtraction problems, children often make addition-for-subtraction errors, but hardly ever make subtraction-for-addition errors. Addition is as natural to them as subtraction is *un*natural.

Piaget (1974/1980) pointed out that a characteristic of preoperational thinking is the primacy of the positive aspect of perception, actions, and cognition. For example, when we show to 4-year-olds two piles of blocks containing 4 and 10, respectively, and ask them which pile has *more*, we are likely to get the correct response. However, if we ask, "Which pile has *less*?" 4-year-olds often look puzzled and do not respond. "More" is a positive term that is easier for them to understand than "less." Less is harder because it expresses the relationship negatively.

Two other examples are presented below from Piaget's research. One concerns how children think about the complementary class, and the second example deals with how they think about quantities of water in a bottle.

How Children Think About the Complementary Class

Materials: A set of cards with pictures of flowers: a rose, a pansy, a tulip, a lily-of-the-valley, and several cards showing primulas; a set of cards with pictures of fruit: a pear, two cherries, a banana, a melon, a bunch of grapes, an orange, and several cards showing apples; two small boxes and labels to place on them.

Procedure

1. In individual interviews, children 4 to about 10 years of age were asked to sort each set of cards by putting them into two boxes.
2. When the dichotomy was made, the children were asked what name should be written on the label for each box.

Findings

Only the findings concerning flowers are given here. All the children said the first group should be called "primulas." For the second group, however, they suggested a variety of labels that could be categorized into the following three levels:

Level 1. At this level the children, mostly 5 years old, said, "Rose(s), pansies, tulip(s), and lilies-of-the-valley," for example (see Figure 6.2a). They named each flower *positively* and *separately* (sometimes in the plural in spite of the fact that there was only one card for each kind of flower).

Level 2. Between 5 and 6 years of age, the children said the label should say, "The others" or "a mixture" (see Figure 6.2b). They described the complementary class *positively*, *as a group*, in relation to the other group ("primulas") but not in relation to a higher-order class ("flowers").

Level 3. Labels such as "all the flowers except the primulas" and "flowers that are not primulas" began to appear among 7-year-olds. As can be seen in Figure 6.2c, these children described the complementary class *negatively* (flowers that are *not* primulas) in relation to a higher-order class (flowers). When children's thinking becomes reversible, the labels they give reflect their ability to "ascend" and "descend" simultaneously in a hierarchical structure.

The Level-2 children can be said to have made progress in two ways: (1) They now put individual objects into a relationship with the other objects and make a second group ("the others" rather than "a rose," "a tulip," and so on), and (2) they put the second group into a relationship with the first group ("primulas"). However, labels such as "a mixture" and "the others" reflect children's thinking that is limited to the two groups. A hierarchical relationship appears at Level 3, when children refer to a higher-order category, namely "flowers."

Figure 6.2. Labels for the complementary class, which are positive in
(a) and (b) and negative in (c).

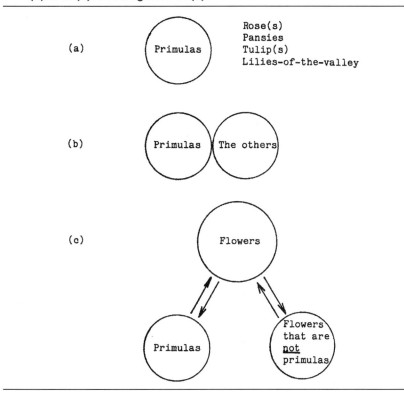

    In the preceding interview, all the flowers were visible on cards. However, only when the children developed reversible, hierarchical thinking did they "see" some of the objects negatively. The experiment described next was conducted with Henriques-Christophides (Piaget, 1974/1980) and involved bottles containing various amounts of water. Water is visible, but the empty part of the bottle is not. We will see that the part-whole relationship stated in terms of the bottle's emptiness is much harder than that stated in terms of its fullness ("a little bit empty" compared with "almost full," for example). This part-whole relationship has the same structure as Figures 6.2c and 6.1b.

How Children Think About the Empty Part of a Bottle

Materials: Five identical, cylindrical bottles 15 cm tall and 3 cm in diameter containing the following amounts of colored water:

Bottle I: 3/4 full
Bottle II: 1/2 full
Bottle III: 1/4 full
Bottle IV: full
Bottle V: empty

Procedure

1. In individual interviews, children 4 to 11 years of age were first asked to describe the amount of water in each bottle. If they used vague terms such as "a lot" and "a little," they were asked to speak more precisely by using the terms *full* or *empty*. The children were then asked to point to (or draw) the bottle that was:

almost full
almost empty
half full
a little bit empty
half empty

2. Some of the questions then asked were the following, all beginning with "Can a bottle be at the same time":

half full and half empty?
almost full and almost empty?
a little full and a little empty?
almost full and a little bit empty?
a little bit full and almost empty?

Findings

Level 0. Four-year-olds had difficulty showing bottles that were more or less *full*, but had even more trouble showing bottles that were more or less *empty*.

Level 1. The most general criterion of Level 1 is children's inability to answer that a bottle can be *half full* and *half empty*. Five- and 6-year-olds continued to have much more difficulty with negative statements (referring to the empty part) than with positive statements (referring to the part of the bottle that was filled). For example, they could point to the bottle that was "a little bit full" but often interpreted "a little bit empty" positively as "a little bit full." The following example illustrates this point:

NIC (5-9) described bottles I–IV correctly in terms of "fullness" but not in terms of "emptiness." He described bottle III as being "even less full [than bottle II]. . . . It has very little. . . . It is all empty, it has a lot of emptiness in it." However, when he was later asked for a bottle that was "a little bit empty," he showed bottle III twice. He vehemently refused to consider bottle I as being "a little bit empty." He drew "half full" as 2/3 and "half empty" as 1/4. When asked if a bottle could be "almost full" and "a little bit empty," he replied, "We would need two bottles [to show them]." (translated by C. Kamii from p. 98, Vol. 2, of the original edition in French; Piaget, 1974/1980, pp. 232–233)

Level 2. The criterion for inclusion at this level is that "half full" and "half empty" are now considered equal. At this level, which spans between 7 and 10 years of age, "almost full" and "a little bit full" were easy, but "almost empty" and "a little bit empty" still caused trouble.

Level 3. At age 11 and above, all the questions were answered correctly without hesitation.

Unlike "the others" in the experiment with flowers, the empty part of the bottle is not visible. The emptiness of the bottle is therefore even harder to logico-mathematize than a mixture of flowers.

Knowledge of water and flowers is physical knowledge, but how we think about them in terms of relationships is logico-mathematical knowledge. Piaget used the terms "logicize" and "logico-mathematize" to refer to our thinking logically about objects. In many other experiments, he (Piaget, 1974/1980) showed that young children generally think about objects and actions positively during the preoperational period. The difficulty of subtraction is part of young children's difficulty in thinking negatively about objects and actions.

WHY WE GIVE WORD PROBLEMS INVOLVING "SUBTRACTION"

It seems appropriate to give subtraction word problems to kindergartners and first graders for two reasons:

1. Research has shown that one-third to one-half of the children in kindergarten and first grade can solve subtraction word problems without formal instruction. Ibarra and Lindvall (1982) reported that, with manipulatives, 37% of the kindergartners they interviewed could solve problems such as "I have 7 flowers. I give you 3 of my flowers. How many flowers do I have left?" Carpenter and Moser (1982) found slightly higher percentages among first graders who had not been instructed in arithmetic.

If many kindergartners and first graders can solve these kinds of problems, similar problems are likely to be good for their further development of logic. Students who can already solve these kinds of problems strengthen their logic by using it. Those who cannot answer these questions develop their logic by *trying* to answer them from time to time. Word problems are like everyday situations, and young children know that if they eat some of their cookies, they will have fewer cookies afterward.

2. Children do not have to use subtraction to solve "subtraction" problems. Kindergartners and primary school–age children tend to use addition whenever possible. Even in third grade, as can be seen in the videotape entitled *Multidigit Division* (Kamii, 1990), Katie used only multiplication and addition to divide 258 M&M's among 22 children. She said that 10 x 22 = 220, and one more 22 made 242. She then asked, "242 plus what is 258?" and wrote as follows before writing the addend that constituted the remainder:

$$\begin{array}{r} 242 \\ \underline{?} \\ 258 \end{array}$$

"Subtraction" Problems from Children's Viewpoint

Mathematics educators generally say that subtraction word problems consist of "separating," "part-part-whole," "comparing," and "equalizing" problems. An example of each is given below:

> *Separating.* You have 7 pieces of candy. You give me 3 of them. How many pieces do you have left?
>
> *Part-part-whole.* There are 6 pieces of fruit in the bowl. Two are apples and the rest are pears. How many pears are there?
>
> *Comparing.* You have 7 pieces of candy. I have only 3 pieces. How many more do you have than I do?
>
> *Equalizing.* I have 3 little candles. I need 7 of them for a birthday cake. How many more do I need?

Gibb (1956) noted almost half a century ago that three-fourths of the second graders in her sample used addition to answer an "equalizing" question. Yet she continued to interpret this type of problem as an application of subtraction. Carpenter and Moser (1982) likewise found that children tended to use addition to answer such questions as "How many more pencils does Kathy need to have 12 pencils?" They nevertheless continued to categorize "equalizing" questions under the heading of subtraction.

From children's point of view, equalizing is an addition problem, or a kind of missing-addend problem. In fact, the preceding four kinds of problems require the making of different kinds of part-whole relationships, as can be seen in Figure 6.3. In "separating," a part is taken away from the whole (Figure 6.3a). "Part-part-whole" (Figure 6.3b) is similar, but neither part is taken away. "Comparing" is harder because it involves two wholes (see Figure 6.3c), and the child has to mentally transport the smaller whole onto the larger whole and make a part-whole relationship out of the two wholes. By contrast, "equalizing" starts with a whole and requires its enlargement into a larger whole (see Figure 6.3d).

To study children's development of the logic of these relationships, I (CK) gave three of the preceding four problems to 183 children in grades 1–5 in a public school in Geneva, Switzerland. (I did not give the part-part-whole prob-

Figure 6.3. The part-whole relationships involved in four kinds of "subtraction" problems.

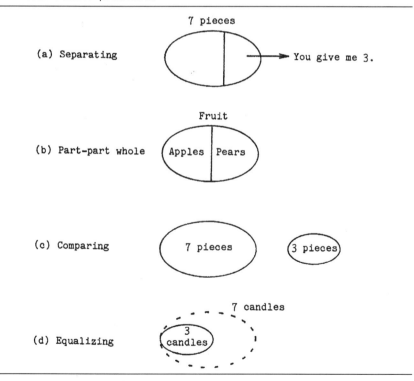

lem because I knew from the class-inclusion task described in Chapter 1 that this kind of relationship is made by age 7 or 8.)

As can be seen in Table 6.1, separating was the easiest of the three problems. Half (52%) of the first graders gave the correct answer, and all the children answered this question correctly by second grade.

The hardest problem was comparing, and only 10% of the first graders gave the correct answer of 4. Half of the second graders had trouble with this problem, and the difficulty persisted among 20% of the third graders. Sixty percent of the first graders gave the answer of 7, indicating that the question they "heard" was "How many do you have?" rather than "How many *more* do you have?" "How many *more*?" is a difficult question to understand, as stated earlier. To understand this question, children have to mentally transport the smaller whole onto the larger whole and make a part-whole relationship out of the two wholes.

Equalizing is easier than comparing because it involves only one whole. Half (46%) of the first graders gave the correct answer. However, almost all the other

Table 6.1. Children's Responses to Three Kinds of "Subtraction" Problems (in Percents)

		Grade level				
		1 $n = 50$	2 $n = 51$	3 $n = 20$	4 $n = 44$	5 $n = 18$
Separating	Correct answer (4)	52	100	100	100	100
	Incorrect answers					
	7	16				
	10	8				
	Miscounting	12				
	Guessing the answer	12				
Comparing	Correct answer (4)	10	53	80	91	100
	Incorrect answers					
	7	60	14	5		
	10	4	10	5	2	
	Others	26	24	10	7	
Equalizing	Correct answer (4)	46	57	95	93	100
	Incorrect answers					
	7	44	28	5	2	
	Others	10	14		5	

half (44%) gave the answer of 7, again attesting to the difficulty of making a part-whole relationship. The question posed was "How many *more* candles do you need?" but the question they "heard" was "How many candles do you need?"

To conclude with the educational implications of this study, it seems good to give so-called subtraction problems from time to time but not to expect or require the use of subtraction. Our purpose is to give to children opportunities to logico-mathematize contents such as flowers and candles. Children must first understand the logic of the question before going on to numerical precision. First graders have trouble with subtraction word problems not because they cannot do the arithmetic but because they do not "hear" the question asked. Once they understand the question, they usually use addition to solve it. Adding is a much better procedure than counting back, which is difficult to do and confusing.

As we saw in Chapter 2 on representation with reference to Figure 2.1, whether children understand certain words and sentences depends on their development of logic (constructive abstraction). If their logic is at a high level, they can understand the words and sentences used in the question (representation). If their logic is at a low level, they can assimilate words and sentences only to their low-level logic.

WHY WE GIVE FEW GAMES INVOLVING SUBTRACTION

Games involve numbers without contents such as apples. In midyear in the early 1980s, Georgia DeClark and I tested first graders individually with a worksheet containing subtraction problems without contents. Neither of us had taught subtraction, but answers to 4 – 2, 10 – 5, and 5 – 1 came *immediately*, without any need to think or count. When we asked about 5 – 3 and 7 – 4, however, fingers came out, and some children counted back. We concluded that when addition has become very easy and "second nature" to children, the corresponding subtraction becomes very easy. (The ease of 2 + 2, 5 + 5, and 4 + 1 can be seen in Table 5.1.) The way to "teach" subtraction is therefore to strengthen children's knowledge of sums.

The only way children can get a sum they do not know on their own is by counting. Counting is therefore necessary for children to learn sums. However, subtraction can be derived from sums, and counting is therefore not necessary to learn subtraction. Counting should be avoided in favor of thinking, and this is why we give many addition games and few subtraction games.

Georgia DeClark and I experimented with subtraction games (see Kamii, 1985), but subtraction games gathered dust on the shelf while addition games were in constant use. The games we now use mix subtraction with addition. In Sneaky Snake (see Chapter 11), for example, each snake is divided into 12 segments that are numbered 1–12. Each player rolls two dice and tries to use addition or subtraction to cover all 12 numbers. If a player rolls a 4 and a 5, for example, he or she can cover either the 9 by using addition or the 1 by using subtraction.

Another kind of game we use involves the partitioning of numbers. In Tens with Nine Cards (see Chapter 11), for example, the object of the game is to find pairs of cards that make 10 (9 + 1, 8 + 2, 7 + 3, and so on). Children at first use addition by trial and error to determine if 8 and 4 make 10, for example. Later, however, they know that they need a 2 to go with an 8. This kind of addition game helps them know answers to subtraction problems.

CONCLUSION

For young children, subtraction is not simply the inverse of addition. For first graders, subtraction is much harder than addition, and we therefore give subtraction word problems but deemphasize subtraction games. We give word problems to encourage children to make part-whole relationships logically, and children usually use addition to get the numerical answer. We emphasize addition games because if children's knowledge of sums is strong and "second nature" to them, they can deduce differences from their knowledge of sums.

CHAPTER 7

Multiplication and Division as Objectives

We advocate first graders' solving "multiplication" and "division" word problems but do not recommend the teaching of multiplication or division. Our reason is that kindergartners and first graders use addition to solve these problems. They are generally not yet able to use multiplication because they cannot think multiplicatively. In this chapter, we first discuss the difference between additive and multiplicative thinking. We then give findings from research showing that children in kindergarten and first grade use addition to solve multiplication and division word problems, and that simple fractions are possible for first graders to invent. The chapter concludes with remarks about factors that make these problems easier or harder.

THE DIFFERENCE BETWEEN ADDITIVE AND MULTIPLICATIVE THINKING

For most mathematics educators, multiplication is only a faster way of doing repeated addition. For researchers such as Piaget (1983/1987), Steffe (1988, 1992), and us (Clark & Kamii, 1996), however, multiplication involves the kind of hierarchical thinking illustrated in Figure 7.1b. As can be seen in Figure 7.1a, the structure of a repeated-addition problem such as $5 + 5 + 5 + 5$ is simple because it involves only *ones* at one level of abstraction. However, a multiplication problem such as 4×5 involves the hierarchical structure shown in Figure 7.1b. As can be seen in this figure, the "4" in 4×5 refers to "4 *fives*." To read "4 $\times 5$" correctly, the child has to be able to transform "5 *ones*" into "one *five*," which is a higher-order unit.

Clark and Kamii (1996) interviewed 336 students in grades 1–5 at a public school in a middle-income neighborhood. Using the following materials and procedure, they found four levels that clearly differentiated between multiplicative and additive thinkers.

Materials: Three "fish (eels)," 5, 10, and 15 cm long (see Figure 7.2); about 100 chips.

Figure 7.1. The structural difference between (a) addition and
(b) multiplication.

(a) 5 + 5 + 5 + 5

(b) 4 x 5

Procedure

1. The child was told, "This fish [pointing to B] eats 2 times what this fish [pointing to A] eats, and this big fish [pointing to C] eats 3 times what the little one [pointing to A] eats. This fish [B] eats 2 times what this fish [A] eats because it is 2 times as big as this one [A]." The interviewer demonstrated by showing that A could be placed on B two times. The interviewer continued, "The big fish [C] eats 3 times what the little fish [A] eats because it [C] is 3 times as big as this one [A]." The interviewer again demonstrated by placing A on C three times.
2. The first question was then posed: "If this fish [A] gets one chip of food, how many chips of food would you feed the other two fish?" The following variations on the question were then posed:
   a. If B received 4 chips
   b. If C received 9 chips
   c. If A received 4 chips
   d. If A received 7 chips

Figure 7.2. The fish (eels) used in the multiplicative-thinking task.

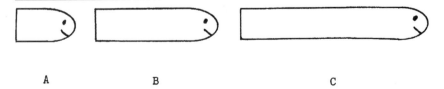

A   B   C

3. If a child answered item b incorrectly, a counter-suggestion was offered: "Another boy/girl told me that if this big fish [C] gets 9 chips, the little fish [A] should get 3 chips because 9 [pointing to the 9 chips rearranged into three groups of 3] is 3 times what this is [pointing to the 3 chips given to A and arranged in one group]. And this fish [B] should get 6 chips because 6 [pointing to 6 chips rearranged into 2 groups of 3] is 2 times what this is [pointing to the 3 chips given to A]. What do you think of his or her idea?" After the child gave an opinion, the interviewer asked for an explanation: "Why do you think your way [or the other person's way] is better?" To avoid suggesting the multiplication tables, care was taken to say, "Nine is 3 times what *this* [A's chips] is," rather than "Nine is 3 times what *three* is."

Findings

It can be observed in Table 7.1 that Level 4B, called *multiplicative thinking with immediate success*, was demonstrated by only 1.7% and 9.2% of the first and second graders, respectively. Level 4A, called *multiplicative thinking but not with immediate success*, was demonstrated by 17.2% and 35.4%, respectively, at grades 1 and 2. Almost all the children at Level 4A were those who benefited from the counter-suggestion in which a multiplicative solution was demonstrated.

The children at Levels 2 and 3 remained additive even after the counter-suggestion. A typical example of Level 2 (*additive thinking with a numerical*

Table 7.1. Number and Percentage of Children at Each Developmental Level by Grade

Level	Grade				
	1	2	3	4	5
1[a]	8 (13.8)	1 (1.5)	—	—	—
2[b]	31 (53.4)	28 (43.1)	8 (13.6)	12 (15.4)	5 (6.6)
3[b]	8 (13.8)	7 (10.8)	13 (22.0)	2 (2.6)	2 (2.6)
4A[c]	10 (17.2)	23 (35.4)	25 (42.4)	42 (53.8)	32 (42.1)
4B[c]	1 (1.7)	6 (9.2)	13 (22.0)	22 (28.2)	37 (48.7)
Total	58 (99.9)	65 (100)	59 (100)	78 (100)	76 (100)

Note: Values enclosed in parentheses represent percentages.
[a]Below additive
[b]Additive level
[c]Multiplicative level
Source: Clark & Kamii (1996)

sequence of +1 or +2) is to give 5 chips to B if A received 4, and 6 chips to C. A typical example of Level 3 (*additive thinking involving +2 for B and +3 for C*) is to give 6 chips to B if A received 4, and 7 chips to C. The children at Level 3 explained that they gave 6 to B because $4 + 2 = 6$, and 7 to C because $4 + 3 = 7$. Level 3 is especially instructive because it demonstrates that if children cannot think multiplicatively, they understand "2 times" as "2 more," and "3 times" as "3 more." As explained in Chapter 2, these children assimilated "2 times" to the knowledge they had, which was "2 more." If children cannot yet make a multiplicative relationship (constructive abstraction), they cannot represent a multiplicative relationship to themselves.

Level 1 (*below additive, numerical thinking*) is even lower than Level 2. For example, if A is given 1 chip, the Level-1 child may give 3 to B and 6 to C. Level-1 children give *more* to B and even *more* to C, but their thinking is intuitive and qualitative rather than numerically precise.

Because this "fish" task is an easy one for the following three reasons, it is useful for the identification of children who cannot yet think multiplicatively:

1. It involves small, easy multipliers such as "2 times" and "3 times."
2. It lets the child show multiplicative thinking with actions (by making 2 groups of 4 and 3 groups of 4, for example) without having to give numerical answers (such as "8" and "12").
3. It includes a counter-suggestion that demonstrates the correct multiplicative solution. Children who reject the multiplicative solution do so because they understand "2 times" and "3 times" additively.

We conclude on the basis of the data shown in Table 7.1 that we can expect first graders to solve "multiplication" word problems with addition but not with multiplication. First graders understand "5 packages of gum, and each package contains 6 pieces of gum" as $6 + 6 + 6 + 6 + 6$ but not as 5×6.

KINDERGARTNERS' AND FIRST GRADERS' ABILITY TO SOLVE "MULTIPLICATION" AND "DIVISION" WORD PROBLEMS

Carpenter et al.'s Research

Carpenter et al. (1993) interviewed 70 kindergartners in six classes in two schools. The classes were socioeconomically and racially heterogeneous and taught by teachers who participated in a program called Cognitively Guided Instruction (CGI; Carpenter, Fennema, Peterson, Chiang, & Loef, 1989). In CGI, children are given a wide variety of word problems and provided with counters to use if they want to. As in our Piagetian, constructivist approach, the children invent their own ways of solving these problems because their teachers do not show them what to do. The entire class, as well as small groups, also exchange ideas about how they solved each problem in a variety of ways.

The 70 kindergartners were interviewed in May with nine questions including "subtraction," "multiplication," "division," and multistep problems. The simple multiplication and division problems were the following three:

1. *Multiplication*. Robin has 3 packages of gum. There are 6 pieces of gum in each package. How many pieces of gum does Robin have altogether?
2. *Measurement division*. Tad had 15 guppies. He put 3 guppies in each jar. How many jars did Tad put guppies in?
3. *Partitive division*. Mr. Gomez had 20 cupcakes. He put the cupcakes into 4 boxes so that there were the same number of cupcakes in each box. How many cupcakes did Mr. Gomez put in each box? (Carpenter et al., 1993, p. 434)

Of the 70 children, 50 (71%), 50 (71%), and 49 (70%), respectively, gave the correct answers to the preceding three questions. The multiplication problem was solved by addition, usually by making three groups with 6 counters in each group. "Measurement division" was also done with counters. Most of the children counted 15 out, arranged them in groups of 3, and counted the number of groups. "Partitive division" was done mostly in two ways. Thirteen children dealt 20 counters one by one into four groups. Twenty-six made four groups and adjusted the number in each group by trial and error.

Olivier et al.'s Research

Olivier et al. (1991) reported from South Africa that their first graders, too, can solve division problems such as 18 cookies to be divided among 3 children and 24 balloons to be divided among 4 children. As can be seen in the drawings in Figure 2.3, some children dealt 1 or 2 cookies at a time to each child. Others estimated the number that each child might get and adjusted their estimation if necessary.

Empson's Research

Empson (1995) took partitive division farther and studied first graders' invention of fractions in equal-sharing situations. For example, she found that, before any instruction in fractions, 14 out of a class of 17 first graders solved the problem of 4 children sharing 10 cupcakes equally. Thirds were more difficult than halves and repeated halving. However, the teacher did not show the first graders how to solve problems and, instead, encouraged them to exchange viewpoints about what they had drawn and why. Many soon became able to divide 7 candy bars among 3 children and 8 pancakes among 6 children.

Our Own Findings

The kindergarten and first-grade teachers we work with have all been giving multiplication and division word problems for several years. The students solve these problems with repeated addition, as can be seen in a videotape entitled *First Graders Dividing 62 by 5* (Kamii & Clark, 2000). The problem in this tape is to find out how many erasers can be bought with 62 cents if each eraser costs 5 cents.

In this videotape, the different ways in which the children drew and wrote reflect their levels of abstraction. The first child drew 62 tally marks, circled 5 of them 12 times, and counted the circles she had drawn. For this child, 62 was clearly 62 *ones*.

The second child, by contrast, wrote many "5s." His procedure was to say "five, ten, fifteen . . ." as he touched each "5" and to stop writing them when he reached "sixty." He then went back and counted the number of "5s" he had written. This child thought about 62 as *groups of fives*. The third child wrote "5 10 15 20 25 30 35 40 45 50 55 60," using an even more efficient way. The last two children were closer to multiplicative thinking than the first child, but all three were using repeated addition.

The first- and second-grade teachers we work with have also been giving fraction problems as described by Empson (1995). We confirm her statement that halving and halving halves are much easier for young children than thirds.

FACTORS THAT MAKE "MULTIPLICATION" AND "DIVISION" WORD PROBLEMS EASIER OR HARDER

The sequencing of objectives is simple in addition and subtraction because children can add cookies to cookies or subtract cookies from cookies by repeating the operation of +1. In "multiplication" and "division," by contrast, some qualitative and quantitative factors make problems easier or harder. These are discussed below.

Multiplication Compared with Division

It is easy for first graders and many kindergartners to move from addition to multiplication problems. From the beginning of the school year, for example, addition and multiplication are not even distinguishable in problems such as: Three people live in my house. How many feet are there in my house?

By contrast, division problems require extra effort in logico-mathematizing reality. When 9 cookies must be divided among 3 children, for example, some first graders have no idea what to do after drawing 9 cookies and 3 children.

Division problems are therefore best introduced after the students have become comfortable with multiplication problems.

When children have no idea what to do with their drawings, it may be good to ask them if counters might help. Counters are often helpful not because they are "concrete" but because they are movable and conducive to the physical action of dividing 9 cookies among 3 children. As explained in Chapter 2, counters and drawings are both symbols, and young children soon go on to prefer using their drawings to solve word problems.

Qualitative Factors

One year, we gave the following division problem that caused difficulty among the less advanced children: "Cody looked outside and saw 8 feet. How many people were outside?" A few children drew 8 circles and 8 people and announced the answer of 8. One child asked if he should count Cody as one of the people.

The question about feet and people seemed especially hard because feet are part of a person. Another cause of the difficulty was that Cody and the people outside were all people, and it was not obvious to everybody that Cody was inside and that his feet were not 2 of the 8. We therefore changed the content to 8 cookies to be divided among 4 children. This problem turned out to be much easier for all the children. Most drew 4 people and proceeded like the first graders in South Africa whose drawings can be seen in Figure 2.3. Others tried giving 2 cookies to each person intending to adjust the outcome if the distribution did not come out evenly.

Quantitative Factors Related to Drawings, Logic, and "Friendly" Numbers

Large numbers obviously make problems harder, but it is important for the teacher to know whether the difficulty is due to a large number per se, or to something else. For example, the following problem involved a class of 19 children: We (the class) will go to the grocery store in groups. Each group will have 4 people. How many groups will we have? _____ Will there be the same number in all the groups? _____

One child took great pains trying to draw 19 stick figures on one side of the paper but ended up with 17 on one side and 2 on the other. Because she wanted to put all 19 people on one side, she erased so many times that it was impossible to tell what was meant to stay there and what was meant to have been erased. When she tried to draw circles around each group of 4 people, she could not deal with the mess on the front and forgot about the 2 people on the back.

By contrast, another child circled 4 people and made 4 groups of 4 people. However, when he went on to count the circles, he counted the 4 circles and 3 people, thereby getting the answer of 7. His problem was one of logic.

Certain numbers are "friendlier" than others, and a large number like 62 is easier to divide by 5 than by 4. Counting by 2s, by 5s, and by 10s is easier than counting by 3s or by 4s. Five bags of candy each containing 5 pieces is therefore sometimes easier to calculate than 6 bags with 4 pieces in each bag.

CONCLUSION

Textbooks do not include multiplication or division problems at the kindergarten and first-grade levels because most authors have traditional views of these operations. However, recent research indicates that young children are capable of using addition to solve multiplication and division word problems. Since children construct multiplication and division out of repeated addition, it is developmentally appropriate to give these kinds of word problems that young children solve with pleasure and ease.

Part III

ACTIVITIES AND PRINCIPLES OF TEACHING

CHAPTER 8

The Use of Situations
Outside the Math Hour

Leslie Baker Housman

A characteristic of a constructivist approach to math education based on Piaget's theory is the use of situations outside the math hour. In my first-grade class I look for math-related situations throughout the day because mathematics grows out of children's logico-mathematization of their reality, and children are motivated to think hard when problems matter to them.

This chapter is divided into four parts. I begin with what happens daily or routinely and go on to less frequent occurrences—what happens monthly and around holidays. In the final section, I discuss what we did with money, which is of special interest to children and rich in possibilities of making combinations such as $10 = 1 + 1 + 1 + 1 + 1 + 1 + 1 + 1 + 1 + 1 = 5 + 5 = 5 + 1 + 1 + 1 + 1 + 1$. Examples appropriate for kindergarten are also presented.

WHAT HAPPENS DAILY OR ROUTINELY

The Morning Routine

At the beginning of each school year, I begin talking with the class about routines and ways in which children can be responsible for themselves. One aspect of making decisions about routines concerns what happens in the morning. I talk to the class about the things that children need to do every day when they come into the classroom, and together we make a list of those duties and post them on the chalkboard for the whole year. Figure 8.1 is an example of such a list. These duties include turning in notes from home, sharpening pencils, and choosing a new book to take home that night. The list may change a little from one year to the next depending on various factors. For instance, one class was fascinated with hand-held pencil sharpeners, so getting pencils sharpened ahead of time in the morning was not an issue that year.

Our list looks very much like a ready-made list I could have posted before the first day of school. However, children are much more likely to follow the

107

Figure 8.1. A list of things to do every morning.

rules *they* made for themselves than the same rules imposed by the teacher. Rather than telling individual children what they need to do, I refer them to the list, thereby reducing my personal authority.

My Daily Letter to the Class.   The students are also responsible for reading a letter I write to them each morning and post on the chalkboard. This letter tells students about special events of the day and what specifically they are to do. An example of a letter follows:

Aug. 29, 1997

Dear First Graders,
    Please read and solve the math problem on your desk.

Love,
Mrs. Housman

I write this kind of letter beginning on the first day of school. I know that many of the children cannot read my letters independently, but these letters send two important messages. The first is that I expect everybody to read. The second message is that nonreaders should ask their peers for help until everybody becomes able to read independently. As a result, my students quickly stop seeing me as the information kiosk. (I say to students, "If you have trouble reading the morning message, what could you do?" Their response is: "Ask a friend.")

The letter later serves as a means of teaching reading and spelling strategies during circle time if I omit some letters in familiar words, as shown in this example:

Nov. 7, 1997

Dear F _ _ st Grad _ _ s,
    Ch _ _ se a ma _ _ game to _ _ ay. We _ _ _ _ have a
v _ s _ t _ _ at 1:45.

Love,
Mrs. Housman

I also use the daily letter as a vehicle for "teaching" children to tell time. For instance, I might write "Please choose a math game. We will clean up at 8:45." Using a large Judy clock (whose hands can be turned with the correct hour-minute relationship because of the gears behind the face), I ask for volunteers to help us know what the clock will look like when it is 8:45. There are usually several first graders who know "where o'clock is," and we start from 8:00. I then ask if anyone notices anything about the space between the 12 and 1 on the clock, drawing the class's attention to the marks for the minutes leading up to the 1. Soon, somebody invariably points out that there are the same number of lines between all the numbers, and this lets me ask how many minutes there are between numbers. Some classes readily agree that there are 5 minutes, and some classes need to count the marks to be sure.

Once we are in agreement, I ask the class how we could get from 8:00 to "5 minutes past eight." Some children immediately say that the long hand has to be on the 1, but others have to count the lines again to be sure. We continue in this manner to find 10 after, 15 after, and so on. Eventually, I might ask, "Does anyone know of a fast way we could count 45 minutes?" and there is always at least one child who says "By fives!" Once we get to that point, I just ask a volunteer each day to set the Judy clock to show the time indicated in my letter to the class, and the rest of the class watches to be sure they agree with the volunteer. The class then begins to do a better job of watching the clock than I do and start to clean up on their own.

This morning routine is obviously helpful for developing reading, language, and time-telling abilities, but those objectives are really secondary. My purpose in organizing our morning this way is to foster the development of autonomy in my first graders. I want them to feel capable and confident in their ability to govern themselves. I don't want to be in charge of my students; I want them to be in charge of themselves. The list of daily responsibilities and my morning letter help the students develop this autonomy.

Committees, Lunch Count, and Taking Attendance.   When I read *Thinking and Learning Together* (Fisher, 1995), I was impressed by the author's explanation of her classroom committees. Fisher explains that rather than having a few helpers responsible for classroom jobs each week or day, she involves the entire class every day through committees, thus fostering a sense of community in the classroom.

I begin each year by choosing one helper a day, called the Big Cheese, while we are getting settled. This may seem like a violation of the principle of reducing the teacher's authority, but I have a different plan. I choose the helpers in alphabetical order and ask children every day if they can figure out why I chose so-and-so today. Sooner or later, someone catches on to my rule, and the children come to know that the choice of the Big Cheese does not depend on the teacher's power.

Once we have had a few days together in the classroom, I start to ask the children what sorts of jobs they see that need to get done. I make a list of the jobs they name such as "Sort books," "Take lunch count," and so on. The list is usually very similar to one I could have made, but children are often much more demanding of themselves than I am. Once the list is completed, I ask the class to help me organize the jobs under the major subject areas: math, reading, and writing. We also have a Clean-Up Committee.

To introduce the idea of "committees," I read the story *Farmer Duck* (Waddell, 1992), and we discuss teamwork. I ask if anyone has ever heard of a *committee*, and we discuss what that means and whether a committee could be more effective than an individual. Over the course of the next few days, the children suggest jobs for each committee, and eventually we narrow the jobs for each committee to the four or five that are most important. Each of the committees is responsible for doing its job every day. Once every nine weeks (a grading period), the children apply for a new committee so that each child will serve on each committee at least once by the end of the year.

Committees help to build a feeling of community in the class so that each child's development of autonomy can be fostered through a feeling of shared responsibility. Serving on classroom committees, children have opportunities to argue their point to make decisions that make sense to them, and to accept responsibilities for the good of the group.

A member of the Math Committee thus becomes responsible for taking the lunch count every morning. I made the grid shown partially in Figure 8.2 so that the child in charge of the lunch count could go around the class with it on a clipboard and record each student's choice. Once finished, the child totals the choices and fills out the form (see Figure 8.3) that goes to the lunch room. He or she also lets me know how many people are absent.

One year, there were six children on the Math Committee. The first group had no problem taking turns each day in spite of the fact that one child did not get a turn each week. This did not bother this group because everyone eventu-

Figure 8.2. Part of the list used for lunch counts and taking attendance.

	1st choice	2nd choice	Sack lunch	Salad bar	Lunch box
Alice					
Allen					
Angela					
Bradley					
Elizabeth					
Ivan					
TOTAL					

ally had a turn. The next group, however, saw this as a terrible injustice and fought every day about it. I tried to engage the committee members in a discussion in hopes of finding a solution, but each was so egocentric that we got nowhere.

I called the class together and asked one of the Math Committee members to explain the problem, thinking that if a solution came from outside the Committee, the children might be more amenable to an outsider's suggestion. However, no matter how reasonable any of their peers' suggestions were, the members of the Math Committee could not be convinced. Finally, the Math Committee said that I should tell them each day whose turn it was to take the lunch count. Recognizing this request as an expression of the children's heteronomy, I responded by putting the basket containing the lunch count tally sheet in the middle of the Math Committee's table each morning before the children arrived. Typically, whoever arrived first took the lunch count, and no one ever complained about this issue again.

The Distribution of Objects

Another job for the Math Committee is fixing snack each day. I leave written instructions on the snack cabinet every day, such as "Goldfish. Each person gets 10." The Math Committee members get out 4 snack baskets, one for each table, and put enough crackers in each basket for every student at every table to have 10. (A "table" consists of desks pushed together.)

Figure 8.3. The form that goes to the lunch room.

1st choice:	_____
2nd choice:	_____
Sack lunch:	_____
Salad bar:	_____
Accountant:	_____
Date:	_____
Class:	_____

Last school year, we had 5 tables with 4 children at each table. By the middle of the year, the children could easily say how many pieces they had to put in the basket because they had worked so much with "4 times." By contrast, we have 4 tables this year—2 with 6 children, 1 with 4 children, and 1 with 3 children. The students have had a much more difficult time this year figuring out how much snack to put in each basket. For instance, early in the school year, if one table needed 20 cookies for each child to have 5, the Math Committee put 20 cookies in every basket and were surprised when some children complained of not having enough or of having leftovers. "Somebody must have eaten too many [or not enough]," the children said, but someone suggested that the Math Committee count out the cookies on each desk before putting them in the basket. This remained the routine through November.

In kindergarten, "just enough cups [or napkins or scissors] for everybody at your table" may be difficult enough. If this is too easy, "just enough for this table and that table" may be a better request.

The Division of Objects

Our class won second prize in a schoolwide pumpkin-decorating contest. Our prize was a plastic pumpkin full of Halloween candy. The children were amazed at how much the candy weighed when I passed this prize around. I asked how many pieces of candy the children thought each person could have. One child instantly yelled out "One hundred!" but most of his peers disagreed.

Quickly, the students agreed that we should try 10 each and see how much was left. When each child had 10 pieces on his or her desk, I asked how many pieces we should take when the bucket was passed around again. Seeing that there was still a lot of candy left, the children agreed that each child should get 10 pieces again. After this round, the bottom of the container was almost visible. Several children said, "Let's try 10 again," but many voiced concern that there were not enough to do that. We decided to try 10 pieces each, but the children began to protest when the bucket became almost empty. They suggested we try 5 pieces, and I asked if we had to put back all the candy that had already been passed out. Amy suggested that each person who had a third turn should give back 5 pieces. The rest of the class agreed, and as luck would have it, there were exactly 25 pieces of candy for each child.

In kindergarten, the teacher may want to make division easier by giving 20 Goldfish for each pair of children, 9 cookies for each group of 3 children, or any other number that seems appropriate.

The Collection of Objects

The collection of such things as parental permission slips prior to a field trip provides a natural opportunity for numerical reasoning. The teacher may ask the following kinds of questions:

Do we have all the slips we need?
How many more do we need to have?
How many children brought their slips back yesterday?
How many brought theirs back today?
How many slips should we have in this pile?

Keeping Records

I post a numbered list to keep a record of all the books we read aloud during the year. When we read book No. 4, I asked the class how many more books we had to read to get to No. 10. Six days before the winter break, we read book No. 70, and Amy commented, "We need 30 more to get to 100." I asked her how she knew that, and she said, "If you count by 10s, it takes three 10s to get to 100, and three 10s is the same as 30." Alvin agreed and said, "It's just like 7 and 3, which is 10. So 70 and 30 must be 100."

I asked the class if they thought we would get to 100 books before the vacation. Most of the class said we would, but a few thought we would have to read too many books every day to reach that goal. I then drew the class's attention to the calendar and asked how many books we would have to read each day to get to 100. "Three!" Albert replied immediately. We counted by 3s and got only to 18 books. Kate suggested that we read 6 books every day. We counted 6 for each day and decided that 36 was more than we needed. Nick then said we should try 5 books. Counting by 5s, we found out that that would be just enough to reach our goal.

When I was recording our 144th book on the list, Meredith announced that we were only 6 books away from 150. When I asked how she knew, she showed how she counted up on her fingers from 144 to 150. Alvin explained that he knew because "If we had read 145 books, it would be 5 more, since 45 + 5 = 50." Therefore, if we've read 144 books, we are 6 away from 150.

Making Sure That Objects Are Not Lost

When we were studying the classification of animals, I asked that families send to school items that could be sorted. Mary's mother sent a box of buttons with a note asking that we be careful not to lose any and that we return the box when we are finished. I read this note to the class and asked how we could make sure not to lose any buttons.

Alvin suggested that we sort the buttons only on a table, since the buttons were more likely to get lost on the carpet. Nick went on to say that each child should count all the buttons before sorting them and again afterward. (There were enough for each child to have his or her own pile to sort.) No one suggested that we count all the buttons together and post that number. I was surprised that they counted the buttons at the beginning and end each time they used them.

To prevent game pieces from getting lost, some kindergarten teachers tape a "list" like Figure 8.4 on a box so that children will know how many markers and dice to look for before putting the box away. When children can read numerals, "4 red markers" may be a more appropriate representation.

Voting

When autonomy is the aim of education, voting takes place frequently, as decisions are made by the children as much as possible. My class has an opportunity every day to choose among several areas in our room in which to work. This is called "workshop time," and the children choose from such activities as working on the computer, painting, building with blocks, reading, and writing. This is every class's favorite part of the day besides recess. One day, when we had a speaker, we did not have time for both workshop and recess. When I explained the situation to the children, they were very disappointed and began to argue among themselves about which they were hoping to do, workshop or recess.

Figure 8.4. A "list" of game pieces that must be returned to the box.

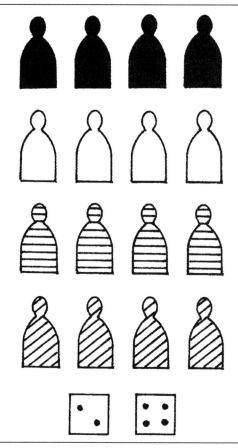

Alba suggested that we vote. I asked the children to raise their hands if they wanted to have workshop. Alba counted 14 hands, and I asked if we needed to count the hands of those who wanted to go outside. Alvin replied that we did not because if 14 people wanted to have workshop, it was impossible to have enough votes for recess. Jack disagreed (he wanted to go outside) and said that we couldn't know for sure without counting. Amy tried to convince him by explaining that 15 and 5 made 20, so 14 and 5 would make 19, meaning that there were only 5 people who wanted to go outside. Jack insisted that it would be unfair not to count the hands and asked everyone who wanted to go outside to raise "your hand." He counted the 5 hands and went on to announce that he changed his mind and wanted to do workshop anyway!

Signing In

When the children arrive in the morning, I often have a sign-in sheet (see Figure 8.5). When they sign in, the children answer a question that is useful not only for learning mathematics but also for the exchange of opinions and experiences. For example, after a unit on light and sound, I asked which they liked better: learning about light or about sound. Before Thanksgiving, I asked whether the children were going out of town for the holiday.

During the morning circle time, we look at the sign-in sheet and count how many people signed in under each answer. Using these numbers, I ask questions such as, "How many people signed in today?" The children share their answers and explain how they arrived at them. Once we agree on the number, we figure out how many people are absent.

The findings from each sign-in sheet are then discussed and recorded in a book about our class.

Three Other Examples

When I introduce a new math game, I tell the class how many people can play it and how many sets of the game are available. I then ask how many children can possibly play the new game at the same time and how many days it would take for each child to have a chance to play.

If a game offers a variety of possible moves, such as Nickelodeon (see Chapter 11) in which children use two numbers to make a total, I ask what the highest possible total is and what all the different ways are of making 11, 10, 9, and so on.

One day, while we were lining up in the lunchroom, Meredith announced that there were 12 children in line. Before I asked a question, Meredith answered it: We had to wait for 7 more.

Figure 8.5. A sign-in sheet.

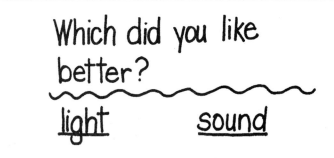

WHAT HAPPENS MONTHLY

At the beginning of each month, the class assembles around an easel to fill in the laminated grid we use as our calendar. We always start with the current day, since the class knows what day of the week it is. After filling in the 5th of January on Monday, for instance, I asked the class where I should write the first. I then asked where the 10th of the month should be, and so on.

Later in the year, I fill in only significant dates, such as a holiday or a child's birthday. The Math Committee is responsible for filling in the rest of the dates. As the calendar begins to fill, I ask the children what they notice. One year, a child observed that "all the numbers in the columns are 7 more." We counted and agreed that this was true. Another child remarked that this was true because there are 7 days in a week.

WHAT HAPPENS AROUND HOLIDAYS

During the Thanksgiving and winter holidays, some fifth graders organized a canned-food drive. Each day, as the children brought in cans, we piled them up in the front of the room. One day, Meredith suggested that the Math Committee count the cans each day so we would know how many we have collected. I taped a sheet of paper on the chalkboard above the stacks, and the Math Committee counted and recorded the number we had each day. The children counted every single can every single day! During the third week of the project, while Alvin was counting the cans, John said, "Just count the new ones!" and began to take some out of Alvin's hands. Alvin protested and no matter how hard John tried to explain the inefficiency of these efforts, Alvin refused to accept John's idea.

DEALING WITH MONEY

Money is a topic in the official curriculum, and I begin by focusing on its social-conventional aspect. I start by asking the children to generate a list of "money words." This gives me a good idea of what kind of knowledge and experience the children have had with money. Next, I show the class my set of Colossal Coins, which are oversized pennies, nickels, dimes, quarters, and half dollars. I hold up each coin, one at a time, and ask what it is called. Most of the children know the names of the coins. I then ask what each is worth. They usually know what a penny and a quarter are worth. They confuse the nickel and dime, and some have not seen a half dollar, or they mistake it for a quarter.

Once we have established these bits of social knowledge, I move into logico-mathematical knowledge. There are several books I use and I usually begin with

26 Letters and 99 cents (Hoban, 1987). This book shows coins equaling 1 to 99 cents. Next, I like to share *Jellybeans for Sale* (McMillan, 1996). In this book jellybeans cost 1 cent each. Children in the book buy different amounts of jellybeans using a variety of coin combinations to pay for them. This gives us lots of opportunities to discuss, for instance, the different ways to make 10 cents.

After reading the book, children take turns "buying" jellybeans from me using the Colossal Coins. When I ask them to come up and buy 10 jellybeans, the first volunteer usually uses 10 pennies. I then ask if someone can think of a way to use different coins. We list all the possibilities until we think we have exhausted them. On subsequent days, I ask volunteers to pay for larger and larger amounts of jellybeans, always asking for more than one way to pay for them. Because I use jellybeans made with construction paper, children can make their own to "buy" from each other throughout the school year.

Bringing Money in for Books

In *Cantaloupes, Cantaloupes* (Atkins & Kuipers, 1990), we read that apples sold "one for a penny," and I asked volunteers to come up with ways to use the Colossal Coins to pay for 9 apples. Kimberly used 9 pennies, and Alvin used a nickel and 4 pennies. Kate then said, "You could use a dime and then you'd get one back." She thus introduced the concept of change, which I had not planned to tackle with my first graders!

I asked the children if it would be right for Kate to pay me a dime and for me to give her a penny. Betty answered Yes and explained that if 9 apples cost 9 cents and Kate gave me a dime, that would be 10 cents. So I would owe Kate a penny because "Ten take away 1 is 9." Many of the children said that they had seen their parents pay for things and get "some money back." I decided to carry this a little further with another problem.

Each child had brought in $5.50 for a book for our next unit, and most of the parents paid by check. When John brought in $6.00 in cash, I did not have any change for him, but Candy brought $5.50 in cash the next day. I told the children how much the book cost and showed them Candy's $5 bill and 2 quarters. The children agreed that that was $5.50. I then showed them John's $5 bill and $1 bill. "That's $6," said Marshall. "That's too much," Meredith remarked. Jerry went on to say, "So you have to give John some change." "Yeah, but how do you know how much?" asked Amy. The other children agreed that that was the hard part.

I wrote "$5.50" on the chalkboard and asked how much two books would cost. "Ten dollars and 50 cents," shouted Kate, and Albert disagreed: "The two 5s make $10 and two 50 cents make a dollar; so that's $11, right?" The class seemed to agree with Albert, and I went on to ask, "So for John and Candy to both get a book, I should have $11?" The children agreed; so I asked them how much money I had. Jack moved to the center of the circle to move the bills and coins as he counted them. "These two 5s are $10. . . . There's this other dollar; that's $11 and 50 cents." Amy then remarked, "You only need $11," and I asked "So how much should I give John back?" Several children shouted "Fifty cents!"

Buying Groceries for Needy Families at Thanksgiving

The teachers of our wing had decided that each child would earn money by doing chores around the house to buy groceries for needy families. On the day the total amount was to be counted in each class, we sat in a big circle on the rug and emptied out all our money. The Big Cheese was the recorder who was to write on the board the amounts counted. We started by counting the bills—the $5 bills by 5s and the $1 bills by ones. Jerry suggested that we count the $1 bills by 5s by making stacks of 5.

I thought we would get stuck when we got to the quarters, but Kate said that, according to her daddy, 4 quarters made a dollar. Since it was only November, I did not ask if anyone could explain why.

John suggested that the class divide itself into small groups and that different groups put all the quarters together, all the dimes together, and so on. When the coins were sorted, the quarter group had several dollars and "3 quarters left." The dime group counted by tens and had over 100 cents. The nickel group counted by 5s, and the penny group counted by ones. The Big Cheese was keeping up with what each group said, and I asked, "How are we going to know how much all of this is?"

Olympia said we could add some to the 3 quarters to make another dollar. I told the children that I knew 3 quarters made 75 cents. Jerry said if we added a nickel to the 3 quarters, that would be 80 cents and proved this by counting by 5s from 5 to 80! We continued to add nickels until we got to 100 cents. Albert said that he knew that 100 cents was the same as a dollar, and we were all satisfied with the result of this hard work. The children had earned about $34.00.

A Penny-Drop Contest

Our school had a penny-drop contest to raise money for a tool shed for our garden. Each class was encouraged to bring in as many pennies as possible to help their hall win the contest. The students were also told that if they rolled the coins into groups of 50 cents before turning them in, they would receive twice the credit for the amount of money turned in. (Contests are not good for the development of autonomy, but they are part of the schoolwide activities in which we feel a need to participate.)

I put a plastic jar in the front of the classroom, and the children put their pennies inside every day. The Math Committee counted the pennies daily, but there were so many by the fourth day that Rosalind said she needed help in counting them. I asked the class what would be the best way to count the pennies.

Carson suggested that we count them by 10s, and the class agreed that that would be the fastest way. The children divided themselves into groups, and I gave each group a pile of pennies. Each group put their pennies in stacks or piles of 10. As these piles were being made, a group gave the left-over pennies to another group who was saying, "We need 2 more," for example. When Carson heard this request, he took 2 from a pile of 10 that had been made, and somebody told him that he could not do this.

As each group finished, it reported how many groups of 10 they had. I recorded this information on the board as follows:

25 stacks of 10
24 stacks of 10
22 stacks of 10
30 stacks of 10

When each group had finished, the children wanted to know how much money they had collected. In retrospect, I should have asked how much they thought there was.

I asked where we should start, and Amy said, "The first group had 25 stacks of 10, and that's . . . $2.50." (She counted by 10s 25 times.) I wrote "$2.50" on the first line and asked what we should do to figure out the next line, "24 stacks of 10." Alvin said, "If 25 stacks made $2.50, 24 stacks should make one less," but Amy disagreed: "It would have to be 10 less because that's one less stack of 10." The class agreed that it would be $2.40, and I wrote this amount in the column of dollar amounts. We figured out the next two groups in the same way, and I wrote "$2.20" and "$3.00" on the board.

John then asked, "But how much money do we have?" and all the children looked a little overwhelmed. So I asked, "What are some things you already know about the numbers up here?" Kate said, "Well, I know that 2 (dollars) and 2 and 2 makes 6, and 3 more would make 9 dollars." I crossed out the numbers she used and wrote "9.00" to the side, as can be seen in Figure 8.6. Kathryn then said "I know that 50 cents and 50 cents is one dollar; so 50 cents and 40 cents would be . . ." and was interrupted by Alvin: "No, 20 is 10 and 10; so if you put one 10 with the 40 cents, that's 50 cents; so that's another dollar." I recorded his argument as shown in Figure 8.6, and Betty exclaimed, "That's 10 dollars!"

"What haven't we added?" I asked, and Albert offered, "The 10 cents left over; so it's 10 dollars and 10 cents." The class agreed, but I think many were disappointed that all of those pennies did not add up to more money.

The group went on to put the pennies in groups of 50 for the coin wrappers. It would have been interesting to have asked how many rolls we would have when we finished, but the class had done enough for one sitting.

Figure 8.6. What the teacher wrote on the board following the statements made by the children.

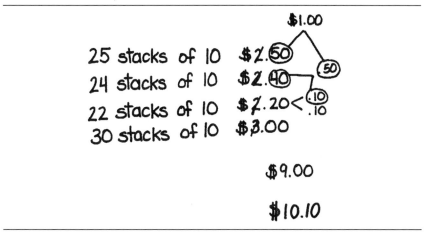

CONCLUSION

In my undergraduate studies, I read about using situations in daily living in *Young Children Reinvent Arithmetic* (Kamii, 1985). When I started teaching, however, I used only word problems, mental arithmetic, and games in my math program. I took for granted that my students were already thinking mathematically in everyday situations and that this was not something we needed to "waste" time on! I didn't realize how negligent I had been in this area until Dr. Kamii asked me to write about math in daily living situations in our classroom. There were only two examples I could think of! Even though I was still not convinced that it was a necessary use of our time, I decided to spend the next school year focusing on math in daily living situations.

As I began to look for math throughout the day, I was struck by several things. First, I couldn't believe how many situations led naturally to a discussion. Second, I found that these discussions took very little time but did a lot to enhance our math program. Next, I was amazed by how readily my students began to recognize the math in their everyday lives. Finally, I was surprised by how something that was previously uncomfortable for me became so natural. Throughout the year, I learned that the children are motivated to solve problems that directly impact their lives. Extending math beyond the scheduled "math hour" helps children recognize math as useful and functional in their everyday lives.

CHAPTER 9

Word Problems

As stated earlier, many authors of textbooks view word problems as *applications* of computational skills. Therefore, in a chapter on addition, for example, we see exercises in producing sums followed by word problems involving only addition.

By contrast, our primary purpose in giving word problems is children's logico-mathematization of reality, and computation grows out of this logico-mathematization. When presented with the following problem, for example, children have to decide whether to use addition and/or subtraction before they work more precisely with numbers: *Grandpa said he grew up in a house where there were 12 feet and one tail. Who could have lived with Grandpa?* Just as our ancestors created mathematics out of the necessity of their reality, today's children should be encouraged to invent arithmetic out of their reality. The use of situations in daily living, which was discussed in Chapter 8, is one way of encouraging children to logico-mathematize reality. Word problems extend their physical and social world beyond the here and now.

The daily math hour in our class generally consists of a word problem and games. However, we sometimes schedule games for the entire hour and sometimes spend the whole hour discussing one or two word problems. In this chapter, we first describe the daily routine, give the general guidelines we follow in deciding what kinds of word problems to give, and conclude with the progress children generally make over the year.

WORD PROBLEMS AND THE MATH HOUR

The word problem of the day is photocopied at the top of a white sheet of paper. The example in Figure 9.1 is Angela's response to the first problem of the year given on September 10: *How many feet are there in your house? Show how you know.* We usually begin the school year at the end of August only with familiar games and wait a few weeks to introduce word problems. Angela's work will often be presented in this chapter so that the reader will have a "feel" for an average child's progress.

When everybody has settled down to begin the day's work, a student or I (LH) read the problem aloud as the rest of the class read it silently. "Does anybody have any questions?" I ask, and the children start working individually. We

Figure 9.1. Angela's response (September 10) to: *How many feet are there in your house?*

usually ask each child to work alone first because we want each person to test his or her own ability and have his or her own opinion about how the problem can be solved. However, if children discuss possible solutions, we do not stop this behavior. Students who ask for help usually need it and learn more through the exchange of points of view than by guessing or copying someone else's work.

As the children work, I circulate around the room talking with individuals in ways that are described later. This is a very important part of our teaching. When the students finish answering the question, they usually compare answers and procedures with neighbors and put their sheets in their math journals. A math journal is a folder with three clips inside, and each child keeps it throughout the year to preserve all of his or her papers in chronological order.

When the word problem is put away, each child selects a game and partner(s) and plays games until the teacher says it is time for the class to assemble in front of the chalkboard to discuss the problem. The whole-class discussion of the word problem takes place at the end of the math hour because some children take much longer than others to finish. Those who have finished should be productively occupied with uninterrupted games while the others take the time they need to solve the problem. I continue to talk individually with those who are still working on the problem. (When a problem is so easy that everybody quickly finishes it, I sit down to play with one or more groups.)

How the Teacher Interacts with Individuals

Our teaching begins with a problem and no suggestions about how to solve it. As I circulate around the room, I first figure out how each child is thinking and formulate questions accordingly. For example, I may say, "Would it help to make a drawing?" but not "Why don't you draw the people's feet?" It is up to each child to decide whether to accept the teacher's idea because children do not develop autonomy (ability to make decisions) by blindly obeying the teacher.

Example 1. The problem one day was the one mentioned earlier about Grandpa and the 12 feet in his house. When I came to Ivan, I saw the paper in Figure 9.2 and noted that Ivan's first answer was "7" (6 Ps + L), and that his second answer was "13" (12 feet + 1 tail). The feet were drawn in pairs, and he had written a "P" for each pair of feet. His representation on paper was thus logical, but he was confused about what to count. As usual, I began the conversation by asking him, "Could you explain to me what you have done?" Ivan answered, "I counted all these lines and got 13."

> *T:* Thirteen what? Thirteen feet? Or 13 people?
> *Ivan:* (Silence)
> *T:* What does the problem ask? (I asked this question because I wanted Ivan to start anew with the question and think more precisely about feet, people, and a tail.)
> *Ivan:* I forgot.
> *T:* (Sending Ivan to the source of information and encouraging self-reliance) Would it help to reread the question?
> *Ivan:* Yes. (He reread the problem and answered.) Who could have lived with Grandpa?
> *T:* Yes. Do you think Grandpa lived with people or with animals?
> *Ivan:* With people, but he had an animal because it says there was a tail.

Figure 9.2. Ivan's response to: *Grandpa said he grew up in a house where there were 12 feet and one tail. Who could have lived with Grandpa?*

At this point, I could have focused Ivan's attention on (1) the number of people in the house, (2) the number of animals, or (3) the number of feet that belonged to Grandpa. I decided to focus on (1) because Ivan had drawn 12 tally marks and had written 6 Ps.

> *T:* You drew 12 lines here (pointing). Do they have something to do with how many people lived with Grandpa?
>
> *Ivan:* Yes. (After counting the Ps he had written) That's 6 people.
>
> *T:* Oh, these 6 people had 12 feet altogether. Was one of those people Grandpa? (This was a big hint, but I was nevertheless giving Ivan the option of rejecting it.)
>
> *Ivan:* Yes (erasing the first "P" and replacing it with a "G").
>
> *T:* So how many other people lived with Grandpa?
>
> *Ivan:* (After counting the remaining Ps) Five.
>
> *T:* I see. And what is this "L" for (pointing to the "L" Ivan had written above something that looked like a tail)?
>
> *Ivan:* That's for Lido, a dog.
>
> *T:* Oh, a dog? Did it have any feet?

Ivan: Oh, yeah! (He circled the tail and the 4 feet above it, and erased two Ps.) That's a dog and 3 people.

T: That makes sense. So Grandpa lived with 3 people and a dog. Thank you, Ivan. Would you like to change your answer?

Note that I never said that a response was correct or incorrect. Instead, I said that I agreed or that something made sense to me (reducing my power and omniscience). I could also have concluded the conversation by asking Ivan, "Does that make sense to you?" The ultimate source of feedback in logico-mathematical knowledge is not what the teacher says but whether something makes sense *to the child*.

Until the very end, I kept asking Ivan to make decisions. Instead of telling him to change his answer, I asked him if *he* wanted to change his answer.

Example 2. I went on to the next child, Vicki, whose paper can be seen in Figure 9.3. Vicki had drawn 12 circles with 2 lines (feet) in each circle, and her answer was "25" (24 feet + 1 tail). I began by asking Vicki to explain what she had done.

Vicki: I drew 12 circles for 12 people and 2 feet for each person. Then, I counted all the feet and got 24. Then I added one to it because there was a tail.

Figure 9.3. Vicki's response to: *Grandpa said he grew up in a house where there were 12 feet and one tail. Who could have lived with Grandpa?*

> *T:* You first drew 12 circles (pointing) for 12 people. Would you like to read the problem to make sure whether there were 12 people or 12 feet? (I wanted Vicki to find out from the print, rather than from me, that the 12 referred to feet.)
>
> *Vicki:* (After reading the first sentence) Oh, it's 12 feet! (She counted the first 12 lines she had drawn and erased all the other lines and circles, and just sat.)
>
> *T:* And what does the problem ask for?
>
> *Vicki:* (After reading the second sentence) One of these people has to be Grandpa. (She labeled the first circle "Grandpa" and counted the other 5 circles.) That's 5 people and a tail. I know, a fish has a tail.

The reader must have noted that Vicki's initial logico-mathematization was at about the same level as Ivan's, but she had more initiative. On rereading the problem, she noticed on her own that one of the 6 people had to be Grandpa. She also recalled on her own that there was a tail in the problem that had to be included in her solution.

Some Principles the Teacher Keeps in Mind in Interacting with Individuals. General principles of teaching such as "Don't show *how* to solve problems" are discussed in Chapter 12. A few principles applying specifically to interactions with individuals working on word problems are given below. The teacher usually begins these conversations by asking children to explain what they have done. Having to justify one's reasoning is beneficial even to a child who produced a correct answer because when we have to explain our own thinking, we think not only about our own thinking but also about how the listener is making sense of what we are saying.

It is important for the teacher always to be diplomatic and supportive, no matter how illogical the child may be. Children who feel respected and supported are more confident about their ability to reason than those who feel on the defensive. Children's confidence is very important because the more confident they are, the more they take the initiative to think. And the more they think, the more they develop their logic.

A way to be supportive in these interactions may be to leave the child temporarily, promising to return. Children often need time to think alone, and hovering over them makes them feel pressured. If the teacher promises to be back, it is, of course, very important to keep this promise.

The teacher sometimes finds herself at an impasse with certain children. One day, for example, the problem asked whether all the small groups would have the same number of children if the class of 21 children went to the store in groups of 4. One child drew, erased, and redrew 21 children, each with arms, legs, eyes, and a mouth, trying to put all of them on one side of the sheet. The child then randomly circled groups of 4 children on her messy paper, leaving some out and unable to tell what had or had not been erased. Knowing that this child had below-average ability, I said, "Thank you. You worked hard on that. We'll see what other people did when we discuss this problem." I thus provided closure because there is no point in pushing children to struggle beyond their limit. They build more taste for mathematics in the long run by stopping their endeavor after making reasonable efforts.

Whole-class Discussion at the End of the Math Hour

A whole-class discussion is a waste of time when the problem is so easy that all the children solved it quickly. When the problem is easy, I skip a whole-class discussion, thereby extending the time allotted to games. Alternatively, I may extend the problem to the next level. For example, if the children easily divided 10 cookies among 4 children, I may ask, "Suppose there were twice as many children—8 of them. How many cookies would each person get?"

The question about who lived with Grandpa was worth a discussion. When all the children had assembled on the rug in front of the chalkboard, I first asked as usual for volunteers to give all the answers they got. "Who wants to tell us their answers?" I asked, and as I called on one volunteer after another, I listed their answers in the upper left-hand corner of the chalkboard, without any comment:

7
3 people and a dog
5 people and a fish
13
6 people and a fish

Children are not afraid of giving wrong answers if they are never put down for being wrong.

"Did anyone else get a different answer?" I asked and went on to the next question: "Is there any answer that seems reasonable or unreasonable to you?" John, one of the two children who raised their hands, explained that it was impossible to have 13 people if there were only 12 feet. This question about the reasonableness of the answers is very important for children's development of number sense. "Does everybody agree with John?" I asked and, having found complete agreement, I erased the "13" on the board.

As usual, I went on to the next question: "Who wants to explain how they got an answer?" Many hands went up, and trying to present a variety of procedures to the class, I called on Angela, whose paper is in Figure 9.4.

Figure 9.4. Angela's response to: *Grandpa said he grew up in a house where there were 12 feet and one tail. Who could have lived with Grandpa?*

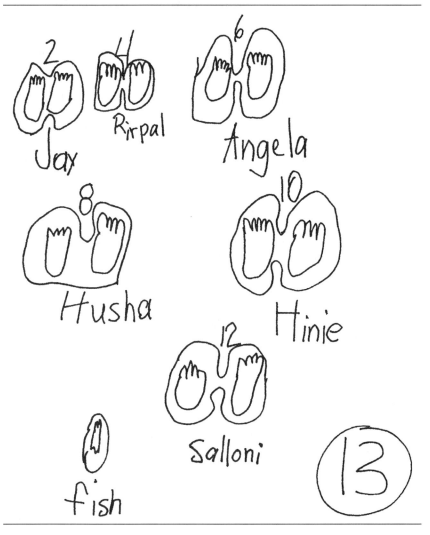

Angela: First, I drew 2 feet.

T: Like this (drawing 2 feet, each with 5 toes)? (Having gone around the room, I knew what Angela had done.)

Angela: Yes, and I circled them, and I wrote "2" on top and "Jay" at the bottom.

I circled the feet and wrote "2" and "Jay" following Angela's description as can be seen in Figure 9.5. My purposes in thus drawing and/or writing by following Angela's statements step by step were: (1) to communicate to Angela what I understood from her description and (2) to make sure that the rest of the class could follow Angela's reasoning. Because the class would have become restless if I had continued to draw all the toes, I asked Angela, "Would it be OK if I drew feet without the toes to save time?"

Angela replied, "Yes, and I drew 2 more feet and circled them. Then I wrote '4' because that's 4 feet, and I wrote 'Rirpal.'" Angela continued in a similar way, and I drew 2 more feet and labeled them exactly as Angela described her procedure. The class could thus see at the end that Angela took care of 2, 4, 6, 8, 10, and 12 feet, and added a fish to have a tail.

Several hands were up by this time, and I did not have to ask "Does anybody have any question for Angela?" I called on Elizabeth, who asked, "Do you mean that Grandpa lived with 6 people and a fish?"

T: (Angela was about to address her answer to me.) Angela, you need to talk to Elizabeth because Elizabeth asked you a question. (Children often talk to the teacher instead of interacting among peers. It is therefore important to redirect their comments to peers.)

Angela: Yes.

(Several hands went up, and Jenna was recognized to speak next.)

Jenna: One of those people has to be Grandpa.

T: What do you think, Angela, about Jenna's question (encouraging Angela to talk to Jenna)?

Angela: I forgot about Grandpa.

T: Would you like to change something in your drawing, Angela?

Angela: Yes, I want to change Jay to Grandpa. That makes 5 people and a fish.

T: So you agree with the person who got this answer (pointing to one of the answers on the board).

I went on to ask, "Did anybody solve the problem in a different way?" and called on Ivan, knowing that his answer was different (3 people and a dog). As

Figure 9.5. What the teacher drew and wrote as she followed Angela's explanation.

Ivan explained how he drew tally marks and labeled them, I followed his procedure step by step on the chalkboard for the entire class to follow. The class agreed
that Ivan's answer was different from Angela's and that it, too, made sense. I
was glad to find out that Ivan did not go back to his earlier, erroneous logico-
mathematization of 12 + 1.

"Did anybody think of a different way?" I again asked and called on Elizabeth, who had written the equation shown in Figure 9.6 (with a "+2" missing).

Figure 9.6. Elizabeth's response to: *Grandpa said he grew up in a house where there were 12 feet and one tail. Who could have lived with Grandpa?*

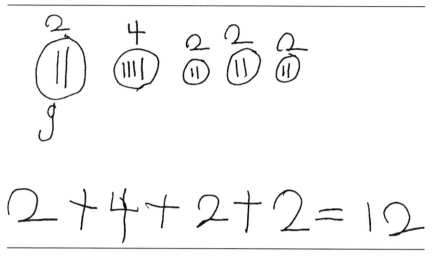

Elizabeth explained that she had drawn 2 tally marks for Grandpa's feet, circled them, and wrote "2" above the circle. She then drew 4 tally marks for a dog's feet, circled them, and wrote "4" above the circle. Then she drew 2 tally marks, 2 more, and 2 more, she reported, as she counted them each time to decide when to stop drawing them. "That's a dog and 3 people," she said, "But I wrote 'Two plus four plus two plus two plus two.'" After drawing all the tally marks and circles Elizabeth specified step by step, I wrote "2 + 4 + 2 + 2 + 2" on the board and asked Elizabeth "Like this?" Elizabeth's answer was: "Yes, but I wrote 'equals twelve.'" I completed the equation as described by Elizabeth, thus writing a complete (corrected) equation on the board.

I thus introduce mathematical signs naturally when the occasion presents itself. Children who want to use this social knowledge do so, and those who are not interested do not. As the more advanced children and I write mathematical signs, more and more children start to use them. (The rationale for this principle of not insisting that children write mathematical signs was discussed in Chapter 2.)

"Did anybody solve the problem in a different way?" I asked again, and the child whose answer was 7 announced, "I disagree with myself. The answer can't be 7." "Oh, so you agree with "3 people and a dog" or "5 people and a fish. OK," I said as I erased the "7" on the chalkboard.

This was a relatively short whole-class discussion. I decided to end it because no one seemed to have any more to say.

Teachers who have been using textbooks at first say that they have trouble inventing word problems. We now discuss some of the guidelines we have conceptualized as we experimented in our classroom.

GUIDELINES FOR CHOOSING AND/OR INVENTING WORD PROBLEMS

We have been collecting word problems, trying out a variety, and building a file with comments about children's reactions and how each might be modified in the future. Some of these problems were created by us, but others were supplied by other teachers. Resources such as TOPS (Greenes, Immerzeel, Schulman, & Spungin, 1980) are also excellent. In selecting word problems, we suggest that teachers give problems that are closely related to children's lives and involve a variety of operations, contents, and situations. At times, it is good to give problems that involve large numbers, those for which there is more than one correct answer, and those that require especially careful logico-mathematization. We will discuss each of these points separately.

Give problems that are closely related to children's lives.

A way to let mathematics grow out of children's lives is to use the situations that come up in and out of the classroom. An example of this principle already given is: *How many feet are there in your house?* Another example is the division of the class into small groups in preparation for a special event. Mentioning individual children by name in the following way stimulates interest: *Kay took 10 cans to be recycled. She was paid a nickel for each can. How much money did she make?*

Another way of relating problems to life is to use holidays. For example, the following problem was given on the day after Halloween: *Russell went trick-or-treating in his neighborhood. He went down 4 streets. Each street had 5 houses on it. How many houses did Russell go to?*

When Valentine's Day approached, one of the problems was: *I went to buy Valentines for the class. There were 5 Valentines in each box. How many boxes did I buy?*

Give problems involving a variety of operations.

For us, as stated in Chapters 6 and 7, there is no clear line of demarcation among the four operations. Young children tend to use addition to solve problems traditionally considered to be "subtraction," "multiplication," and "division" problems. For example, the problem about the number of feet in each child's house was solved with addition. The question about Grandpa and the 12 feet was also solved with addition. The next day's problem was solved additively too (see Angela's work in Figure 9.7): *We planted 12 pole bean seeds. Seven of them sprouted. How many did not sprout?* The important thing in word problems is children's logico-mathematization of reality and not the specific operation they use.

Division problems such as the following already mentioned can lead to fractions: *If 4 children want to share 10 cupcakes, how can everybody have the same amount?* Halves come easily to children who simply externalize their mental images in drawings.

Some problems are much more open and can be answered with a variety of operations. For example, when asked, "Write what you know about 10," children can write as many answers as they can think of such as $4 + 6 = 10, 5 + 5 = 10, 3 + 7 = 10, 11 - 1 = 10, 20 - 10 = 10$, and so on.

The following well-known problem about chickens and pigs also requires trial and error and much more than simple addition or division: *Carl looked at the pigs and the chickens in the farmer's barnyard. He counted 8 heads and 22 feet. How many pigs and how many chickens were in the barnyard?*

In May, the children were given the following multistep problem involving characters from a children's book read in class: *When Rosa, Leora, Jenny, and Mae opened the envelope Leora's mother gave them, they saw 5 dimes, 8 nickels,*

Figure 9.7. Angela's response (in October) to: *We planted 12 pole bean seeds. Seven of them sprouted. How many did not sprout?*

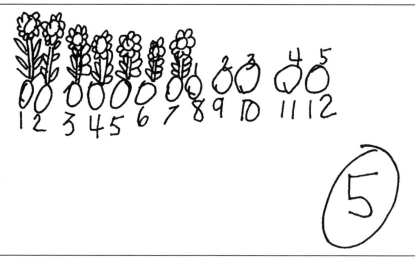

and 10 pennies. How could the girls divide the money so each girl gets a fair share? Some children tried to give the same kinds of coins to all four girls, but others gave 25 cents to each child without thinking about what kinds of coins to give.

Many operations can thus be mixed in a single problem. At the beginning of first grade, giving problems involving a variety of operations means that we give an addition problem one day, a so-called subtraction problem the next day, and a division problem on the subsequent day.

Give problems involving a variety of contents and situations.

The preceding examples have illustrated a variety of contents such as people's feet, seeds, and coins. Variety can also be enhanced by using children's literature as already mentioned in a few examples. Children love stories involving kings, queens, and animals, and books such as Burns (1992) and Sheffield (1995) give excellent specific recommendations. Our children's reactions to *One Gorilla* (Morozumi, 1990) were presented in Chapter 2.

At times, give problems involving large numbers.

It is obviously important to adjust the numbers in word problems so that children can be successful in solving them. We therefore generally give small numbers at the beginning and gradually increase them to the 20s and beyond. For first graders, numbers above 25 seem to be as vague for a long time as our understanding of the federal budget. However, we give numbers up to 100 ($1.00) toward the end of the school year as long as most children seem able to deal with them (10 dimes = $1.00, for example).

Large numbers as such do not necessarily cause trouble by the middle of the school year. Young children love big numbers, and big numbers consist simply of more + 1 + 1 + 1 + 1. . . . Therefore, numbers beyond 25 are not necessarily as hard as authors of textbooks assume. For example, we gave the following problem in the middle of the year: *We will each plant two seeds. If 16 seeds come in a packet, how many packets will I need to buy?* Two times 21 (for 21 students) and 42 divided by 16 cause trouble mainly because less-advanced first graders draw circles or tally marks, erase them incompletely, redraw them, and deal inaccurately with the mess on their papers. Advanced first graders draw neatly and with a good organization from the beginning, as can be seen in the example in Figure 9.8. Bradley did not need to erase anything and easily got the answer of 3 packets.

Problems involving exact multiples of 10 encourage children to use higher-order units (10s) and numerals. For example, one day in February, we gave the following problem based on a children's book, and many average students like Angela solved it with numerals as can be seen in Figure 9.9: *Mr. Higgins made*

Figure 9.8. Bradley's response to: *We will each plant two seeds. If 16 seeds come in a packet, how many packets will I need to buy?*

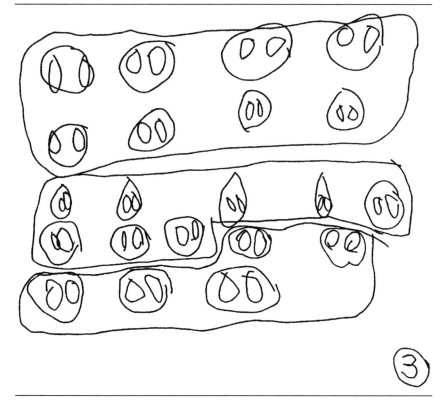

three trips to the clockmaker. On each trip, he spent $10.00 on a clock. How much money did he spend on clocks?

On the next day, a similar problem was given with $12.00 rather than $10.00 for each clock: *That silly Mr. Higgins! He made three more trips to the clockmaker. This time, he spent $12.00 on each clock. How much money did he spend this time?* Most of the children, like Angela, went back to counting by ones using circles and tally marks. Angela wrote numerals, but she was thinking about *ones*, as can be seen in Figure 9.10.

Most first graders deal with 12 + 12 + 12 as 12 ones, plus 12 ones, plus 12 ones. There is an occasional exception by February such as Bradley, whose calculation can be seen in Figure 9.11. After doing 12 + 12 = 24 by counting tally marks, he separated 10 from the next 12, and added 10 to 24 and 2 to 34. Figure 9.12 indicates that Lauren did something similar a month later. She did 11

Figure 9.9. Angela's response (February 26) to: *Mr. Higgins made 3 trips to the clockmaker. On each trip, he spent $10.00 on a clock. How much money did he spend on clocks?*

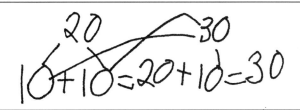

+ 11 by adding the two 10s first and then adding two ones to 20. These inventions are rare in first grade, but they do occur when students are challenged.

At times, give problems for which there is more than one correct answer.

Who could have lived with Grandpa? is an example of a problem that can be answered in more than one correct way. Below are four other examples:

Figure 9.10. Angela's response (February 27) to: *That silly Mr. Higgins! He made 3 more trips to the clockmaker. This time, he spent $12.00 on each clock. How much money did he spend this time?*

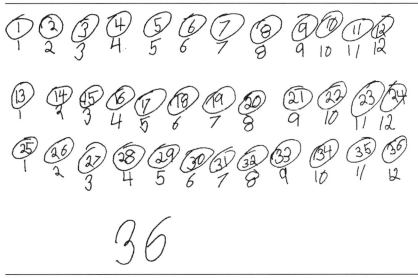

Figure 9.11. Bradley's response to: *That silly Mr. Higgins! He made 3 more trips to the clockmaker. This time, he spent $12.00 on each clock. How much money did he spend this time?*

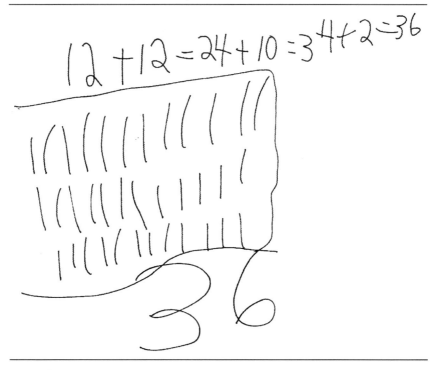

- *Curious George was collecting bicycle and tricycle wheels. He had collected 15 wheels. How many bicycles and tricycles can he make?*
- *You throw 3 beanbags. How can you get a score of 10? (This problem was accompanied by a picture of a board in which four holes had been made for beanbags to go through. The four holes were labeled "1," "2," "3," and "4," respectively.)*
- *How many ways can you make 30 cents using pennies, nickels, and dimes?*
- *I have only pennies and nickels in my pocket (lots of them!). I reach in my pocket and pull out 3 coins. How much money could be in my hand?*

At times, give problems that require especially careful logico-mathematization.

The problem about who could have lived with Grandpa is an example of one that requires careful logico-mathematization. Below are other examples:

Figure 9.12. Lauren's response to: *This is half of my blocks. How many blocks do I have altogether?*

I think its 22 be cause 10+10=20. And then there is 1 from each 10 and then you add 1+1=2 2+20=22.

- *There are 6 boys in front of Lee and 3 girls behind him. How many children are in the line? How many of our classmates are not in line?* (Some children do not think about Lee and simply add 6 and 3.)
- *Mr. Andrews has decided to buy some plants for his factory. He is going to buy 2 corn plants, 3 rubber tree plants, 4 aloe vera, and 1 flowering plant or a cactus. How many plants will he buy?* (Some children add 2 rather than 1 for "1 flowering plant *or* a cactus.")
- *Fern is having a party. Five of her friends will come. Mrs. Arable will bake cupcakes. Each child will have two cupcakes. Mrs. Arable will also bake one for Wilbur. How many cupcakes will she bake?* (Some children think that there will be only 5 children at the party.)
- *If the moms who came to cook yesterday had wanted us to work in 4 groups, would there have been the same number of children in all the groups?* (Some children think the question asks how many children will be in each group.)

- *I am going to sell cookies for 5 cents each. It cost me 75 cents to make the cookies. How many cookies will I need to sell to make a profit?* (The answer of 15, which is often given, is incorrect.)

THE PROGRESS CHILDREN MAKE OVER THE YEAR

Two aspects of children's progress seem noteworthy. One has to do with the ways in which children logico-arithmetize the contents presented in the problem. The other deals with the ways in which children represent objects and numbers on paper. Each of these aspects is discussed below.

Logico-arithmetization

In general, the logico-mathematization of reality is never a problem for the advanced children from the beginning of the year. (Logico-mathematization is broader than logico-arithmetization. Mathematics includes geometry and algebra, and algebra is preceded by arithmetic.) Average children make errors, as we have already seen, and there is usually at least one child in the class who is developmentally so slow that he or she needs help every day for a long time even to get started. We never tell these children what to do and push them to do their own thinking by posing questions or asking if a drawing, counters, or play money might help. Almost all of them become able to solve problems—before the winter break in some cases, and around February in others.

The difference between the top and the bottom of the class at the end of the year is not in their logic but in their numerical thinking. For example, the following problem was given in May when we made the videotape already mentioned (Kamii & Clark, 2000): *In the school store, erasers cost 5 cents each. Howard has saved 62 cents in his jar. How many erasers can he buy?* All the children approached this problem logically, and almost all of them got the correct answer of 12. However, the great majority drew 62 tally marks, circled 5 of them many times, and counted the number of circles. By contrast, the advanced children wrote "5, 5, 5, 5, 5 . . ." or "5, 10, 15, 20, 25. . . ." The majority of the first graders were thus reasoning by *ones*, but the advanced students were reasoning by *fives*.

As stated earlier with respect to the problem about Mr. Higgins's purchase of three clocks at $12.00 each, a few children had also invented 10s and did "24 + 12 = 24 + 10 = 34 + 2 = 36."

Representation

Word problems are by definition given with language, and children must represent to themselves their interpretation of language. For example, when they hear or read *"How many feet are there in your house?"* children may evoke a mental image of the people in their house. As stated in Chapter 2, children are free to use counters to solve problems in the classroom, but they usually choose to draw on paper. The reason is that children prefer to use their own ideas projected onto a blank sheet of paper—an action that is impossible with counters.

On September 10, when the problem asked for the number of feet in each child's house, all the children in the class except about five drew pictures, either of people (as Angela did in Figure 9.1) or of legs and/or feet (as Elizabeth did in Figure 9.13). The more advanced children drew tally marks.

Most of the children were thus representing the *objects* they were thinking about (such as people and legs), but the more advanced children drawing tally marks were representing *ones* (numbers). Feet and people are contents, but numbers such as *ones* are contentless (the results of constructive abstraction as explained in Chapters 1 and 2, especially with reference to Sinclair et al.'s [1983] study). Angela even drew details such as hair, arms, hands, and clothes, which

Figure 9.13. Elizabeth's response (September 10) to: *How many feet are there in your house?*

were irrelevant to the problem. Elizabeth, by contrast, drew only legs, suggesting that she focused only on the parts of the body that were relevant (empirical abstraction within a logico-mathematical framework).

We do not say to children that details such as arms, hands, and hair are irrelevant to the problem because these details are relevant to the children who draw them. However, tally marks and circles soon begin to increase spontaneously, and pictures become rare by spring. First graders thus think more and more numerically and less about the specific contents as they logico-arithmetize them. However, this progression is very gradual, and children go back and forth between drawing tally marks one day and drawing pictures on many subsequent days.

A parallel development is the appearance of numerals on children's papers. Numerals are first used to label groups of objects or tally marks or to represent the act of counting. In Figures 9.4 and 9.7, we can see that, in October, Angela started to use numerals to represent the act of counting objects. She was beginning to use numerals, but it was still important to her to draw toes in great detail in Figure 9.4, and leaves and flowers in Figure 9.7.

As their numerical reasoning becomes stronger, first graders begin to use numerals as independent signs. In December, Angela surprised us by writing equations (see Figure 9.14). Before writing these equations, she had connected the 1 cent with another 1 on the tree, 2 cents with another 2, and so on. She also drew tally marks below each numeral to get the total cost of all the ornaments. After getting the total of 35, she spontaneously wrote the equations for the doubles that she knew very well and $10 + 5$, which was easy for her.

The fact that Angela wrote equations does not imply that she wrote them consistently. She continued to use tally marks until the end of the school year and occasionally drew pictures until February 11, when the problem asked how many children had played in the snow if there were 22 boots left by the door to dry.

Children first seem to write numerals for numbers that are easy for them, such as 5 and 10. As can be seen in Figure 9.9, Angela used only numerals on February 26, when the problem involved exact multiples of 10. On the next day, when the problem involved 12s, she used numerals but went back to the addition of *ones* (refer to Figure 9.10). While she often continued to use tally marks, she consistently used "equations" ($5 + 5 = 10 + 5 = 15 + 5 \ldots$) when a problem involved nickels.

Angela also wrote equations without tally marks when the numbers involved in a problem were small and easy for her. For example, she wrote "$3 + 4 = 7$" when presented with the following problem in February: *Six people get on an empty elevator. Three get off at the next floor, and 4 more get on. How many people are on the elevator now?* In April, she wrote "$1 + 10 = 11 + 5 = 16$" when the problem was: *Marilee put 1 cent in her jar the first day. She put 10 cents in*

Figure 9.14. Angela's response to: *How much are the ornaments on this tree worth?*

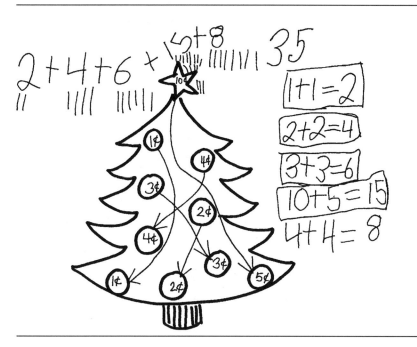

on the third day. Now she has 16 cents. How much did she put in her jar the second day?

Children thus seem able to choose for themselves the tools that work best for them. Just as they give up crawling on their own when they can walk, they give up pictures and tally marks when they decide that numerals work better for them.

CHAPTER 10

Games Involving Logic, Spatio-Temporal Reasoning, Small Numbers, and Numerals

This book is about arithmetic, and not about geometry or physical knowledge. However, some young children have not yet developed sufficiently to differentiate number from other aspects of knowledge and cannot yet enjoy arithmetic games. The lack of differentiation between space and number was seen in the conservation-of-number task in Chapter 1 and our explanation of why nonconservers do not conserve. There is also little differentiation between physical and logico-mathematical knowledge (between empirical and constructive abstraction) among less-advanced children. Since these children prefer activities involving physical knowledge, these kinds of games are presented at the end of this chapter. Number concepts develop out of the undifferentiated relationships young children have been making since infancy.

This chapter is devoted to games involving logic, spatio-temporal reasoning, small numbers, and numerals. Those involving addition and subtraction are presented in Chapter 11. Although the games described in Chapter 10 are generally more appropriate for kindergarten than for first grade, some like Make the Biggest Number and Animal Olympics are intended for first graders. Most kindergartners can play addition games that appear in Chapter 11 such as One More, Piggy Bank, and Double War (with cards up to about 5).

This chapter is divided into two parts. In the first part are games involving logical relationships between and among pictures and spatial relationships among objects. In the second part are those involving small numbers and/or numerals. Both begin with card games and proceed to board games, and a few games involving physical knowledge and whole-class activities appear at the end of the chapter.

We invented some of these games, but most were found in classrooms, described at conferences, or photocopied from various sources and passed around. Modifications of the games are included based on observation in classrooms. Information on commercially made games and materials is provided in the Appendix, as is a list of catalogs through which games may be purchased. To avoid wordy expressions such as "he or she," "his or her," and "himself or herself," we alternate between "he" and "she" from game to game in this chapter and Chapter 11.

GAMES INVOLVING PICTURES AND OBJECTS

Card Games

Drug stores and discount stores often carry commercially made cards such as *Snap*, *Fish*, and *Animal Rummy*, attesting to their popularity. Below are three games that can be played with these cards. The number of players we recommend is two to four unless otherwise specified, but three is generally ideal for maximizing children's opportunities for mental activities. Details such as how to decide who goes first are not given because, for children's development of autonomy, it is best that players make this kind of decision through negotiation.

CONCENTRATION

Materials: 6 or more pairs of picture cards. Regular playing cards can also be used. The following 6 pairs, each pair in the same color, are good for beginners because the large differences among the pairs facilitate perceptual discrimination: kings, queens, 2s, 4s, 6s, and 10s.

Play: The cards are arranged, face down, in neat rows (3 rows of 4 cards each, for example). The players take turns turning two cards over trying to make pairs that match. (It is more advantageous to turn one card over after another than two cards simultaneously.) If a player succeeds in making a pair, he can keep it and continue trying to make more pairs. If he fails, the two cards that do not match are returned to their face-down positions. The person to the left is the next player. (For the development of children's autonomy, it is better that children make this kind of decision through negotiation. When games are first introduced, however, some young children are too heteronomous to engage in such negotiations.)

The winner is the person who collects the greatest number of cards (or pairs of cards).

Concentration is the easiest of all card games, and one that even many 3-year-olds can play. It is easy because (1) the children do not have to hold any cards, and (2) they do not have to make relationships between more than two cards at a time. Because this is an easy game, it is a good one for first graders who are introduced to math games for the first time. Young children count cards rather than pairs of cards at the end. Some only compare the height of the stacks.

This game can be made harder by adding more pairs of cards (for example, A through 5, then A through 6, and so on). Another modification for more advanced children is Huckleberry Hound (see Chapter 11), which involves addition.

ANIMAL RUMMY

Materials: Nine (or more) sets of 4 cards each of *Animal Rummy* cards. Regular playing cards or any picture cards mentioned earlier in this chapter can also be used.

Play: Seven cards are dealt to each player to begin the game. The remaining cards constitute the drawing pile, which is placed face down in the middle of the table. The top card of the drawing pile is turned over and placed next to it, face up, to begin the discard pile. The object of the game is to make 2 sets of 3 identical cards first.

The first player begins by taking a card either from the discard pile (which in this case has only one card in it) or from the top of the drawing pile. She tries to make a set of 3 identical cards and then discards one card, face up, on the discard pile. In other words, each player begins a turn by taking a card and ends the turn by discarding one, thereby having 7 cards again.

The turns proceed clockwise (or in some other order agreed on by the players), until someone wins by having 2 sets of 3 identical cards.

When this game is first introduced, it is desirable that all the players arrange their 7 cards face up in front of them because (1) children can then offer advice to each other, (2) young children often do not notice advantageous or disadvantageous possibilities, and (3) young children do not play competitively anyway.

This is a great game of logic in which children begin each turn by deciding whether it is more advantageous to take the card they can see in the discard pile or one they cannot see in the drawing pile. Many levels of logic can be observed, and some children cannot "see" the advantage of taking a card that is visible in front of their eyes!

Many levels of logic can likewise be observed when children decide which card to discard. For example, having noticed that the next player has 2 monkeys, some children avoid discarding a monkey. By contrast, those at a lower level cannot "see" the next player's monkeys (which are visible) because they cannot make these kinds of relationships.

MAKING FAMILIES

Materials: Five or more sets of 4 cards that are the same, such as those mentioned earlier in this chapter. Playing cards can also be used.

Play: This game is similar to Go Fish, but all the cards are dealt, and there is no "pond" or drawing pile. When all the cards have been dealt, the first player begins by asking someone for a card in an attempt to make a family of 4 of a kind. For example, Brenda may say, "Josh, do you have an elephant?" If Josh has one, he has to give it to Brenda. As long as a player gets a card asked for, he can continue asking for more. If Josh says, "I don't have any," the turn passes to Josh because he said "I don't have any."

Play continues until all the cards have been put down in groups of 4. The person who makes more families than anybody else is the winner.

Making Families is a better game than Go Fish because it makes logical deductions possible. For example, if three people are playing Making Families, and player B has said to player A that he does not have an elephant, A can deduce that C *must* have all the elephants that A does not have. When there is a drawing pile, by contrast, A cannot know whether the other elephants are in C's hand or in the drawing pile. Advanced 5–year-olds can make this kind of deduction and make many families with spectacular speed.

Board Games

Below are seven board games that encourage children to think strategically and make spatial and temporal relationships. All of them are 2–player games and encourage children to decenter (that is, to make spatial and temporal relationships from another point of view and to coordinate that perspective with one's own).

TIC TAC TOE

Materials: A Tic-Tac-Toe set (see Photograph 10.1) or a board made on paper by drawing two vertical lines and crossing them with two horizontal lines.

Play: One player takes the Xs, and the other, the Os. The players take turns placing one of their pieces in a space that is empty. The object of the game is to get 3 of one's pieces in a line first, vertically, horizontally, or diagonally. The boy in Photograph 10.1 may or may not anticipate that unless he puts an X between the two Os, the girl will win.

Tic Tac Toe can be made harder by using a 5 × 5 board, and the person who gets 4 in a line first wins. Another modification is to use two boards.

QUARTETTE

Materials: A board with 16 squares (see Figure 10.1); 8 poker chips or checkers, 4 each of two colors.

Play: Each player takes 4 poker chips of the same color. The chips are arranged as shown in Figure 10.1 to begin the game.

Photograph 10.1. Tic Tac Toe

The players take turns moving one of their chips either vertically or horizontally (but not diagonally) into any unoccupied adjoining square. Squares, whether vacant or not, must not be jumped over, and a player must always make a move when her turn comes.

The winner is the first player to get her 4 pieces in a straight, unbroken line, horizontally, vertically, or diagonally. Young children do not have any strategy at the beginning, and some even play so that both partners get a straight line of chips!

Figure 10.1. The beginning of Quartette.

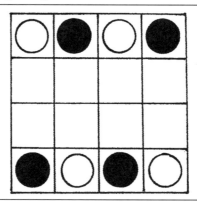

THE SPIDER GAME AND TAPATAN

Materials: The gameboards shown in Figures 10.2 and 10.3; 6 poker chips (3 each of 2 colors).

Play: In The Spider Game, each player takes 3 chips of the same color and places them on the spiders closest to him. The object of the game is to get one's chips in a straight line first. (One of one's 3 chips has to be in the center to make a straight line.)

The first player slides one of his chips along any line to the next vacant point. The other player then takes his turn.

In Tapatan, each player also takes 3 chips of the same color but tries to be first to get 3 in a line horizontally, vertically, or diagonally. The players begin by taking turns placing chips on any of the 9 points (or circles) that are vacant. When all 6 chips are placed, the players take turns sliding from one point to the next along a line. They cannot jump over another marker, and 2 markers cannot be on the same point.

Tapatan offers more possibilities of making a straight line with 3 chips, as it is not necessary to have a chip in the center.

PENTOMINOES

Materials: Two sets of 12 pentominoes in two different colors (available through catalogs such as those of Cuisenaire Dale Seymour Publications, ETA, and Nasco; see Appendix); a board with a 10" × 10" grid on it for a competitive game (a 15"

Figure 10.2. The board for The Spider Game.

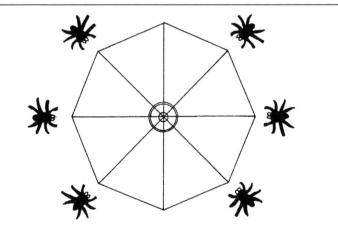

Figure 10.3. The board for Tapatan.

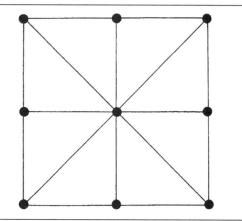

× 15" grid for a noncompetitive game). (As can be seen in Figure 10.4, the pentominoes come in a variety of shapes, but each pentomino is made by putting 5 squares together.)

Play: Each player takes 12 pentominoes of the same color. The person who begins the game puts down one of her pieces anywhere, making sure that it fits inside the lines on the board.

The players take turns putting a pentomino down in such a way that the new piece does not touch any pentomino of one's own color, and every new piece

Figure 10.4. A pentomino touching another pentomino of another color.

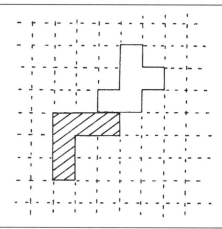

touches at least one inch of the opponent's piece (see Figure 10.4). In this game, "touching" means "sharing at least 1 inch of a line."

The winner is the first person to use up all 12 of her pieces. When using the 10" × 10" board, whoever gets stuck first is the loser.

A 15" × 15" grid is best for kindergartners because they become frustrated with a 10" × 10" grid and do not play this game competitively anyway.

TRAP THE KING

Materials: The gameboard shown in Figure 10.5; 2 "kings" (blocks) of different colors; 60 counters.

Play: The two kings (blocks) are placed on the marks that look like asterisks to begin the game. The object of the game is to entrap the opponent's king so that it will be unable to move.

The players take turns by first moving one's own king to any adjoining unoccupied space (by one space, horizontally, vertically, or diagonally) and then placing a counter on any unoccupied space. Play continues until one of the kings is trapped and cannot move horizontally, vertically, or diagonally into an adjoining square.

The squares that have asterisk-like marks are treated as any other square once the game begins.

This game is similar to Quartette and Checkers, but because children place a counter on each square as they move, these objects help them recall where they have been and where they are going. The counters thus facilitate strategic thinking.

Figure 10.5. The board for Trap the King.

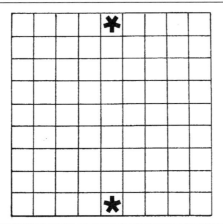

CHECKERS

Materials: A checkerboard; 12 black checkers and 12 red ones.

Play: The players decide who will use which color and arrange their respective checkers on the black squares in the first three rows near them. The object of the game is to move one's checkers to the three rows on the opposite side first and to eliminate or block the opponent's checkers.

The players take turns moving their checkers forward, one square at a time, diagonally to an adjacent black square. Checkers cannot be moved backward or to a red square.

A checker can jump an opponent's if the square beyond it is vacant. When a checker is jumped, it is eliminated from the board and captured by the person who made the jump. A player cannot jump her own checker.

On reaching the last row on the opposite side, a checker is "kinged" by placing a previously captured checker of the same color on top of it. A king can move or jump either forward or backward.

NINE MEN'S MORRIS

Materials: The gameboard shown in Figure 10.6; 9 markers for each player (in two different colors).

Play: The players take turns putting one marker on the board at a time at any unoccupied point (where lines meet or cross). When both players have

Figure 10.6. The board for Nine Men's Morris.

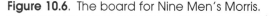

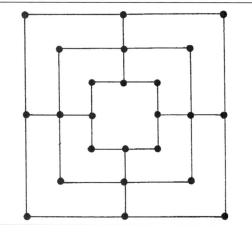

put all their markers on the board, they take turns sliding one marker along any line to an unoccupied adjacent point. When a player makes a line of 3, he takes one of the opponent's pieces off the board. The opponent's pieces taken must not already be in a line of 3 unless there are no other markers left on the board.

The winner is the first player to reduce the number of the opponent's markers to 2.

GAMES INVOLVING SMALL NUMBERS AND/OR NUMERALS (WITHOUT ADDITION OR SUBTRACTION)

Card Games

The use of regular playing cards is assumed in the following card games unless some other material is specifically mentioned. If the sequence of A, 2, 3, 4 is a problem, the teacher may want to white out the "A" and change it to "1."

Flinch cards or *Rook* cards can also be used if children can read numerals. *Flinch* cards consist of 10 sets of numeral cards going from 1 to 10, all in the same color. In *Rook*, there are 4 sets of 4 different colors, each set going from 1 to 14.

LINE-UP (OR CARD DOMINOES)

The face cards (J, Q, and K) are removed from the deck before the remaining cards are dealt to all the players. The children take turns putting down one card at a time trying to make a matrix in the middle of the table consisting of 4 rows (hearts, diamonds, spades, and clubs) going from 1 to 10 in order.

If the first player puts down a 1 of spades, for example, the second player can put down a 2 of spades or a 1 of any other suit. If the second player puts down a 2 of spades, the third player can put down a 3 of spades or a 1 of any other suit. All the numbers have to be placed in order within each suit, without skipping any.

Anyone who does not have a card that can be played must pass. The first player to use up all her cards is the winner.

This game can be modified by beginning with the 10s and proceeding in descending order. Another modification is to begin with the 5s and go both up and down. A game for very young children should use cards going only up to 5.

Children do not have to know how to read numerals to play this game, and many kindergartners learn to recognize numerals by playing this game. The teacher may want to white out the small symbol below each numeral if children persist in counting them and saying that the "2" says "4," the "3" says "5," and so on.

In this game, there are too many cards for young children to hold, and we recommend that they be aligned face up in front of each player. Many do not think of any strategy anyway, even when all the cards are visible! Many kindergartners and first graders help each other when a player does not notice in her own hand a card that can be used.

This is a game of logic for those who think about it. Most children do not sort or seriate their cards, but more-advanced children do. Advanced children are thus able to anticipate that to be able to play a 9 and a 10 of hearts, for example, it is better to play a 5 of hearts than to play a 5 of another suit.

When children can make many relationships simultaneously, they want to change the rule to: "Put down all the cards one can on each turn." This is a good change because when children become able to think fast, they do not like games that move too slowly.

WAR

It is best to have only two players at the beginning and later increase the number when children can easily compare more than two numbers. All the cards are dealt (see below to decide which cards to use). Without looking at the cards, each player keeps his pile face down. The players then simultaneously turn over the top cards of their respective piles. The person who turns up the larger number takes both cards. The winner is the person who has collected more cards than the other at the end.

If there is a tie, each player turns over the next card, and the person who turns up the larger number takes all 4 cards. (This is a simplification of the conventional rule, which children often insist on following.)

In this game, children compare numerical quantities and judge which of two numbers is "more." It is best at first to use cards from two decks going up to 4 or 5 only and later use 4–8 or 6–10, for example. Cards going up to 4 or 5 are educationally not very valuable because numbers up to 4 or 5 are *perceptual numbers*, as stated in Chapter 1. These small perceptual numbers can be distinguished at a glance even by some birds. Comparing a "2" with an "8" is likewise of little educational value because the judgment can be made by perceptual discrimination.

First graders at times want to take a peek at their cards and choose the next card they want to play. When they decide to change the rule to "Everybody can choose a card," many believe that a 10 beats a 3 more than a 4 because a 10 is stronger!

War becomes more interesting when it is modified into an addition game, Double War, which is presented in Chapter 11.

CRAZY EIGHTS AND *UNO*

Materials: A deck of playing cards or *UNO* cards.

Play: Crazy Eights begins by dealing 5 cards to each player and placing the remaining cards face down as the drawing pile. The top card is turned over and placed face up beside the drawing pile. The players try to win by getting rid of all their cards first.

Each person puts, face up on the upturned card, a card that matches it either by number or by suit. For example, a 2 of hearts can be matched either with a 2 of any other suit or with a heart of any other number. All 8s are "crazy" ("wild") and may be played on any card. Whoever plays an 8 tells the next player what suit ("picture" or "symbol") to play next.

If a player cannot match a card or play an 8, she must take cards from the drawing pile until one is found that can be played. When the pile is used up, she passes.

UNO is very similar but has instruction cards saying "Draw four [cards]," "Skip [the next player]," and "Reverse [the direction in which the turns are taken]."

I DOUBT IT

The 40 cards 1 through 10 are dealt. No one lets the others see his cards. The first player puts a 1 in the middle of the table, face down, saying "One." The second player then places a 2 on top of the first card, also face down, saying "Two." A player who does not have a card that is needed in the sequence uses another card trying to get away with this substitute.

Anyone who thinks that a false card has just been played says "I doubt it." If the doubt is verified, the person caught must take all the cards on the table and add them to his hand. If the doubt is not verified, the accuser has to take all the cards. Play continues until one person wins by getting rid of all his cards.

THE CLOCK GAME

The entire deck is used. Twelve cards are arranged, face down, like the face of a clock as shown in Photograph 10.2a. The easiest way is to begin with the 12-o'clock and 6-o'clock positions and then the 9-o'clock and 3-o'clock positions. The dealer continues to put cards down around the clock, one at a time, face down, until there are 4 cards in each of the 12 positions. The remaining 4 cards are placed in the center of the clock in a face-down pile, and the top card of this pile is turned over to begin the game.

If the turned-over card is a 3, for example, the first player places this card in the 3-o'clock position as shown in Photograph 10.2a. The second player then

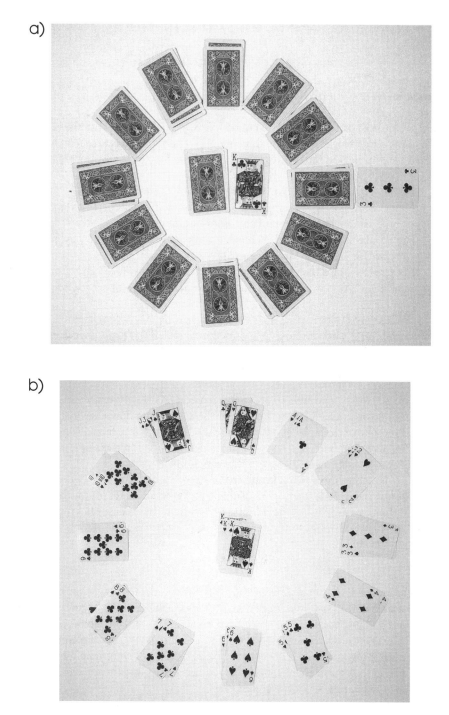

Photograph 10.2. The Clock Game

turns over the top card of the pile in the 3-o'clock position. If, for example, this card is a 10, she places it in the 10-o'clock position. The top card in the pile in the 10-o'clock position is then turned over by the third player, and the game continues.

If a player turns up a king (a 13), she has to put it in the center of the clock as shown in Photograph 10.2a. The next player then takes the top card of the face-down pile in the center, and the game continues until all the cards have been arranged as can be seen in Photograph 10.2b.

The person who has to put the fourth king in the center of the clock is the loser. Many children enjoy playing this game alone as Clock Solitaire.

BEFORE OR AFTER

All 40 cards 1–10 are dealt, and the players keep them in a face-down stack. The first player turns over the top card of his stack and discards it in the middle of the table. The next player turns over the top card of his stack and tries to use this card to make a pair with a number that comes immediately before or after it. (If there is a 5 on the table, for example, a pair can be made with either a 4 or a 6.) If a pair can be made, the second player can take both cards and keep them. If not, the card turned over has to be discarded in the middle of the table.

Play continues until pairs cannot be made any more. The winner is the person who collected more pairs than anyone else.

SPEED (OR SPIT)

This is a two-player game. The dealer places 2 cards in the middle of the table, face down. She then deals 5 cards, face down, next to each of these 2 cards as shown in Figure 10.7a.

The rest of the cards are dealt to the two players, face down. Each player then draws 5 cards from those that have been dealt.

To begin the game, the players count to three and simultaneously turn over the 2 cards that were placed in the middle of the table (see Figure 10.7b). The object of the game is to be first to use up all 14 of one's cards by placing on these 2 cards, one at a time, a number that comes immediately before or after the number that can be seen. For example, if a 5 and a 9 are up (Figure 10.7b), the cards that can be played are a 4 or a 6 (on the 5), or an 8 or a 10 (on the 9). If a 4 is placed on the 5, then either player can put a 3 or a 5 on the 4. Speed is important in this game.

Each time a card has been used, the player can take one from her pile to have 5 cards again.

Figure 10.7. The cards in Speed (or Spit).

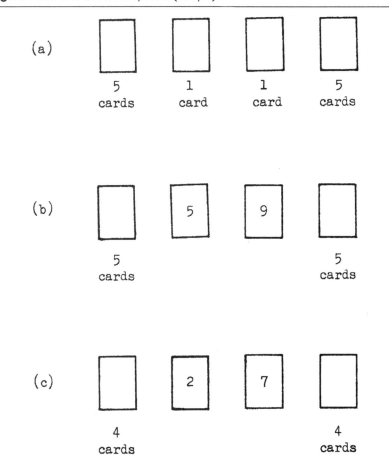

(a)   5 cards   1 card   1 card   5 cards

(b)   5 cards   5   9   5 cards

(c)   4 cards   2   7   4 cards

If neither player has a card that can be played, the top card of each 5-card stack in the middle of the table is turned over simultaneously and placed face-up on top of the two center piles (see Figure 10.7c).

MAKE THE BIGGEST NUMBER

Materials: 50 cards, 5 each of the numerals 0 to 9.

Play: All the cards remain in a box, face down. Each player draws 2 cards and tries to make the biggest two-digit number possible. The person who makes the biggest number takes all the cards that were played in this turn. Play continues until the box is empty. The winner is the one with the most cards.

Make the Biggest Number aims only at strengthening children's *social knowledge* of place value and does not attempt to teach the logico-mathematical knowledge of "tens and ones." As stated in Chapter 2, the great majority of first graders cannot *think* "one ten" and "ten ones" *simultaneously*. This game merely involves the social knowledge that 32 is more than 23, for example, because 32 comes after 23 in our system of writing.

ANIMAL OLYMPICS

Materials: 39 cards numbered 1–39. (The name of this game came from the fact that the commercially made cards had animals on them.)

Play: Eight cards are dealt to each player, in a face-down row. The players are not allowed to look at the cards received. The remaining cards are placed in a face-down stack. The object of the game is to be first to get 8 cards in the correct order, face up, from the lowest number on the left to the highest number on the right as shown in Figure 10.8a.

The first player takes the top card of the face-down stack and trades it for one of his face-down cards. If the number drawn is large, a good place for it is as shown in Figure 10.8b. If the number is small, the other end of the line is a good place (see Figure 10.8c). If a 22 is drawn, the middle of the row is a good place for it (see Figure 10.8d). The first player then gives the replaced card to the next player, and it is the second player's turn to decide which one of his cards should be replaced.

A person loses the game if, for example, he has the arrangement in Figure 10.8e and receives an 8. Once a card has been turned over, it has to remain face up.

Another version of this game is to give a choice at the beginning of each turn: A player can either accept the card given or discard it in the discard pile and take the top card of the face-down stack.

Thirty-nine is a large number for most first graders, and we have tried to reduce the maximum number to 20. This modification did not work because there were then not enough cards for children to work with. Therefore, this game has to be introduced later in first grade, when children's number sense goes up to 39.

Board Games

FIFTY CHIPS

Materials: A board for each player divided into 50 squares (5 squares × 10 squares, see Photograph 10.3); 50 chips for each player; a 6-sided or 10-sided die with dots or numerals.

Figure 10.8. The cards in Animal Olympics.

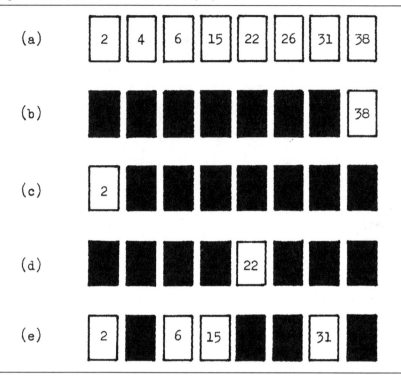

Play: The players take turns rolling the die and putting the corresponding number of chips on their boards. The winner is the first one to fill his board.

This game can be made harder by using two dice, in which case it becomes an addition game. It can also be made easier by using smaller boards with 20 or 30 squares. Some children suggest that each player has to fill up and then empty her board.

Young children have trouble even putting the chips in the spaces! Also, they reveal their low-level spatial organization by not filling up the board in any organized way.

Hop to It

Materials: A board such as the one shown in Photograph 10.4; a 6-sided or 10-sided die with dots or numerals; a marker for each player.

Photograph 10.3. Fifty Chips

Play: The players take turns rolling the die and moving their markers the corresponding number of steps on the path. The winner is the first person to reach the tree.

The players must agree on the rule about how to end this game. Some think that the exact number has to be rolled to reach the goal, but others say that either the exact number or a larger one is acceptable.

This game can also be played with two dice, in which case it becomes an addition game. The commercially made *Candy Land* is a much easier version of a path game, and *Chutes and Ladders* is harder than Hop to It. The path can also be spiral (see Photograph 10.5) or zigzag (see the numerals in Photo-

Photograph 10.4. Hop to It

Photograph 10.5. Dinosaurs

graph 10.6) with various themes such as dinosaurs or Star Wars. In these games, the rule can stipulate that if one lands on a picture, one must take an instruction card and follow the instruction on it. Below are examples of instructions that can be written on cards:

> Run forward 4 spaces.
> Go forward one space.
> Run back 4 spaces.
> Go back 2 spaces.
> Move any player back or forward to 18.
> Go to see the cat at 5.
> Run to the dog food dish.

The difference between Fifty Chips and a path game is that the number of spaces covered remains visible in Fifty Chips. In Hop to It, for example, the number of steps taken disappears as soon as the steps have been taken. Fifty Chips is therefore a better game for children whose number concepts are not yet strong.

Photograph 10.6. Star Wars

TRACK MEET

Materials: The board shown in Figure 10.9 representing a track field divided into 52 segments, with the starting line, which is also the finish line; 2 markers; 2 dice (1–6 or 1–10 with dots or numerals).

Play: Each player takes a marker and one of the dice. Each player rolls her die, and the one with the higher number moves. For example, if a player rolls a 5 and the other, a 3, the one with the 5 moves 5 spaces, and the other player remains at the starting line.

Play continues, and the winner is the one who gets her marker across the finish line first.

This game is like War in which two numbers are compared. The rule could state that the player who rolled the larger number advances by one step, but such a game would be too slow and boring.

A similar game can be played using Unifix cubes to add. Unifix cubes offer the advantage of remaining visible.

Figure 10.9. The board for Track Meet.

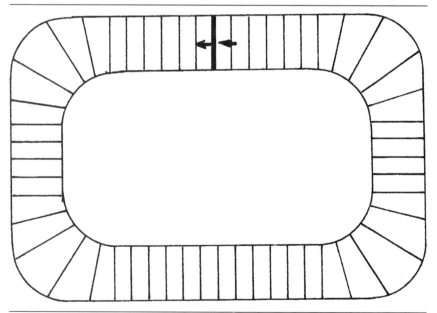

BINGO

Materials: A commercially made Bingo set.

Play: Bingo boards are divided into 25 squares in a 5 × 5 arrangement. Each square is numbered, and the numbers are randomly arranged. Each player's board is different.

The Bingo set contains 99 or 100 pieces of wood, plastic, or cardboard bearing numerals. On each piece is a numeral from 1 to 100 or 99. These pieces are placed in a sack and mixed. A caller reaches into the bag, takes these pieces out one at a time, and calls out the number drawn. The player who has this number speaks up and puts a chip on his board, on the number called. The caller then places the piece drawn on a master sheet on which all the numbers are written. This game is therefore good for the acquisition of the social knowledge of numerals.

The winner is the first player to fill a row, a column, or a diagonal and say "Bingo!" (Four corners is also a win in some games, and children can also try to make a "T" or a "Z" to win.) The win is verified by checking his numbers against the master sheet.

CROSSING

Materials: The board shown in Figure 10.10; 9 chips (3 each of three different colors); a 1–6 die.

Play: Each player takes 3 chips and chooses one of the three sections on the board in which to place her chips.

The first player rolls the die and may move any of her chips forward by that number of squares. Once a chip has been touched, it must be moved.

If a player lands on a "black-dot" square, the chip must be returned to Start.

The exact number must come up for each chip to land on Finish. The first player to get all of her chips to Finish wins.

In this game, advanced children begin to remember combinations that make 10. If they are on 8, for example, they begin to say "I need a 2." They later learn more difficult combinations such as "If I am on 6, I need a 4." To avoid black-dot spaces, advanced children also move to the square before or after a black dot and use the remaining moves on another chip. For example, if they roll a 3, they may move 2 spaces in one lane and 1 space in another lane.

Physical-knowledge Games

The movement of objects belongs to physical knowledge. All babies and very young children develop their logico-mathematical knowledge as they act

Figure 10.10. The board for Crossing.

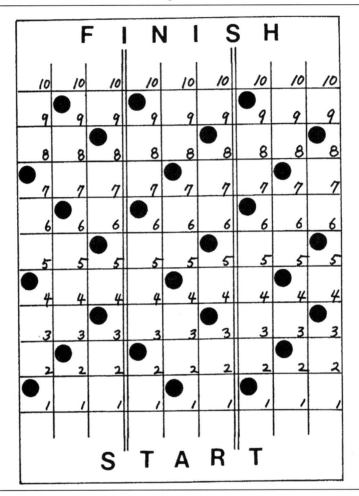

on objects to produce desired effects (Kamii & DeVries, 1978/1993). The following games are therefore especially good for slow-developing children who are not yet interested in card games and board games that involve only logico-mathematical knowledge.

PICK-UP STICKS

Materials: Commercially made pick-up sticks or about 30 Japanese chop sticks (see Photograph 10.7).

Photograph 10.7. Pick-Up Sticks

Play: Each player begins by holding all the sticks in one hand and releasing them so that they will scatter on the floor. He then tries to pick up as many as possible, one at a time, without making any other stick move. If he makes one stick move, this is the end of the player's turn.

The next player gathers all the sticks and begins his turn. The winner is the person who picks up more sticks than anybody else.

This game can be modified into an addition game by stipulating, for example, that the red sticks are each worth 2 points (or 5 points).

In this game, children first categorize all the sticks into "those which are not touching any stick" and "the others." Within the second category, they seriate the sticks from the easiest to the more and more difficult ones to pick up.

BOWLING

Materials: About 12 empty plastic bottles with some sand in them; a ball.

Play: Each player arranges all the plastic bottles behind a line in any way she considers advantageous and rolls a ball from a certain distance. The person who knocks over more "pins" than anybody else is the winner.

This game is especially good for children to devise ways of keeping score as can be seen in Kamii (1982). Children also think about the different ways in which they arrange the pins and what kind of arrangement is most advantageous (spatial reasoning).

MARBLES

This is also an aiming game. All the marbles are placed in the middle of a circle taped on the floor. A player rolls a marble from a distance outside the circle, trying to knock as many marbles out of the circle as possible. The person who rolls more marbles out of the circle than anybody else is the winner.

This game, too, can involve score keeping and addition, but very young children are interested only in counting how many marbles went out of the circle. If they say, "I got 4 out, and you got 5," this is often two isolated observations that do not involve a comparison!

THE BALANCE GAME

Materials: A pizza plate or a large piece of cardboard; a 6-sided die with dots or numerals on it; a plastic bottle (with some dirt or sand inside); 20 (or more) plastic-bear counters of the same color for each player. As can be seen in Photograph 10.8, 3/4-inch round stickers are randomly placed all over the pizza plate.

Play: The materials are arranged as shown in Photograph 10.8. Each player takes 20 (or more) plastic bears of the same color. The players take turns rolling the die and placing the corresponding number of bears on the stickers.

Whoever makes the plate fall is the loser. The first person to use up all her counters is the winner.

This game can be modified for children to learn numerals. For this modification, the teacher writes a numeral 1–6 on each sticker and places the stickers randomly all over the plate. Each player rolls a regular die with dots on it and places a bear on a sticker indicating the number rolled.

This game can also be modified into an addition game by using two dice. The teacher should write the numerals 2–12 on the stickers if two 6-sided dice are used. If two 10-sided dice are used, the numerals must go from 2 to 20.

In this physical-knowledge activity, children represent the middle of the circle to themselves and think about balance in relation to distances from the middle.

Photograph 10.8. The Balance Game

A Whole-Class Game

GUESS MY NUMBER

The leader thinks of a number within a certain range (between 1 and 10 or 1 and 20 in kindergarten, and between 1 and 30 in first grade, for example), and the rest of the class tries to guess it. As one person after another takes a guess, the leader responds by saying "It's more" or "It's less." If the number in the leader's head is 20, for example, and the first guess is 30, the leader says "No, it's less." The person who guesses the number correctly is the leader of the next round.

This game can also be played by a small group or by two children.

To teach the ">" and "<" signs as required by the official curriculum (social knowledge), we wrote "> 5," "< 30," and so on, on the board. We also provided small chalkboards so that pairs of children could play this game by writing their responses. The children wrote "m 5" for "more than 5," "l 30" for "less than 30," and so on, attesting to their wisdom about how to communicate clearly and efficiently!

CHAPTER 11

Games and Other Activities Involving Addition and Subtraction

The games involving addition and subtraction are presented under the following three headings: (1) those involving only addition, (2) those involving partitioning numbers, and (3) those involving addition and subtraction. Three whole-class activities are presented at the end of the chapter.

The games within each category do not necessarily appear in order of difficulty because most easy games (such as One More, Double War with addends up to 4, and Piggy Bank) can be modified as the children become able to handle larger addends. For example, Piggy Bank is easy when children have to find 2 cards that make 5, but the total can be increased to 6, 7, 8, 9, 10, or more. Addends on dice can also be made easier by changing the 5 and the 6 to a 3 and a 4 (thereby making a die show 1, 2, 3, 3, 4, and 4) or harder by replacing a 6-sided die with one that has 10 sides.

Unless otherwise noted, all the games are for two to four players, but 3 is ideal to maximize opportunities for mental activity. Only the essential rules are given in this chapter, and how to decide who goes first, for example, is not specified. For the development of children's autonomy, it is best that children make these kinds of decisions through negotiation. Many other good games invented by teachers can be found in Wakefield (1998).

GAMES INVOLVING ADDITION ONLY

Two Addends up to 4, then to 6 or More

Random Addends

ONE MORE

Materials: A gameboard such as the one shown in Figure 11.1 (with numbers 2–7); a die; transparent chips of 4 colors (10 each in 4 different colors if there are 35 numbers on the board).

Play: This is about the easiest addition game for kindergartners. Each player first takes all the chips of the same color.

Figure 11.1. The board for One More.

5	2	6	3	4	7	3
3	7	5	4	6	2	5
4	7	2	5	3	7	6
6	5	6	7	6	4	3
2	7	3	6	2	5	4

The players take turns rolling the die and placing a chip on the number rolled plus one, anywhere on the board. For example, if a person rolls a 4, she puts a chip on a 5. The person who uses up all her chips first is the winner.

This is a better game than one like Bingo, in which children have individual boards, because when children have their own boards, they are not likely to supervise each other. Transparent chips enable the players to see the number covered.

DOUBLE WAR AND COIN WAR

Number of Players: Two.

Materials: Thirty-two playing cards, 8 each from two decks going from 1 to 4. Larger numbers can gradually be added when the game becomes too easy. Face cards can be used as 10s late in first grade.

Play: Double War is a modification of War (see Chapter 10). All the cards are dealt, face down, so that each player will have two stacks. Without looking at their cards, the players simultaneously turn over the top cards of their stacks (see Photograph 11.1.). The person whose total is greater takes all 4 cards. The one who has more cards at the end is the winner.

If there is a tie, 4 more cards are turned over, and the person whose total is greater takes all 8 cards.

Double War can be modified into Triple War, in which the total of 3 cards is compared with the total of the opponent's 3 cards.

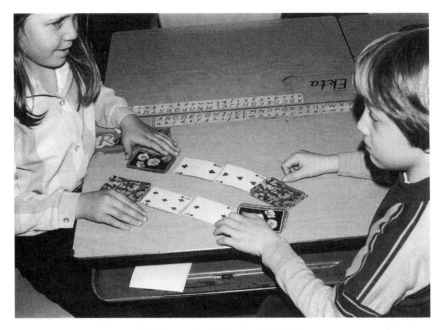

Photograph 11.1. Double War

Coin War is another possible modification. A set that works well consists of the following 44 cards: cards showing 1, 2, 3, 4, 5, 6, 7, 8, 9, and 10 pennies (2 cards of each kind, making 20 cards); cards using a nickel to show 5, 6, 7, 8, 9, and 10 cents, such as a nickel and 5 pennies to show 10 cents (4 cards of each kind, making 24 cards).

DINOSAURS AND OTHER PATH GAMES

The boards in Photographs 10.4–10.6 are homemade and easy to modify. Two dice can be used when children are ready for addition. The players take turns rolling the dice and taking the number of steps corresponding to the total. The first player to reach the goal is the winner.

The end of the game often leads to negotiations to decide (1) if a player has to roll the exact total to land on the goal and (2) if a player can use only one die.

As stated in Chapter 10, Star Wars (refer to Photograph 10.6) is similar to *Chutes and Ladders* (commercially made) in that it has a zigzag path. Children often move backward when they are not paying attention to the numerals.

COVER-UP

Number of Players: Two.

Materials: The board shown in Figure 11.2a (the numbers have to go from 2 to 12 if two dice numbered 1–6 are used); 22 poker chips; 2 dice.

Play: The players, sitting on opposite sides of the board, take turns rolling the dice. The two numbers that came up are added, and the number corresponding to the sum is covered with a poker chip on one's side of the board. If a number is already covered, the turn is wasted. The player who covers up all the numbers on his side first is the winner.

This game can be changed to Doubles Cover-up, which can be seen in Figure 11.2b. One die is used for Doubles Cover-up, and the number rolled is doubled. This game can be made harder with a 10-sided die and correspondingly larger numbers on the board.

Figure 11.2. Boards for Cover-up and Doubles Cover-up.

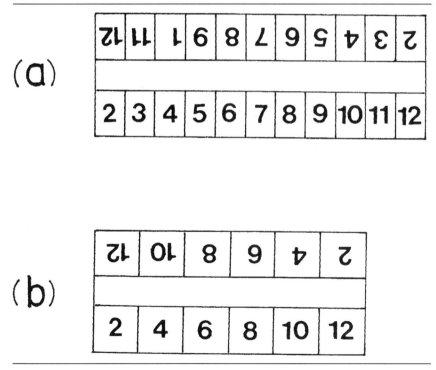

FIVE-PLUS BINGO

Materials: Four gameboards with numbers 6–11 scattered over them such as the ones in Figure 11.3 (there are 6 of each number; all the boards should have numbers that are scattered differently); a die (with numerals 1–6); about 25 transparent chips for each player.

Play: The players take turns rolling the die and announcing the sum of the number rolled and 5. For example, if a 1 turns up, the sum is 6. Whoever has a 6 on her board covers it. The winner is the first person to get 6 in a row vertically, horizontally, or diagonally.

This game can be shortened by requiring only 4 or 5 numbers in a row to be covered. Covering four corners is another way of playing this game.

DOUBLES

DOUBLE *PARCHEESI*

Double *Parcheesi* uses the commercially made *Parcheesi* board shown in Photograph 11.2. Each player selects one of the 4 colors and places the markers in the circle of the same color as shown in the photograph. (Using only 2 of the 4 markers is best in first grade, but most first graders use only one marker at a time anyway.) The object of the game is to move all of one's markers around the board to Home. Double *Parcheesi* is different from *Parcheesi* in that the players

Figure 11.3. Boards for Five-plus Bingo.

7	9	6	8	10	11
8	9	10	7	11	6
7	8	11	6	9	10
6	11	7	11	7	10
10	9	8	8	9	6
9	10	11	7	6	8

7	10	8	11	6	9
8	6	9	7	11	10
9	10	7	11	8	6
6	11	8	9	7	10
10	7	6	8	8	9
9	11	11	6	10	7

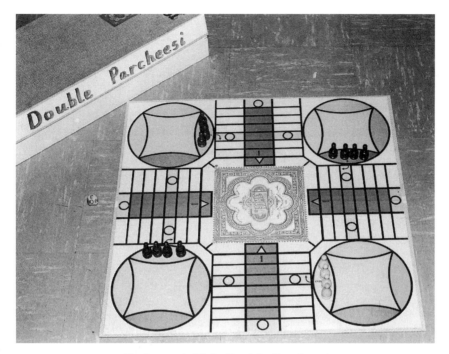

Photograph 11.2. Double *Parcheesi*

double the number shown by the die. A 6-sided die is used first and an 8- or 10-sided die, later.

If a marker lands on a space already occupied, the one already there is sent back to its starting point. There are 12 safety spaces (indicated by small circles) where a marker is safe from being sent back.

This game was invented because doubles are generally easier for children to remember than sums of two different numbers. Children who know doubles very well add 5 and 4, for example, by adding 1 to 4 + 4 or subtracting 1 from 5 + 5. The *Parcheesi* board has a long path, and children like the idea of moving fast.

SQUARE-OMINOES

Materials: 60 Color Tiles on which numbers 3–9 are written on the sides as shown in Figure 11.4 (the four numbers on each tile should be different, and there should be about the same number of 3s, 4s, 5s, and so forth); paper and pencil for score keeping.

Play: All the tiles are scattered, face down. Each player takes 3 of them and stands them up so that others cannot see the numbers on them.

Figure 11.4. Tiles and a score sheet used in Square-ominoes.

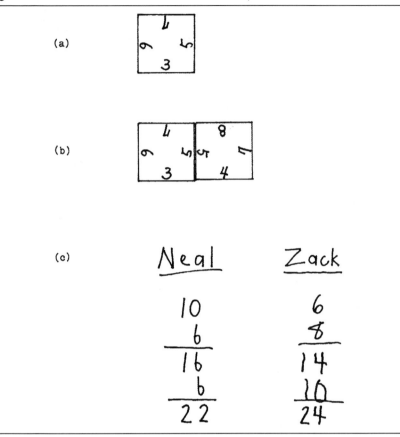

One tile is turned up and placed in the middle of the table to start the game (see the example in Figure 11.4a). The players take turns laying down one tile at a time, matching a number. In the example in Figure 11.4b, the player matched the 5s and got 10 points. (He could have matched the 7s to get 14 points!)

The sheet of paper is passed around for each person to keep his score up to date. Figure 11.4c is an example of a score sheet.

Whenever a tile is played, it is replaced with one from those that are face down, so that the player will have 3 tiles again. A player who does not have one that can be played must pass.

This game can be made easier by (1) putting smaller numbers on the tiles and (2) changing the point system so that if two 4s are matched, the player gets only 4 points.

More Than Two Addends

TAKE TEN

Materials: A commercially made board shown in Photograph 11.3 or a similar home-made board; 66 round cards bearing the numerals 1 through 7, in the following quantities:

1 – 22 cards	5 – 4 cards
2 – 16 cards	6 – 2 cards
3 – 12 cards	7 – 2 cards
4 – 7 cards	Joker – 1 card

Play: The object of the game is to make 10 with 4 cards in a row, horizontally, vertically, or diagonally.

All the cards are placed face down in the box, and each player takes 3 cards. Each in turn places a card on any circle that is unoccupied on the board. She then replaces this card with one from the box to have 3 cards again.

When a player completes a row of 4 cards that make 10, she collects the 4 cards. The Joker can be used for any value. (The child who is putting down a 2 in Photograph 11.3 knew that his opponent was holding the Joker and decided to block him.)

The player who collects more cards (or more sets) is the winner.

Photograph 11.3. *Take Ten*

PUT AND TAKE

Materials: 32 brown chips (worth 1 point each), 40 white chips (worth 2 points each), 20 orange chips (worth 5 points each); a large, 12-sided die bearing the following instructions: "Take 1, Take 3, Take 5, Take 7, Take 8, Take 9, Take 11, Put 2, Put 4, Put 6, Put 10, and Put 12"; a bowl (the "kitty").

Play: Each player takes 8 brown and 5 white chips (totaling 18 points). The rest of the chips remain in the kitty to begin the game.

The players take turns rolling the die and following the instruction that came up. For example, if "Take 8" comes up, the player takes from the kitty chips that are worth 8 points (8 brown ones, 4 white ones, or one each of three different colors, for example). If "Put 6" comes up, the person has to put into the kitty his own chips totaling 6 points (an orange and a brown chip, for example).

The first player to get a total of 30 points is the winner.

If a large 12-sided die cannot be found, instruction cards or a spinner can be used instead.

HUCKLEBERRY HOUND

Materials: The deck of 34 cards shown in Photograph 11.4. These cards are out of print, but the teacher can write the following numbers on any other cards that come in sets of 4 pictures. (Sets of 2 pictures work well too.)

1 (point): on 2 different sets (of 4 cards)
2 (points): on 2 different sets
3 (points): on 2 different sets
4 (points): on one set
5 (points): on one set
10 (points): on 2 cards

Play: This is a Concentration game. All the cards are arranged, face down, in neat rows. The players take turns turning over 2 cards, trying to make pairs that have the same picture. A player can keep playing as long as she is making pairs. When she fails, the 2 cards must be returned to their face-down positions, and the turn passes to the next player. The winner is the person who got the highest total number of points.

It is best to take out the 10-point cards when this game is first introduced.

THE SANDWICH GAME

Number of Players: Two.

Materials: A gameboard with 12 squares horizontally and 14 squares vertically as can be seen in Figure 11.5a (the 4 squares in the middle are marked as shown);

Photograph 11.4. *Huckleberry Hound* cards

44 pennies or counters that have different colors on their sides; paper and pencil for score keeping.

Play: One player is heads (or red) and the other is tails (or yellow). Each takes 22 pennies or counters and places 2 of them in the center of the board as indicated in Figure 11.5a. The players take turns putting down one penny at a time, trying to "sandwich" the opponent's pennies between 2 of one's own. Figure 11.5b is an example of "sandwiching." Each time a sandwich is made, the penny or pennies sandwiched are turned over (see Figure 11.5c). Each time a penny is turned over, it earns 2 points (or 5 points).

A sandwich can be made horizontally, vertically, or diagonally. Two sandwiches can be made at the same time in two directions (see Figure 11.5d). The person who placed the penny indicated by the arrow earns 6 points in this example.

A similar game can be played with *Othello* (commercially made) by stipulating that each disc flipped earns 2 points (or 5 points).

EVEN DOMINOES

Materials: A set of dominoes; paper and pencil for score keeping.

Play: The object of the game is to make points by making even-numbered sums (such as 6 + 2 and 5 + 3 as shown in Figure 11.6).

Figure 11.5. The board and arrangement of pennies in the Sandwich
   Game.

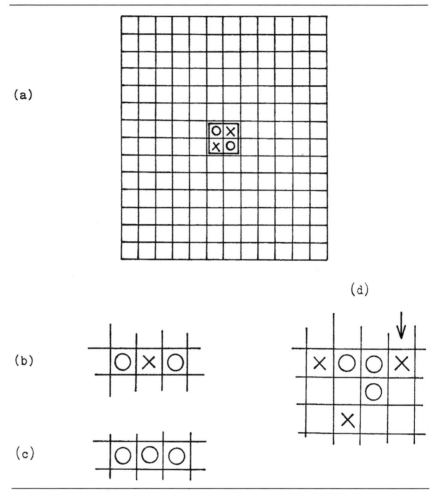

All the dominoes are turned face down, and each player takes 5 dominoes.
One domino from the face-down pile is placed in the middle of the table.

The players take turns placing a domino so that the two ends touching make
an even number. After each turn, players draw another domino to have 5 again.

A player's score is the total of all the totals made. The first player to reach
40 (or 70) is the winner.

Figure 11.6. The placement of dominoes in Even Dominoes.

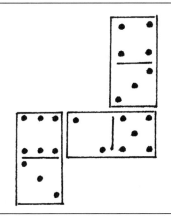

GAMES INVOLVING PARTITIONING NUMBERS

Partitioning 5 into Two Numbers

PIGGY BANK

Materials: The following 30 cards:

7 cards showing 1 penny
7 cards showing 2 pennies
7 cards showing 3 pennies
7 cards showing 4 pennies
2 cards showing 5 pennies (it is best to exclude these two cards until the children become familiar with this game).

Play: All the cards are dealt, and each player keeps all the cards received in a stack, face down, without looking at them. The game involves players putting money in the bank, but this can be done only with 2 cards that make 5 cents.

When a turn comes, each player turns over the top card of his stack. The first player always has to discard this card in the middle of the table, face up, because one card cannot make 5 cents with 2 cards. If the second player turns over a 3, and sees a 2 on the table, he can take the 2 and bank 5 cents. If, on the other hand, the second player turns over any other number, he has to discard it in the middle of the table, face up.

Play continues until all the cards have been used. The winner is the person who has collected the most cards (or has saved the most money).

This game can, of course, be modified to make a total of 6, 7, 8, or more. Regular playing cards can be used, and the teacher needs to select appropriately larger numbers.

Partitioning 10 into Two Numbers

TENS WITH NINE CARDS

Materials: 36 playing cards going up to 9.

Play: The first 9 cards of the deck are arranged as shown in the example in Figure 11.7. The object of the game is to find all the pairs of cards that make 10, such as 9 and 1, 3 and 7, and two 5s in this example. After taking all the possible pairs, the first player fills up the empty spaces with cards from the deck, and the turn passes to the next player.

The same game can be made harder by arranging all the cards face down and changing the game to Tens Concentration.

FIND 10

This game is like Piggy Bank, but cards going up to 9 are used, and the object of the game is to make 10 with 2 cards.

DRAW 10

This game is played like Old Maid, but cards going up to 9 are used, and the object of the game is to find 2 cards that make 10.

Figure 11.7. The arrangement of cards in Tens with Nine Cards.

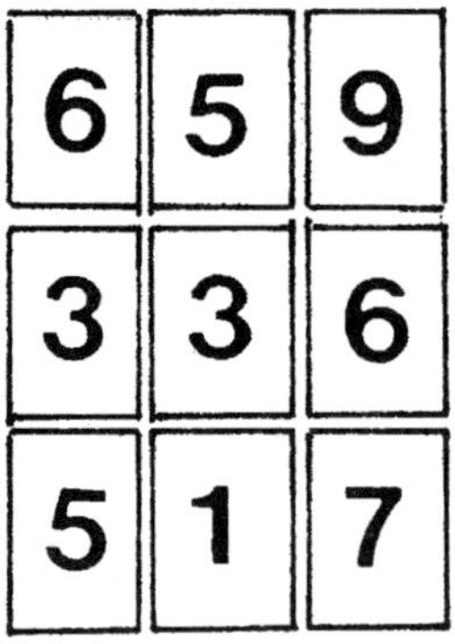

One card is removed from the deck at random, so that there will be a card without a mate at the end of the game. All the other cards are dealt.

Each player goes through the cards received and discards in the middle of the table all the pairs that make 10 (6 + 4, for example).

The players then hold their cards like a fan and take turns letting the person to one's left draw one of them at random without looking at them. If the person who drew a card can use it to make 10 with one of her own cards, the pair can be discarded in the middle of the table. If a pair cannot be made, the card drawn is kept, and the person to the left draws a card by chance.

Play continues until one person is left holding the odd card and loses the game.

TENS AND *TENS AND TWENTIES*

Materials: The commercially made game that can be seen in Photograph 11.5.

Play: All the triangular pieces are placed face down in the box. Each player takes 6 pieces, turning them up, and the other pieces remain in the box.

Play begins with one piece from the box turned up and placed in the middle of the table. In turn, each player tries to put down one of his pieces by putting

Photograph 11.5. *TENS*

together two numbers written on the same color that make a total of 10 (see Figure 11.8 for an example). If a player does not have a piece that can be played, he takes one from the box and tries again. If he still cannot use a piece, the turn passes to the next player. The winner is the first person to use up all his pieces.

GO 10

Go 10 is like Go Fish, but playing cards going up to 9 are used, and the object of the game is to make 10 with 2 cards. All the cards are dealt. (There is no "pond" in this game.) The players ask specific people for specific numbers. For example, John may say to Katie, "Do you have a 5?" If Katie has a 5, she has to give it to John. John then lays this 5 and his 5 in front of himself, face up.

A player can continue asking for cards as long as she gets the number requested. If a player is told "I don't have any," the turn passes to the person who said "I don't have any."

The person who makes the greatest number of pairs is the winner.

ADD-UP-TO-10 BINGO

Materials: A 10-sided die bearing the numbers 1–10 or 0–9; a board for each player such as the one in Figure 11.9 with numbers 0–9 or 1–10 written randomly in a 5-by-5 arrangement; (For example, if the die goes from 1 to 10, the numbers 0–9 on the board might appear with the following frequencies indicated in parentheses: 0(1), 1(1), 2(2), 3(4), 4(4), 5(2), 6(4), 7(4), 8(2), 9(1). There are more 3s, 4s, 6s, and 7s than other numbers because 7+3 and 6+4 are harder to remember than combinations such as 5+5 and 9+1. The numbers must ap-

Figure 11.8. How a triangle can be placed in *TENS*.

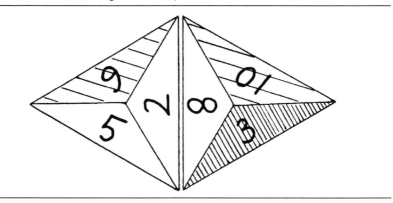

Figure 11.9. A board for Add-up-to-10 Bingo.

7	4	6	3	7
2	9	4	5	2
3	6	7	1	0
5	3	6	8	4
8	4	7	3	6

pear with the same frequencies on all the boards but scattered over the boards differently. If the die goes from 0 to 9, the numbers on the board must vary from 1 to 10.). Also, 20 transparent chips for each player.

Play: The players take turns rolling the die and placing a chip on a number that makes 10 with the number rolled. For example, if the number rolled is 8, a 2 must be covered. The winner is the first person to cover a line of 5 numbers, vertically, horizontally, or diagonally.

Partitioning Various Numbers

PUNTA

Materials: 60 cards, 10 each of numbers 1–6; 2 dice.

Play: All the cards are dealt. The players take turns rolling the dice and announcing the total. All the players try to make this total in as many ways as possible. For example, if 5 and 4 were rolled, the players can do 6 + 3, 6 + 2 + 1, 5 + 3 + 1, and so forth. The first player to use up all his cards is the winner. First graders at first do not notice the advantage of saving for later use the cards that have small numbers.

SHUT THE BOX

Materials: This game can be played with 9 cards numbered 1 through 9, but children have a strong preference for the commercially made box called *Shut the Box* or *Wake Up Giants*; 2 dice. (Pieces can be flipped up or down when a commercially made box is used. These actions appeal to young children much more than turning cards over.)

Play: If cards are used, the 9 cards are arranged in a line in sequence from 1 to 9, face up. The players take turns rolling the dice and turning down as many cards as they wish to make the same total. For example, if a 6 and a 2 were rolled, a player can turn down the 8; the 1 and the 7; the 2 and the 6; the 3 and the 5; or the 1, the 3, and the 4. The player keeps playing until it is impossible to make a total with the remaining numbers. The numbers left unused are added and recorded, and the next player takes a turn.

The points left at the end of each turn are added to the player's previous total. The player who reaches 45 points first is the loser.

NICKELODEON

Number of Players: Two.

Materials: A board like the one in Figure 11.10a; 20 transparent chips (10 each of the same color); 2 rings.

Play: Each player takes 10 chips of the same color. The object of the game is to be first to make a line of 3 chips of the same color, horizontally, vertically, or diagonally.

The first player places both rings on any two of the six numbers in the row outside the square (2 and 6, for example) and covers with a chip a number that corresponds to the total (an 8 in this case).

The second player then moves one of the rings to another number (from 2 to 5, for example) and covers the total with one of her chips (an 11 in this case because 5 + 6 = 11).

The players take turns moving only one of the rings and covering a number that corresponds to the total.

Figure 11.10b is a harder version of Nickelodeon, with addends ranging from 3 to 8 and correspondingly larger totals. This game can, of course, be modified to use addends going from 1 to 12 and a larger board having 6 columns and 6 rows, for example.

TIC TAC TOTAL

Number of Players: Two.

Materials: A laminated board such as the one in Figure 11.11 with even numbers on one side and odd numbers on the other side; a Vis-à-Vis marker (with ink that washes off) for each player.

Figure 11.10. Two boards for Nickelodeon.

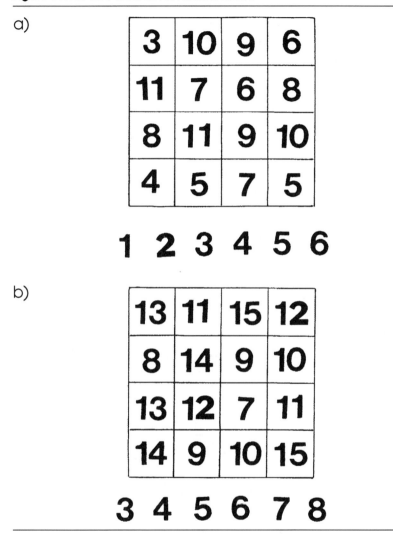

a)

3	10	9	6
11	7	6	8
8	11	9	10
4	5	7	5

1 2 3 4 5 6

b)

13	11	15	12
8	14	9	10
13	12	7	11
14	9	10	15

3 4 5 6 7 8

Play: This game is played like Tic Tac Toe. The players first decide what the target number will be. If the target number is 13, they write "13" after "TIC TAC," and the game comes to be called "Tic Tac 13." The players then decide who will use even numbers and who will use odd numbers.

The players take turns choosing and writing a number in one of the nine spaces. The one who is first to make a total of 13 with three numbers in a line (vertically, horizontally, or diagonally) is the winner.

Figure 11.11. A board for Tic Tac Total.

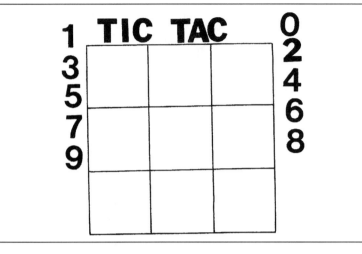

FOXES BOXES

Materials: A laminated small board like the one in Figure 11.12 for each player; a Vis-à-Vis marker (with ink that washes off) for each player; 20 numeral cards (2 each of 0–9).

Play: Each player takes a board and a marker. The cards are placed face down in a stack. The object of the game is to make the number at the top of a column by adding the four numbers entered in the column.

Figure 11.12. A board for Foxes Boxes.

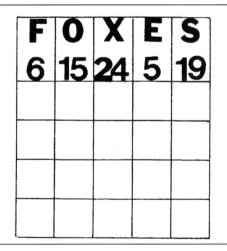

The players take turns turning over the top card of the face-down stack and reading it. Each player writes this number in an unused space in any column. For example, if a 5 is announced, a good place for it is *not* the column with 5 or 6 at the top.

The winner is the first person to make the total at the top of the column and say "Foxes boxes!" The number at the top must be made by adding the four numbers entered in all four boxes.

GAMES INVOLVING ADDITION AND SUBTRACTION

SNEAKY SNAKE

Number of Players: Two.

Materials: A gameboard like the one in Figure 11.13; 2 dice; 24 chips.

Play: The object of the game is to be first to cover all 12 numbers on one's snake. The players take turns rolling the dice and covering a number. The two numbers rolled can be added, or one number can be subtracted from the other. If there is no sum or difference that can be covered, the player must pass.

ALL BUT 7

Number of Players: Two.

Materials: The gameboard shown in Figure 11.14; 2 6-sided dice; 40 transparent chips (20 each in two different colors).

Play: The players take turns rolling the dice. If a sum of 7 is rolled, the player puts a chip in his rectangle. If any other sum is rolled, that number is covered up with a chip. Addition or subtraction can be used to cover up numbers. The winner is the first player to cover up all the numbers without getting more than 7 chips in his rectangle.

SALUTE!

Number of Players: Three.

Materials: A deck of playing cards with the face cards removed.

Play: The cards are dealt to 2 of the 3 players. The 2 players hold the cards received in a face-down stack. Simultaneously, both take the top card of their

Figure 11.13. The board for Sneaky Snake.

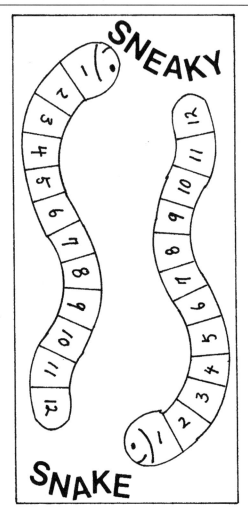

respective piles saying "Salute!" and holding the cards up next to their ears in such a way that each player can see the opponent's card but not his own.

The third player announces the sum of the 2 cards, and each of the other 2 players tries to figure out the number on his own card (by subtracting the opponent's number from the sum that has been announced). The one who announces the number correctly first takes both cards.

The winner is the person who collects more cards.

Figure 11.14. The board for All but 7.

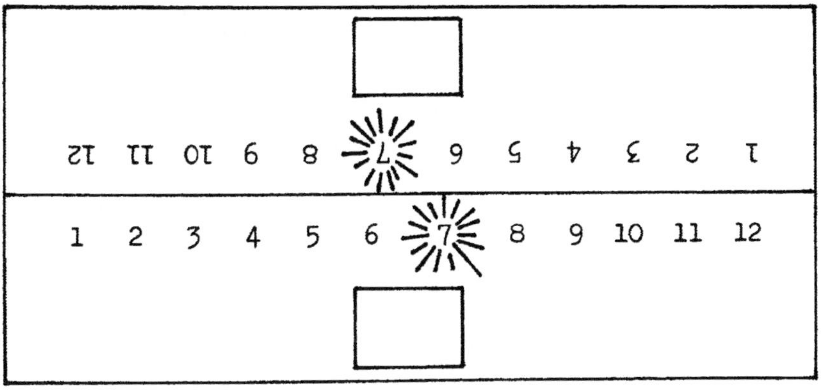

This is a difficult game for first graders, and we recommend introducing it late in the school year.

24 GAME PRIMER, ADD/SUBTRACT

Materials: A commercially made game available through most catalogs. Examples can be seen in Figure 11.15.

Play: Twelve to 24 cards are placed in a stack in the middle of the table, face up. The players all try to make the target number (3 in Figure 11.15a) by choosing one of the two wheels (the one that permits 8–5 in this case). Addition or subtraction can be used in this game. The person who says "I got it" first and can justify her choice wins the card. All the numbers in a wheel must be used once and only once.

The cards are marked "o," "oo," or "ooo" according to difficulty. The one in Figure 11.15b is harder and is marked "oo." A card with "o" wins 1 point, a card with "oo" wins 2 points, and a card with "ooo" wins 3 points. The winner is the person who gets the highest total number of points.

OTHER ACTIVITIES FOR THE WHOLE CLASS

MAGIC NUMBER

All the members of the class stand in a circle, and the teacher says, for example, "The magic number is 20 counting by 2s." She starts by saying "2,"

Figure 11.15. Two cards from *24 Game Primer, Add/Subtract.*

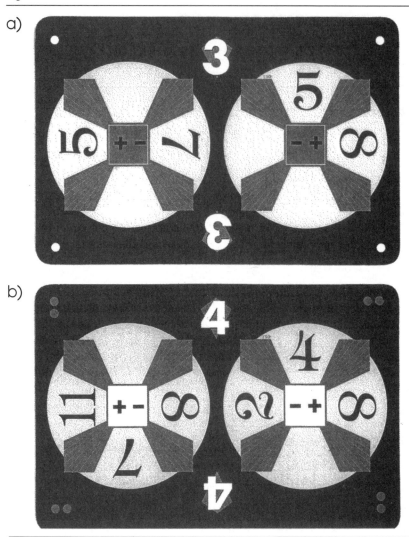

and the children to the left say, successively, "4," "6," "8," and so on. The person who says "20" has to sit down and is eliminated for the rest of the round.

The person to the left of the child who sat down starts counting by 2s again and the children say "2, 4, 6, . . . 20." The child who said "20" has to sit down and is eliminated. The game continues until only 2 people remain standing, and one of them has to say "20" and sit down.

This is an excellent game for children to learn the social knowledge of counting by 2s, 5s, and 10s. The end point can be gradually extended to 30, 50, and beyond.

THE BALANCE BOXES

The teacher draws a balance like the one in Figure 11.16a that has a number on one side and two empty boxes on the other. He says, "Tell me what numbers could go in the boxes." As the children raise their hands, he calls on them, one at a time, and records all the combinations such as "a 5 and a 5" and "9 and 1" (see Figure 11.16b). He, of course, encourages the rest of the class to say

Figure 11.16. Examples of what the teacher draws and writes in The Balance Boxes.

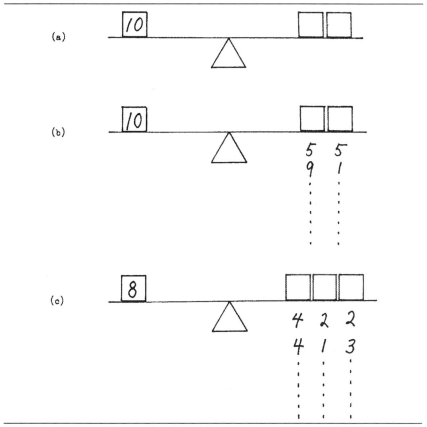

whether a combination makes sense. If someone later says "1 and 9," he also encourages the class to say that this combination has already been given.

This game can be modified with different numbers in the box on the left and 3 boxes on the right as shown in Figure 11.16c.

There are many commercially made balances intended to teach arithmetic, and it is important to differentiate those balances from the activity just described. A balance uses weight, which is physical knowledge, but numerical equality is logico-mathematical knowledge. Children cannot learn sums by making weights balance. Our activity uses the *drawing* of a balance only to communicate a problem for children to solve by thinking numerically.

TIC TAC TOTAL

This game is played like the Tic Tac Total that was described earlier in the chapter, but it is played by the entire class divided into two teams. We at first thought that each team should discuss and decide what number its representative will write on the board and where. We later changed our minds when we found out that the children with less-advanced abilities merely carried out the decisions of those with more-advanced abilities. All children learn more from the results of their own decisions as long as group members are encouraged to be kind to each other.

CHAPTER 12

General Principles of Teaching

According to Piaget's constructivism, children acquire logico-mathematical knowledge as well as the morality of autonomy by *constructing them from the inside*, in interaction with the environment, rather than by *internalizing* them directly from the outside. Educators who believe that children learn these by direct internalization from the environment try to facilitate this internalization. Those who understand that only surface bits of knowledge and behavior can be learned by absorption from outside try to foster the construction of knowledge and moral values in a deeper and broader sense from within.

Children's development of autonomy cannot be fostered only during the math hour or an hour set aside for moral development. Children who govern themselves all day long can also play math games without getting into fights. Those who are considerate of others all the time are likewise considerate when ways of solving word problems are discussed. This chapter will therefore begin with some general principles of teaching that flow from autonomy as the aim of education. Children's relationships with adults will be discussed first, followed by relationships among children. More specific principles focusing on arithmetic will be presented in conclusion. In Chapter 13 are principles of teaching related specifically to games, and Chapter 8 gives many examples of how a teacher fosters children's development of autonomy throughout the day.

AUTONOMY AND CHILDREN'S RELATIONSHIPS WITH ADULTS

In Chapter 4, we stated that the most general implication of autonomy as the aim of education is that children must learn to make decisions by discussing relevant factors and making decisions for themselves. Another way of expressing the same general idea is: We must *reduce our adult power as much as possible and exchange points of view with children*. In other words, we must let children make as many decisions as possible and avoid using reward and punishment to enforce the decisions we impose on them.

Adult power is pervasive in most classrooms even in situations that seem unrelated to adult power. For example, when children ask if they can go first to start a game, it is natural for teachers to say yes. Most teachers are not aware that they are exercising power when they give this kind of permission. A better response is "You need to ask the people you are playing with."

Reducing adult power *as much as possible* does not mean that the teacher gives up his or her power completely. The teacher's role in three kinds of situations is discussed below: (1) when rules must be made, (2) when children need to judge at what point an act becomes excessive (e.g., when noise becomes excessive), and (3) when decisions must be made.

When Rules Must Be Made

Children are often greeted on the first day of school with a list of rules such as "Do *not* talk when the teacher is talking to the class." It is better to wait until a problem arises and ask the class, "What can we do about this problem?" Children often make the same rules that adults impose, but they are much more likely to respect a rule *they* made. If they have lived through the problem of not being able to hear the teacher, they are likely to remember why they made *their* rule.

Class meetings (Nelsen, 1981) are excellent for promoting self-government and developing children's ability to take relevant factors into account. There are many ways of conducting class meetings, but their purposes are: (1) to clarify the problem that seems to exist, (2) to discuss possible solutions, and (3) to agree on a solution, usually by majority vote. Below is an example of a class meeting, and many others can be found in this chapter, Chapter 13, and DeVries and Zan (1994).

One day in the lunchroom, some children shot spitballs that landed in people's food. After stopping the spitball fight and returning to the classroom, the teacher asked the class if anyone objected to the spitballs. Some responded that they did not like spitballs in their milk, their hair, and so on. The class made a rule against spitballs and went on to discuss what should be done if someone broke the rule.

Two of the suggestions were: "Send them to the principal's office" and "Make them write sentences." The teacher responded, as one of the group like any other member of the community, that she would not vote for those ideas because they were not related to shooting spitballs. The final decision was that the person would have to sit alone in the lunchroom for a week and would not be allowed to have drinking straws.

The teacher was in control in this situation. However, she reduced her power *as much as possible* and had only one vote in the final decision.

The reader may have noted in Chapter 8 that the teacher makes many decisions without any negotiation, such as what word problem to give each day. However, she consciously strives to reduce her power and encourages children to make as many decisions as possible.

When an Act Becomes Excessive

A common problem is that when children play games, the noise level goes up, and the teacher next door complains. Unlike shooting spitballs, talking excitedly is not an undesirable behavior in itself. Noise becomes a problem only when it becomes too loud for other people. Making a rule would not help in such a situation because there is no clear-cut criterion of what makes the behavior excessive.

In a traditional school, the teacher next door usually complains privately to the teacher of the noisy class and expects him or her to control the noise level. For children's development of autonomy, however, it is much better that the teacher next door come to the noisy room and personally explain that the noise prevents her from being heard. This face-to-face communication is the best way for children to become aware of the consequence of their noise (of which they have been unaware).

Children become considerate when they can decenter and take other people's perspectives. Another person's perspective is easier to imagine when specific people tell them, in effect, "*You* bother *me*." The teacher's reminder about a specific person's complaint is much more conducive to children's decentering than a general statement such as "The noise bothers the people next door." Children construct moral rules from within, out of positive, personal relationships with specific people.

When Decisions Must Be Made

Some decisions are too trivial to warrant a vote or too complicated to negotiate. For example, whether to go outside for recess is not open to negotiation if the principal makes this decision for the whole school depending on the weather. However, teachers often make decisions that unnecessarily emphasize their power. For example, when a teacher wants a note delivered to the office, he or she usually chooses one child for this privilege. For children's development of autonomy, it is better to have a system that uses chance or alphabetical order. The teacher can have cards on hand with each child's name on a card. If one of the cards is drawn at random, the decision can be made by chance. The cards can be used throughout the day whenever one, two, or more children have to be chosen for an attractive or unattractive task.

If a snowball fight results in a broken car window, and it is impossible to determine who caused the breakage, the class may decide that it could either raise money to pay for the damage or ask the owner if the damage is covered by insurance. The class may in the end decide to ask the principal or school lawyer to make a decision, but going through a debate about what to do is in itself good for children's development of autonomy. Children who have thought hard about how to make restitution are likely to be more careful in the future. Thinking about the group's responsibility contributes to the development of a sense of community. A feeling of community grows as problems, decisions, and feelings are shared by the entire class, including the teacher. Schools too often reinforce children's heteronomy by imposing ready-made rules such as "No snowball fights."

AUTONOMY AND CHILDREN'S RELATIONSHIPS AMONG PEERS

If children are to exchange ideas critically with others, it is necessary to have an atmosphere of consideration and respect for others. The following discussion deals with the fostering of respect and consideration and the resolution of conflicts.

Respect and Consideration for Others

When individual children give answers to a math problem, the class often reacts with a chorus of "Disagree!" (We never suggest to children that they react in unison, but they spontaneously begin to say "Agree!" or "Disagree!") Sensitive children's feelings are sometimes hurt when disagreement is expressed.

There are many ways to handle these kinds of problems, and teachers usually handle them privately. If conditions permit, it is possible to call the class's attention to the problem *they* caused. The teacher might say to the entire class, "So-and-so's feelings are hurt because we shouted at him [or her]. Can we think of a way we can do something about this problem?" The class is usually totally unaware of the sensitive child's feelings, and the teacher can use his or her power to ask children to decenter and take responsibility for the problem they caused. Children come up with suggestions such as "I think we should talk with a soft voice when So-and-so talks." They can be touching in their response when the teacher skillfully presents this kind of problem as the *group's* problem. A feeling of community develops when each member's ideas and feelings are respected, and the group feels responsible for the welfare of its members. Children who are treated respectfully usually deal with others respectfully.

Conflict Resolution

When two children are in conflict in class, teachers often separate them or tell them to "stop it." These solutions may solve the problem for the time being, but children do not learn how to deal with a conflict next time. It is better to ask them to step outside for 5 minutes to "talk it over to come to an agreement."

In a kindergarten room one day, a child raised his hand while the teacher was reading a book. His request to the teacher was: "Can you wait a minute because Tom and I have a problem we have to talk about before we can go on?" This is a sign of autonomy on the child's part and of a good relationship with the teacher. Children rarely take such initiative. The teacher asked the two children to step outside to work out an agreement.

Stepping outside does not lead to a resolution unless children have had some education in conflict resolution. The important point for the teacher to keep in mind is to bring children's feelings out honestly rather than trying to sweep them under the rug "nicely." Games are good partly because they predictably give rise to conflicts and become occasions for children to learn to resolve conflicts. Children often come to the teacher saying, "So-and-so is cheating," expecting the teacher to solve the problem. Teachers usually believe that it is their duty to tell children what to do in such a situation. For the development of children's autonomy, however, it is better to ask, "What have you done to solve your problem?"

The usual answer at first is "Nothing." The teacher may then ask, for example, "Have you told So-and-so that it's not fair if only one person chooses cards [in War]?" This is sometimes enough of a push for children to get started in conflict resolution. However, they often come back to report, "He said he doesn't care if it's unfair." The teacher may then have to make another suggestion such as, "Do you think it might be good to say to him that if *he* cheats, *you* should be able to cheat, too?" (In War, incidentally, it is interesting to observe what children do when they *choose* the card they want to play. If Child A turns over a 5, for example, Child B can win by putting down a 6. However, young children often choose to play a 10 because a 10 is stronger than a 6!)

Another solution the teacher may suggest is: "Do you think the best thing might be to say to So-and-so that you won't play with him if he cheats?" Note that the teacher is always asking the child to decide whether an idea is worth a try. Children do not feel responsible for solving their own problems if they merely do whatever the teacher suggests.

If Child A wants to play the game one way but Child B wants to play it differently, the teacher can ask, "Do you think it might be a good idea to suggest to So-and-so that you'll play the game *his* way if he will then play it *your* way?" When the teacher thus makes it clear that children's conflicts are *theirs* for them to resolve, we soon overhear conversations between two children such as: "I'm going to tell on you." "Go ahead. Mrs. So-and-so will only say we have to solve our own problem."

AUTONOMY AND CHILDREN'S LEARNING OF ARITHMETIC

For the development of autonomy in a math class, it is essential first of all that teachers capitalize on children's intrinsic motivation to learn. After discussing the importance of intrinsic motivation, we go on to the desirability of encouraging children to do their own thinking by *not* showing them how to solve problems, and *not* saying that an answer is correct or incorrect. The chapter will conclude with the desirability of letting computation grow out of everyday situations and word problems and recognizing the desirability of games over worksheets.

Use Intrinsic Motivation

Teachers who use worksheets often dispense stickers or smiley faces. These devices make children feel good but are mild forms of bribery that reinforce children's heteronomy. None of these rewards is necessary when everyday situations, word problems, and math games are used. Children *choose to* engage in these activities and *try to become increasingly better at them*. Some children even ask if they can take playing cards to the lunchroom, but they never ask if they can take a worksheet to the lunchroom.

In games, motivation is intrinsic partly because games are a natural form of activity in childhood. When they are bored, with nothing to do, children are delighted when a specific game is suggested. Before the advent of television, they used to play street games in their spare time (Opie & Opie, 1969).

Children are also willing to work on word problems everyday without any rewards. They welcome the challenge of word problems and are proud to show off their ways of solving them. When they engage in an activity for the pleasure of the activity itself, children are likely to repeat it. When they have mastered an activity, they go on to something else that is more interesting to them.

Do Not Show *How* to Solve Problems

In traditional math education, the teacher shows children *how* to add, subtract, multiply, and divide and then gives similar practice problems. By contrast, we do not tell children what to do and, instead, give problems so that children will use what they know to invent new ways of solving them. In kindergarten, for example, when children can play a board game such as Hop to It (see Chapter 10) with one die, we give them 2 dice and observe what they do. If they cannot figure out what to do, we do not show them how to add two numbers.

In light of the 60 years of research by Piaget and his collaborators all over the world, it is clear that children construct logico-mathematical knowledge by making relationships out of the relationships they created before. In arithmetic, therefore, we can expect them to *invent* a way of dealing with two "fives" on two dice, for example, if they have constructed a solid notion of "five." If they cannot invent a way, this is because the problem is still too hard for them.

By struggling to figure out a way of dealing with problems, children create new relationships (by constructive abstraction). Relationships that a child has created from within are not forgotten like relationships fed from the environment. A relationship created by the child also serves as a foundation for later inventions. Following are three specific ways in which the teacher can promote children's making of relationships.

Ask Questions Instead of Showing What to Do.   Most first graders have no trouble solving problems such as: *How many feet are there in the teacher's house if 3 people live in it?* When children seem not to have any idea what to do, the teacher can help the logico-arithmetization of people and feet by asking questions such as: "What does the question ask?" "What do you know about the people in the house?" "Would it help to read the problem again?" "Would it help to use counters [or draw a picture]?" Note that the teacher is asking questions, and it is up to the child to decide whether a suggestion is worth taking.

Give Problems at the Appropriate Level.   Children invent new solutions by using what they already know. This means that the teacher must know what children know to decide what kind of question to give from day to day. The teacher thus pushes children with challenging questions but is always ready to return to an easier level if the majority seem frustrated. This is why it is impossible to write a constructivist textbook or recipe for the teacher to follow day by day.

As stated in Chapter 7, the following problem was the first division problem we gave in first grade one year: *Cody looked outside and saw 8 feet. How many people were outside?* This problem turned out to be difficult for the less-advanced children, who drew 8 circles for 8 people, for example. We hypothesized that this problem was difficult to logico-arithmetize because feet are part of people and difficult to separate.

A few days later, we asked how many cookies each child would get if 8 cookies were to be divided among 4 children. This question involving the same numbers turned out to be much easier, and all the children solved it successfully. The difficulty of a problem thus depends not only on the numbers involved but also on the specific objects and situation that must be logico-arithmetized.

Ask Each Child to Solve Problems on His or Her Own.   We strongly believe in social interaction for the reasons given in Chapter 3. However, social interaction is more productive when each child has his or her own idea to exchange with others. In so-called cooperative groups, the child with the most advanced abilities often does all the work, and the others merely go along and copy somebody else's answer. In our classroom, by contrast, children are encouraged to compare answers and procedures when they have their own answers. Each child's struggle to arrive at an answer is important for the construction of logico-mathematical knowledge.

Do All Children Really Invent Solutions?   Some children's inventions are truly new, as they invent solutions to which they have never been exposed. However, many children "catch on" to their more-advanced peers' arguments and start to imitate them. We think that even the latter group is inventing arithmetic for the following reasons: Children who do not understand the explanation of more-advanced children are free to reject more-advanced ideas. When the less-advanced children finally understand a higher-level idea, this can be said to be an invention for these children. We never know when a child will invent higher-level logic and are delighted when a child finally invents counting-on, for example.

As Piaget (1945/1951) pointed out in connection with babies' becoming able to imitate Piaget's actions (of touching his eyebrow, for example), children have to make spatial relationships to be able to imitate others. Even at the end of second grade, there are a few students who do not understand "one 10," in spite of all the discussions they heard every day. By observing children who cannot understand higher-level arguments, we become convinced that children who finally become able to understand them have invented new relationships through constructive abstraction.

Do Not Say That an Answer Is Correct or Incorrect

In traditional math education, part of a teacher's role is to give feedback about the correctness of each answer. However, we avoid saying that an answer is correct or incorrect and instead ask, "Does everybody agree?" The source of feedback in logico-mathematical knowledge is inside each child, that is, whether something *makes sense*. If everybody agrees that an answer makes sense, the child who gave the answer can know that it must be correct.

Some readers may be wondering what the teacher would do if the entire class agreed with an incorrect answer. Our answer is that that never happens. If it did happen, the teacher would know that the question was too hard for the class and go on to something else.

In traditional teaching, when the teacher says that an answer is correct, all thinking stops because there is no need to think any more. If, however, the teacher does not express any opinion, children are motivated to keep thinking. When a scientist constructs a new theory (such as the heliocentric theory), there is no teacher or higher authority to reinforce its truth! Children should likewise be self-reliant in deciding what makes sense and what does not.

Let Computation Grow Out of Everyday Situations and Word Problems

As stated in Chapters 5, 6, and 7, our ancestors developed mathematics as they coped with practical problems they wanted to solve. Children, too, invent arithmetic as they deal with situations in daily living. We therefore use these situations and extend them in word problems. Many examples of this principle were presented in Chapters 8 and 9.

Recognize the Superiority of Games over Worksheets

It is necessary for children to repeat adding the same numbers if they are to remember sums and build a network of numerical relationships (refer to Figure 5.2). Repetition in games is much better than with worksheets for many reasons. The fact that children are intrinsically motivated in games was discussed earlier in this chapter. Seven other reasons are given below.

First, feedback is immediate in games because children supervise each other. By contrast, worksheets are usually returned the next day, and children cannot remember and do not care about what they did yesterday.

Second, when worksheets are used, truth is decided by the teacher, and children get the message that truth can come only from the teacher. In a game, by contrast, the players decide whether an answer is correct. If one child says that 2 + 2 is more than 2 + 3, for example, children try to convince each other and arrive at truth by themselves. In logico-mathematical knowledge, children are bound to arrive at truth if they argue long enough because there is absolutely nothing arbitrary in logico-mathematical knowledge.

Third, games can be played at many levels in a variety of ways, but worksheets encourage children to crank answers out mechanically. In playing Put and Take (see Chapter 11), for example, some children can make 6 only with 6 chips that are each worth one point. Others say that they can make 6 either with 3 2-point chips or with a 5-point chip and a 1-point chip.

Fourth, having to write answers interferes with the possibility of remembering sums. Children are much more likely to remember sums when they are free to think "2, 3, and 5," for example, without stopping to write "5." Some first graders have to think to make a "5" look different from an "S."

Fifth, children are more likely in a game to construct a network of numerical relationships (refer to Figure 5.2). If a player rolls a 3 and a 3, and the next roll is a 3 and a 4, for example, there is a high probability that the answer will be deduced from 3 + 3 = 6. When children fill out worksheets, by contrast, they approach each problem mechanically as a separate and independent problem.

Sixth, children choose the specific games they want to play, but they can seldom choose the worksheets they get. If children can choose an activity that appeals to them, they are likely to work harder. In life outside school, adults constantly make choices, and children need to learn to make wise choices within limits.

Our seventh and last point is that children do not develop sociomorally by sitting alone filling out worksheets. They are well behaved when they are filling out worksheets, but working alone precludes the possibility of sociomoral development. In games, by contrast, children have to interact with others, make decisions together, and learn to resolve conflicts. As stated in Chapter 4, sociomoral education takes place every minute of the school day, whether or not educators are aware of it. By giving countless worksheets, we unwittingly reinforce children's heteronomy, thereby preventing the development of their autonomy.

CHAPTER 13

Principles of Teaching with Games

The teacher's role is crucial in maximizing the value of math games. For example, if the teacher corrects papers at his or her desk while children are playing, children quickly get the message that games are not important enough for the teacher to bother with. If games are unimportant to the teacher, children's attention drifts to other activities. If the teacher plays with children but constantly corrects their errors, children are prevented from developing confidence and initiative. When they feel that the teacher is in charge, they are not likely to supervise their peers either.

Teachers ask a variety of questions related to games, and this chapter attempts to answer these frequently asked questions. They are listed first and addressed one by one.

> What do you do about losing control of the class?
> How do you choose games?
> How do you introduce new games?
> Do you assign games and partners?
> Do you let children change game rules?
> What do you do when children cannot remember how to play a game?
> How do you handle competition?
> What's a good way to store games?
> What do you do with children who "goof off"?
> What's the best thing for the teacher to do while children are playing games?

What do you do about losing control of the class?

If a teacher has been using his or her power to control the class, fights break out soon after the introduction of games, and chaos ensues. These are manifestations of children's heteronomy. It is normal for all young children to be heteronomous at an early age, but, as discussed in Chapter 4, traditional education unfortunately reinforces this heteronomy. In Chapter 12 we suggested ways teachers can transfer the power of control to the children (autonomy). Here we focus specifically on control related to games.

The personalities and dynamics of each class are different, and there is no recipe that will bring success to all teachers. There are, nevertheless, a few principles. As pointed out in Chapter 12, the first principle is to have many class meetings to discuss problems so that the children can think hard to decide on ways of solving *their* problems. The first class meeting related to games may be held to anticipate what the class will do when games are introduced. "Can you think of any problem we might have?" and "What do you think we can do about that problem?" the teacher may ask.

The next meeting may be held to review and evaluate what happened. "Who liked this game?" and "Did anybody have any problems?" the teacher may ask. However, it is sometimes necessary to stop everything and have a class meeting about the screaming and arguing that have erupted.

The important point to keep in mind is that the teacher should refrain from preaching or giving solutions to children so that they will begin to take the initiative of coming up with *their* solution. The teacher is there to help children figure out how they can solve *their* problems, rather than to solve problems for them. As stated in Chapters 4 and 12, children respect the rules they make for themselves much more than the same rules given by an adult.

Another point to remember in these discussions is that problems must be discussed without mentioning specific names. A conversation about "one person" and "the other person" leads to a more general discussion that is applicable to everybody in the class.

If class meetings are frequently held about all kinds of problems that come up throughout the day, children soon learn to govern themselves while playing games, too. Problems are often "too hot" to settle during a game, and it is sometimes best to put the game away and see if, in a class meeting afterward, someone else in the class has an idea about how to handle the situation next time.

Some of the solutions accepted by the group may be unworkable. For example, in deciding who goes first in a game, children often agree on "Eeney, meeney, miney, mo." This solution predictably results in someone's figuring out where to start to always be the one to start the game. The teacher thus knows that "Eeney, meeney" is not a wise solution. However, it is important that the children discover for themselves that their solution led to another problem.

When a decision is found not to have been wise, it is time for another class meeting. The children are likely to make a better decision the second time around because they will take into account the outcome of the first decision.

Conflicts are bound to emerge when children play games. In a traditional classroom, it is the teacher's responsibility to take care of children's conflicts, and teachers often separate the children. When autonomy is the aim of education, however, the teacher works hard to encourage children to resolve their own conflicts. Practical ways of accomplishing this were discussed in Chapter 12.

Children are enthusiastic and excited when they play games, and it is natural for the class to be well behaved but noisy. Our approach to the problem of noise was also discussed in Chapter 12.

How do you choose games?

The appropriate games for kindergarten are generally those in Chapter 10 that do not involve addition. However, kindergartners are able to play easy addition games described in Chapter 11 such as One More, Piggy Bank, and Double War with addends up to 4. Some even come to know all the combinations that make 10 (9 + 1, 8 + 2, and so on) and all the doubles up to 6 + 6. Some games in Chapter 10 such as Animal Olympics are difficult even for some first graders.

To choose games for first graders, it is best to consult the sequence of objectives in Chapter 5 and to choose and modify the games in Chapter 11 accordingly. Generally speaking, subtraction games should wait until January for reasons stated in Chapter 6. Strategy games such as Foxes Boxes and Nickelodeon become attractive after the spring vacation.

The teacher should always accommodate a range of levels for two reasons. First, every class obviously has a range of developmental levels. Second, some games that seem too easy can serve to encourage practice, and repetition is necessary for children to remember various combinations such as "3 + 3 = 6" and "3 + 4 = 7."

First graders like large numbers, and it is not hard for them to add 12 to 36, for example, by counting by ones. While 36 + 12 is not undesirable in itself, counting by ones day after day does not encourage children to think. In such a situation, it is best to change the addends or put the game (such as Square-ominoes) away.

Some groups quickly get tired of games, and a new one stimulates interest and serious play. Other groups are happy with the same game for a long time. A game can also be attractive to one group one year but not to another group the next year. Again, there is no recipe we can offer, and the teacher should experiment and judge how each group of children is thinking and feeling. A path game can appear to be a different game to young children if the stickers are changed from planets to dinosaurs, for example.

How do you introduce new games?

Some games, such as Double War and Cover-up (see Chapter 11) are so simple that a demonstration with one child in front of the entire class is sufficient. The overhead projector can be used for this purpose with transparent cards or gameboards. However, the best way to introduce most games is to involve children in actually playing the new game.

When a game such as the Sandwich Game (see Chapter 11) is very complicated, it may be necessary for the teacher to play with every single child. When the game is simpler, however, the teacher can demonstrate it with one or two children and tell the class to learn it from these "experts." The teacher can, of course, play with 2 or 3 small groups, and tell the rest of the class to learn it from those in the know.

We found out one year that some children were not choosing some of the games simply because they did not know how to play them. Unless children know how a game is played, they do not have the possibility of choosing or rejecting it. We therefore decided to ask all the children to play each new game at least once during the week in which it is introduced.

Do you assign games and partners?

We generally prefer to let children choose the games they want to play and the partner(s) with whom they want to play. Our reasons are that (1) choosing and making decisions are part of autonomy, and children need to learn to make wise decisions and (2) children learn more when they are engaged in activities of their own choice that they enjoy.

However, children often do not make wise choices. For example, first graders who are still counting-all toward the end of the year often choose hard games such as Foxes Boxes (see Chapter 11). This game is not harmful, but time is better spent playing Cover-up or a similar game in which two small addends come up randomly. We have used a "log" to deal with this kind of problem.

A log is a form for each week with "Monday," "Tuesday," and so on listed in the left-hand column (see Figure 13.1). The other two columns are entitled "Game(s) Played" and "Partner(s)." Children usually complete this form after playing games, but the teacher can prescribe "Animal Olympics" and "Emily" for Tuesday and "Five-Plus Bingo" and "Jennifer" for Thursday, for example. This is a way to let children choose games most of the time but not always. Children usually choose someone at a similar developmental level, but it is sometimes necessary to assign partners who are at about the same level.

Another way is to limit the choices on certain days to three games or five games. If the choices are among very easy, very hard, and in-between, children often make more appropriate choices than when there are too many to choose from.

Some first graders play War with great pleasure and frequency when it has become much too easy for them. Rather than outlawing War in such a situation, the teacher might bring this problem up in a class meeting. "Today, I saw some people [who remain anonymous] playing War and wondered what the class thought about this game," the teacher might say. He or she might also ask, "Why do you think I want you to play math games anyway?" The group is likely to conclude that playing War is not the way to become competent in math.

Figure 13.1. A log indicating that, on Tuesday and Thursday, the teacher wants a child to play specific games with specific partners.

Name_____ Date_____

	Game(s) Played	Partner(s)
Monday		
Tuesday	Animal Olympics	Emily
Wednesday		
Thursday	Five-Plus Bingo	Jennifer
Friday		

Do you let children change game rules?

Some modifications of games are introduced by the teacher, and others are initiated by children. For example, Double *Parcheesi* is best introduced with a die going up to 6. When many children know most of the doubles up to 6, it is time for the teacher to introduce a die going up to 8 or 10.

The rules of a game belong to social (conventional) knowledge, and every convention can be changed by agreement among the members of the group. Therefore, when children say that they want to change a rule of a game, we usually say that they must ask the other members of the group if they agree to the proposed change.

The changes children suggest are usually wise and appropriate. In Line-up (or Card Dominoes, see Chapter 10), for example, the rule states that a player can put down only one card at a time. Kindergartners are happy to follow this rule at the beginning of the year, but there comes a time every year when someone asks, "Can we put down all the cards we can?" Our reaction, as usual, is, "You have to ask the other children what they think." The other players are usually glad to change the rule because they, too, have become impatient with a game that moves too slowly. By the middle of the year, most children have become able to make many relationships simultaneously.

While the modifications children suggest are usually wise and appropriate, this is not always the case. For example, children sometimes change Double *Parcheesi* to a regular *Parcheesi* game in which the number rolled is not doubled. When this happens in first grade, the game becomes much too easy and devoid of any necessity for addition. The teacher should intervene when such a modification of a rule takes place. For children's development of autonomy, the best way to intervene is to refer them to the written rule rather than telling them the rule.

What do you do when children cannot remember how to play a game?

Neither children nor adults can remember all the rules of all the games. We therefore write the essential parts of each game on a card and tape it on the gameboard or put it in the box. These rules can be photocopied to reduce their size. These written rules provide excellent opportunities for children to practice reading. Being able to read written rules makes children less dependent on the teacher.

How do you handle competition?

Some teachers dislike games because some children boast when they win. Boastfulness is a symptom of children who already have personality problems, and this problem disappears when the teacher is casual about winning and losing. Winning becomes "no big deal" when the teacher simply asks "Who won?" and then asks, "Would you like to play this game again or a different game?"

The possibility of winning is a uniquely desirable characteristic of games because this possibility serves to organize the small-group activity. In games, each group can function without the teacher because everybody knows that there is a beginning and an end and rules about how to get to the end. If competition did not exist, there would be no need for rules, and the activity would not remain organized.

Four-year-olds are generally incapable of competing in games because they are not cognitively advanced enough to compare their performance with other children's performance in a game (Kamii & DeVries, 1980; Piaget, 1932/1965). When they are between 5 and 6, however, they begin to play games competitively and begin to think, for example, that Musical Chairs is no fun if there are as many chairs as children.

Five- and 6-year-olds do not become competitive overnight and play games with an amusing mixture of competitive and uncompetitive ways. When they win in Line-up (or Card Dominoes, see Chapter 10), for example, they dislike not being able to play and ask others, "Can I have some of your cards [to be able to continue playing]?"

Remnants of uncompetitiveness continue to manifest themselves in first grade, especially in certain games such as Tens with Nine Cards (see Chapter 11). First graders like to help others in this game if they find a pair that makes 10. When this happens, the teacher needs to say, "Let's let everybody do his or her own thinking. You can say that there is a possibility, but let's not say which cards a person can take." This remark is desirable because it informs the child who cannot find any pair that a possibility of making 10 exists. If the advanced students do the thinking for their less-advanced peers, the educational value of the game is reduced to zero.

What's a good way to store games?

A good system of storage facilitates choosing games and returning all the pieces to their designated places. We use three kinds of equipment for storage. The gameboards made with laminated Manila folders are stored in a filing crate that holds hanging files so that all the Nine Men's Morrises can be found and returned to the file labeled "Nine Men's Morris," for example.

Cards, chips, and dice are placed in a set of 18 drawers (see Photograph 13.1) originally made to store fishing equipment that we found in a discount store. We put the name of each game in front of each drawer so that the child who chooses that game can take the drawer and return it after using its contents. A set of cardboard jewelry boxes or transparent plastic boxes can be used in a similar way.

Other games that come in large boxes or require more space are stored on shelves. When the children throw games on the shelves leaving a mess behind, the teacher can ask the class what they think of the way the games have been returned to the shelves. He or she can also ask, "Do you think people will be able to choose games easily tomorrow?" Straightening out the mess is the

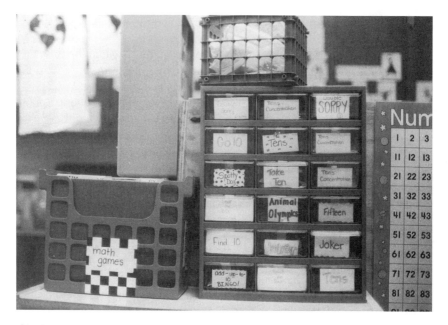

Photograph 13.1. A Set of Drawers Used to Store Cards, Chips, and Dice

children's responsibility. Since *they* played with the games, it is *their* responsibility to return them to the shelves thinking about the next persons who will use them.

The problem of missing game pieces is a topic that is appropriate for a class meeting. If children are not given any solution and, instead, are asked to think together to solve the problem, they gradually construct their own rules and remember them. When everybody feels responsible about not losing the pieces, children remind each other when a chip is left on the floor, for example. The need for a class meeting arises less frequently as children become more careful about these small objects.

Many games become too easy after a while. Easy games that nobody wants to play are put away and replaced by more difficult ones that come out of the teacher's cabinet. The labels on the set of 18 drawers are changed as old games are retired and new ones are introduced.

What do you do with children who "goof off"?

Even with attractive games whose difficulty levels are perfect for the class, there are times when children "goof off" and begin to discuss their plans for an after-school activity, for example. One of the solutions we have tried is to move games from the floor to children's desks. Sitting on the floor is conducive to lying down, relaxing, and feeling free to do anything one pleases. Sitting at a desk sometimes prevents these temptations but not always.

The best solution we have found has been, again, a class meeting. The teacher might ask, "Why do you think I set a time aside every day for math games?" Somebody is likely to say, "Because you want us to learn math." In the final analysis, we find that all children want to become competent, and games are a natural activity for all young children. How to relate their general desire for competence to daily efforts is an art, and each teacher works with his or her own personality and the personalities of the children. We therefore experiment with different solutions each year. Some classes do not present the problem of attention that drifts.

What's the best thing for the teacher to do while children are playing games?

There are many different things the teacher can do, but playing with individual children or a small group is the most useful activity for the teacher. The reason is that playing games with children is the best way to assess their level of numerical reasoning.

Some of the questions the teacher can keep in mind while playing a game with a child are: Is the child counting-all or counting-on? Does he or she count-on from the larger addend (using commutativity)? Which sums are in the child's memory (with no need for counting)? Which doubles does the child know? Which combinations that make 10 does the child know? Does the child use knowledge of doubles (such as $3 + 4 = [3 + 3] + 1$) and of 10s (such as $8 + 5 = [8 + 2] + 3$)?

In Double War (see Chapter 11), for example, when a child turns over two 3s and the teacher, a 3 and a 2, many children start to count the symbols on the cards. In this situation, the teacher can ask, "Is there a way to know without counting?" Some children instantly say "Oh, yeah!" but others say no. The teacher can then say, "Hmmmm. We both have a 3." This remark serves as a big hint to higher-level children but not to those at a lower level. These questions are good not only for instructional purposes but also for assessment. We get insight into children's level of reasoning by observing how they react to hints.

The teacher can go on to say, "Somebody last year said that the two 3s were the same; so all she had to do was to compare her 3 with my 2." Some children have no idea what the teacher is talking about. They count their 3 and 3, and the teacher's 3 and 2, and then conclude that $3 + 3$ is more than $3 + 2$. This kind of information about a child's level of logic is usually impossible to get in an interaction with more than one child.

Another valuable activity for the teacher is to circulate in the class observing which games are currently popular and who is playing which game at what level. These observations can lead to the modification of a game if it seems too easy or to the conclusion that a game was prematurely introduced. The teacher can also pick up a variety of problems such as Double *Parcheesi* played without doubling the numbers rolled. These problems are often best presented at a class meeting, as stated before.

Part IV

RESULTS

CHAPTER 14

Evaluation

The progress of Leslie Housman's first graders was assessed by individually interviewing them in January and May. Most of them had been in a constructivist kindergarten. To compare the outcome of our teaching with that of traditional instruction, we also interviewed 37 children in May in two first-grade classes in a nearby school. This school served a population similar to ours but was using a textbook series and workbooks. Throughout this chapter, the two groups will be referred to as the "Constructivist" and "Textbook" groups.

Each child was interviewed in four sessions—two sessions with word problems and two with computational problems. The findings about word problems will be discussed first and followed by the results concerning computation.

CHILDREN'S ABILITY TO SOLVE WORD PROBLEMS

The 13 word problems given in two sessions can be seen in Table 14.1. These problems were typed on a sheet of paper, and each child was asked, "Would you like to read the first problem, or would you like me to read it?" The questions were given in the order in which they appear in Table 14.1 and reread to the child as many times as necessary. A sheet of paper, a pencil, and about 50 counters were provided, and the child was told, "You can use any of these if they help you figure out the answers."

The numbers used in the word problems were generally small, and our focus was on children's logico-arithmetization of each situation described with words. We asked the child to explain each answer unless we knew that the procedure was easy and obvious to all the children (e.g., Question 1 in Table 14.1). The problems varied in difficulty from one requiring the simplest addition (Question 1) to one involving more than simple multiplication (Question 12).

The results of the word-problem interviews can be seen in Table 14.1. The findings are summarized below.

Overall Comparison of the Two Groups

The first point that can be made is that the Constructivist group did better on all the word problems, with statistical significance for all the questions ex-

Table 14.1. Percentage of Children in the Constructivist and Textbook Groups Giving the Correct Answers to Word Problems

	Const. $n = 21$	Text. $n = 37$	Diff.	Signif.
1. Let's pretend you had 3 sticks of gum. If I gave you 9 more, how many sticks of gum would you have?	90	84	6	n.s.
2. If you had 4 little candles, and you wanted 7 candles for a birthday cake, how many more would you need to get?	86	38	48	.001
3. You had a bunch of stickers. You gave 4 of them to me, and now you have 5 left. How many stickers did you have to begin with?	86	41	45	.001
4. You have 8 marbles. You have 4 more than I do. How many do I have?	86	70	16	n.s.
5. I am getting soup ready for 4 people. So I have 4 bowls. If I want to put 3 crackers in each bowl, how many crackers do I need?	86	22	64	.001
6. I have 18 cookies that I want to give to 3 children. If I want everybody to get the same number, how many would each child get?	86	38	48	.001
7. You had 7 pieces of candy. You gave some of them to me. Now you have 4 pieces left. How many pieces of candy did you give me?	95	54	41	.001
8. There are 5 people at the table. If you want to give 3 graham crackers to each person, how many graham crackers would you need?	76	32	44	.001

9. I have 15 cents. Do I have enough money to buy a pencil and an eraser?
    Pencils cost 5 cents each.
    Erasers cost 8 cents each.
    Notebooks cost 12 cents each.
	76	54	22	.05

10. I have 21 cents. If bubblegum costs 5 cents a piece, how many pieces of bubblegum can I buy?	86	43	43	.001
11. Mints cost 3 cents each. Candy canes cost 4 cents each. If I want to buy 3 mints and 2 candy canes, how much money do I need?	62	11	51	.001
12. Marilyn wants to buy 3 small boxes of raisins. At Bruno's a box of raisins costs 20 cents. At Winn Dixie, they sell 3 boxes for 50 cents. Which store should Marilyn go to to get a better price?	24	0	24	.001
13. David had 3 small packages of crackers. Each package had 6 crackers in it. He ate 15 crackers. How many crackers does he have left?	67	27	40	.001

cept the easiest two, namely, Questions 1 and 4. Question 1 was the following addition problem that was so easy that 90% and 84%, respectively, answered it correctly: *Let's pretend you had 3 sticks of gum. If I gave you 9 more, how many sticks of gum would you have?*

Question 4 was an addition/subtraction problem: *You have 8 marbles. You have 4 more than I do. How many do I have?* This problem was solved correctly by 86% of the Constructivist group and 70% of the Textbook group. "More" is a difficult word for first graders when used in questions such as "How many *more* does A have than B?" and "How many *more* do you need?" However, when a specific number is mentioned as in "You have *4 more* than I do," it is not a hard word.

Level of Performance Within Each Group

The second point that can be made is that at least two-thirds of the children in the Constructivist group answered all the questions correctly except the hardest two, namely, Questions 11 and 12. By contrast, the 13 questions varied greatly in difficulty for the Textbook group, and the success rates ranged from 0% for Question 12 to 84% for Question 1.

Question 11 was answered correctly by 62% of the Constructivist group and 11% of the Textbook group: *Mints cost 3 cents each. Candy canes cost 4 cents each. If I want to buy 3 mints and 2 candy canes, how much money do I need?*

The Textbook group's incorrect answers were usually 5 (given by 32%) or 7 (given by 24%). The other incorrect answers were: 8, "10 more," 11, 12, 13, 14, 16, 20, 24, 32, and 34. When asked to explain these answers, the Textbook group was either unable to justify them (e.g., "I just knew it") or explained that 3 (mints) and 2 (candy canes) made 5 or that 3 (cents) and 4 (cents) made 7.

In the Constructivist group, one child gave the answer of 5, and one gave 7. The other incorrect answers were 8, 11 (given by 2 children), 13, 19, and 21. When asked to explain these, 5 (24% of the total group of 21) of the 8 who had given incorrect answers changed them to the correct one.

Self-correction is a general characteristic of the children in the Constructivist group. When asked to explain their incorrect answers, children in the Constructivist group often corrected themselves while trying to justify their thinking. By contrast, those in the Textbook group seldom corrected themselves. The ability to generate a better answer is an indication of more-advanced logic.

Question 12 was the most difficult of the 13 questions. It was the following and was answered correctly by only 24% of the Constructivist group and none of the Textbook group: *Marilyn wants to buy 3 small boxes of raisins. At Bruno's a box of raisins costs 20 cents. At Winn Dixie, they sell 3 boxes for 50 cents. Which store should Marilyn go to, to get a better price?*

Forty-three percent of the Textbook group answered that Bruno's had a better price because 50 cents was more than 20 cents. Forty-seven percent sat silently without any response for a long time and were relieved to be asked, "Would you like to skip this question?"

Thirty-three percent of the Constructivist group also compared 20 and 50 cents, but the other incorrect answers showed slightly better logic such as 40 vs. 50 cents, 40 vs. 150 cents, and 60 vs. 150 cents. When asked to explain their answers, 14% of the Constructivist group changed them to the correct one.

Comparison of the Two Groups with Respect to Each Type of Problems

The 9 questions not discussed so far (Questions 2, 3, 5, 6, 7, 8, 9, 10, and 13) also consistently revealed the superiority of the Constructivist group's logic. Findings from these questions are discussed below under three headings: Addition/subtraction, "multiplication," and "division" problems.

Addition/subtraction Problems. Question 2 was the following "equalizing" or missing-addend question that was answered correctly by 86% of the Constructivist group and 38% of the Textbook group: *If you had 4 little candles, and you wanted 7 candles for a birthday cake, how many more would you need to get?* This type of question is generally answered correctly by only half of the children in second grade, as documented in Chapter 6. The reason for this difficulty is that this kind of logic of part-whole relationships is hard for all children until 7 to 8 years of age. Eighty-six percent of the first graders in the Constructivist group nevertheless answered this question correctly.

The incorrect answers given by the Textbook group demonstrate their lower level of logic. Their incorrect answers were mostly 11 (4 + 7, given by 27%) and 7 (given by 19%).

Question 3 also involves the logic of a part-whole relationship and was answered correctly by 86% of the Constructivist group and 41% of the Textbook group: *You had a bunch of stickers. You gave 4 of them to me, and now you have 5 left. How many stickers did you have to begin with?* Forty-one percent of the Textbook group gave the incorrect answer of 4, revealing their inability to make a part-whole relationship.

A part-whole relationship was again involved in Question 7: *You had 7 pieces of candy. You gave some of them to me. Now you have 4 pieces left. How many pieces of candy did you give me?* Ninety-five percent of the Constructivist group and 54% of the Textbook group answered this question correctly.

The incorrect answers given by the Textbook group were mostly 4 (given by 32%), 11 (7 + 4, given by 8%), and 7 (given by 5%). These children simply could not put the numbers into a logical relationship.

Question 9 is a simple addition problem with irrelevant information. The children in both groups generally ignored the irrelevant information, and 76% and 54%, respectively, gave the correct answer.

"Multiplication" Problems.   Question 5 was a "multiplication" problem, which 86% of the Constructivist group answered correctly with repeated addition: *I am getting soup ready for 4 people. So I have 4 bowls. If I want to put 3 crackers in each bowl, how many crackers do I need?*

This multiplication problem was answered correctly by only 22% of the Textbook group and produced the greatest difference of 64 percentage points between the two groups. Since the first-grade textbook does not include multiplication problems, the Textbook group was at a disadvantage. The incorrect answers most frequently given by this group were: 4 (given by 35%), "one more" (4 is one more than 3, given by 11%), and 9 (given by 11%). The answers of 4 and "one more" indicate that these children did not have the logic of repeated addition.

A similar multiplication problem was Question 8: *There are 5 people at the table. If you want to give 3 graham crackers to each person, how many graham crackers would you need?* The percentages getting the correct answer were 76 and 32, respectively, for the two groups. Most of the incorrect answers given by the Textbook group were: 5 (given by 19%), 8 (5 + 3, given by 16%), and 3 (given by 8%). These incorrect answers again show that it did not occur to these children to add 3 or 5 repeatedly.

A much more complicated multiplication problem was Question 13: *David had 3 small packages of crackers. Each package had 6 crackers in it. He ate 15 crackers. How many crackers does he have left?* The percentages of 67 and 27, respectively, getting the correct answer are not surprising. The large variety of unexplained incorrect answers given by both groups (0, 1, 4, 6, 8, 9, 10, 11, 12, 13, 18, 20, 21, 36, and "2 boxes") defied our effort to identify common errors.

"Division" Problems.   Question 6 was a (partitive) "division" problem, which 86% of the Constructivist group solved with repeated addition: *I have 18 cookies that I want to give to 3 children. If I want everybody to get the same number, how many would each child get?*

Thirty-eight percent of the Textbook group gave the correct answer, and 22% gave the answer 3. Examples of the other incorrect answers are 1, 5, 15, and 18.

Question 10 is a (quotitive) division problem that 86% of the Constructivist group solved with repeated addition: *I have 21 cents. If bubblegum costs 5 cents a piece, how many pieces of bubblegum can I buy?*

Forty-three percent of the Textbook group succeeded in answering this question. The incorrect answers given by this group were the following, justified with statements such as "I just guessed it," and "I thought it in my brain": 1, 3, 5, 8, 10, 15, 17, 20, 21, 26 and 105.

In conclusion, the Constructivist group proved to be far superior in solving word problems. Some children in the Textbook group could solve most of these word problems, but the proportion who succeeded was significantly higher in the Constructivist group. It can therefore be concluded that when first graders are encouraged to do their own thinking, they are much more likely to develop their potential for logical thinking.

There were three children in the Constructivist group (14% of the 21) who started the school year at a very low level and continued to have difficulty in putting numbers into logical relationships. These children did not give correct answers to our word problems, but their logic nevertheless developed over the year to the point of producing partial success or complete success some of the time.

CHILDREN'S KNOWLEDGE OF SUMS AND DIFFERENCES

The children's ability to add and subtract was evaluated in two sessions. The problems given in the first session are in the left column of Table 14.2. Those given in the second session are in the right column of the same table and in Table 14.3. The questions were given in the order in which they appear in these tables.

For reasons stated in Chapter 5, Table 14.2 includes many doubles (such as 3 + 3) and combinations that make 10 (such as 2 + 8). Questions like 6 + 1 and 1 + 4 involving the addition of 1 were not given because previous research had informed us of the ease of +1 problems (see Table 5.1). Because we deemphasize subtraction for reasons stated in Chapter 6, Table 14.2 includes only a few subtraction problems.

The interviews took place with the child and the interviewer sitting next to each other on two sides of the table. Both had a photocopied form showing all the problems in the left-hand column. The child was given a ruler to use as a marker and was asked to slide it down to the next problem after giving each answer. The ruler thus served to hide each subsequent problem and to let the interviewer know exactly when each problem was exposed. No pencil or counters were provided in these sessions.

The interviewer recorded each child's responses with shorthand so that each session could be recreated from the notes that were taken. For example, one dot per second was recorded to indicate the child's silence. The final answer was always circled. "CO" or "CA" was used to indicate "counting-on" or "counting-all." An "F" was recorded if the child counted openly on fingers, and an "f" was recorded if this counting was not so obvious.

Table 14.2. Percentage of Children in the Constructivist and Textbook Groups Giving the Correct Answers Within 3 Seconds

	Const. $n = 21$	Text. $n = 37$	Diff.		Const. $n = 21$	Text. $n = 37$	Diff.
2 + 2	100	100	0	5 + 5	100	100	0
2 + 8	90	59	31	6 + 6	100	73	27
7 + 3	95	59	36	5 + 3	76	76	0
8 + 6	48	11	37	8 + 2	95	92	3
3 + 3	100	95	5	9 + 9	48	41	7
2 + 9	90	68	22	5 + 6	76	35	41
10 + 10	100	95	5	3 + 7	81	49	32
5 + 7	48	22	26	7 + 8	38	11	27
2 + 3	86	81	5	8 + 5	43	22	21
4 + 4	100	89	11	7 + 7	67	49	18
5 + 8	52	14	38	4 + 6	57	27	30
9 + 5	57	38	19	7 + 4	81	32	49
4 + 3	76	54	22	8 + 8	67	16	51
7 + 6	43	14	29				
4 + 9	57	30	27				
4 + 5	71	51	20				
10 - 5	86	84	2				
4 - 2	81	73	8				
8 - 4	71	57	14				
10 - 8	52	27	25				
12 - 6	62	41	21				
7 - 2	52	51	1				
10 - 6	43	27	16				

The criterion for inclusion in Table 14.2 was that the correct answer be given within 3 seconds *without counting*. Therefore, the child's response was included in Table 14.2 if, for example, the record for "5 + 7" was ". . *12*." If the record showed "6 7 8 . . . . . *12*," however, this response was not included in Table 14.2 because the child counted to get the answer. By writing "6 7 8 . . . . . *12* (or CO5)" or "8 9 10 11 *12* (or CO7)," it was possible to know later whether the child counted-on from 5 or from 7 (with commutative reasoning).

Table 14.3. Percentage in the Constructivist and Textbook Groups Giving Correct and Incorrect Answers When at Least One Addend Was a Two-Digit Number

	Constructivist	Textbook		
	$n = 21$	Algorithm taught $n = 19$	Algorithm not taught $n = 18$	Total $n = 37$
$10 + 7 = 17$	52	37	39	38
$\begin{array}{r} 22 \\ +7 \\ \hline 29 \end{array}$	71	37	56	46
$= 11^*$	0	32	0	
$\begin{array}{r} 28 \\ +31 \\ \hline 59 \end{array}$	19	37	11	24
$= 14^*$	0	26	0	
$81 + 12 = 93$	38	32	11	22
$= 12^*$	0	21	0	
$\begin{array}{r} 13 \\ +8 \\ \hline 21 \end{array}$	76	37	61	49
$= 12^*$	0	32	5	
$\begin{array}{r} 27 \\ +13 \\ \hline 40 \end{array}$	48	5	33	19
$= 13^*$	0	21	0	

*Common incorrect answers that result when all digits are added as ones.

The findings about sums and differences with numbers up to 10 are summarized below. The addition of two-digit numbers is discussed later.

Addition and Subtraction with Addends or Minuends to 10

The first observation that can be made from Table 14.2 is that the Constructivist group did better on all the items except three, where differences were zero. The second point that can be made is that if a problem was easy for the Textbook group, it was also easy for the Constructivist group, and if it was hard for the Textbook group, it was sometimes hard for the Constructivist group. Both groups easily and quickly produced correct answers to the following doubles: 2 + 2, 3 + 3, 4 + 4, 5 + 5, and 10 + 10. Another problem that was easy for both groups was 8 + 2. (Problems involving +1 are very easy, and those involving +2 are next, as can be seen in Table 5.1.)

The two groups differed the most on 9 items that produced differences of 30 percentage points or more. These items were: 2 + 8, 7 + 3, 8 + 6, 5 + 8, 5 + 6, 3 + 7, 4 + 6, 7 + 4, and 8 + 8. These can be categorized into the following three groups: (1) a relatively difficult double, 8 + 8; (2) combinations that make 10, namely, 2 + 8, 7 + 3, 3 + 7, and 4 + 6; and (3) combinations such as 8 + 6, 5 + 8, 5 + 6, and 7 + 4 that allowed the use of doubles (e.g., 5 + 6 = [5 + 5] + 1) and combinations that make 10 (e.g., 8 + 6 = [8 + 2] + 4).

The results concerning 8 + 8 can be explained by the fact that the Constructivist group played many games in which they doubled single-digit numbers. The Constructivist group's superior knowledge of combinations that make 10 can also be explained by the many games they played in which they tried to find two numbers that made 10. When they encountered problems such as 5 + 8, the children in the Constructivist group changed them to (5 + 5) + 3 or to (8 + 2) + 3.

Both groups did very well on 8 + 2, but only the Constructivist group did well on 2 + 8. Ninety percent of the Constructivist group answered 2 + 8 and 2 + 9 within 3 seconds, but the percentages for the Textbook group were 59 and 68, respectively. These percentages indicate that more children in the Constructivist group used the logic of commutativity (Gréco, 1962).

We gave very few games involving subtraction because (1) subtraction is much harder than addition, as explained in Chapter 6, and (2) we believe that the way to render subtraction easy is to strengthen children's knowledge of sums. It can be seen in Table 14.2 that the Constructivist group nevertheless did as well as or slightly better than the Textbook group on the kinds of subtraction problems we stress (the inverse of doubles, the inverse of adding two numbers that total 10, and the inverse of +1 and +2).

Addition with Two-digit Numbers

Table 14.3 presents percentages of children who gave correct and incorrect answers when at least one of the addends was a two-digit number. Speed was not a criterion for inclusion in this table.

By the time each child reached this part of the interview, it was easy to tell who would have difficulty. For example, if a child had been counting on fingers all along, it was clear that 28 + 31 would be discouraging or too hard. When difficulty was evident, the interviewer asked, "Would you like to skip this one?"

If the child persisted in trying, this question was repeated as soon as frustration was observed.

Two points can be made from Table 14.3. One concerns the harmful effects of teaching the algorithm of aligning and adding each column. The second point deals with the emergence of the idea of *tens*.

As stated in Chapter 5 with reference to Table 5.4, one of the teachers of the Textbook classes had taught the rule for adding two-digit numbers that do not require "carrying." This teaching resulted in answers such as $22 + 7 = 11$, $28 + 31 = 14$, $81 + 12 = 12$, $13 + 8 = 12$, and $27 + 13 = 13$. These answers were obtained by treating all the digits as *ones* (for example, $22 + 7 = 11$ because $2 + 2 + 7 = 11$). None or almost none of the children in the groups who had not been taught the conventional algorithm produced such absurd answers. The differences with respect to these kinds of answers were statistically significant ($p < .05$) between the groups who had and had not been taught the algorithm. These findings support the conclusion reached several years ago based on many data (Kamii, 1994) that teaching conventional algorithms as recommended by most textbook series is harmful to children's numerical reasoning. The algorithm makes computation efficient for adults, who already know that the first "2" in "22" means "twenty." For young children, who are not sure of *tens* and *ones*, however, the conventional algorithm reinforces their tendency to think about all the digits as ones. After being taught the conventional algorithm, one-fifth to one-third of the first graders began to get totals that were smaller than, or the same as, one of the addends.

The last question, $27 + 13$, is informative because it involves "carrying." The Textbook class that had *not* been taught the algorithm did better than the Textbook class that had received this instruction because the former simply counted-on from 27. In the class that had been taught the algorithm, many of the children got the answer 13 by treating all the digits as *ones*, or made statements such as "10 for $7 + 3$, and 3 for $2 + 1$."

The Textbook class that had *not* been taught the algorithm behaved similarly to the Constructivist group in that, unless they skipped a problem, they got the correct answer by counting-on. The percentage getting the correct answer therefore tended to be high when the second addend was a small, one-digit number (such as $22 + 7$ and $13 + 8$). There were, however, differences between the two groups. One of them was in the speed with which they answered $10 + 7$. Thirty-eight percent of the Constructivist group gave the correct answer instantly, indicating that 10 and 7 were composite higher-order units for them. These children did not need to count-on or stop to think. The percentage instantly giving the correct answer in the Textbook group was 5 (one child in each class).

In the Constructivist group there were 3 children who were beginning to reason about *tens* and *ones*, but no one in the Textbook group thought in this way. To do $13 + 8$, for example, one child in the Constructivist group said, "That's

10, and 3 + 8 = 11; so 10 + 11 = 21." These children also added 27 and 13 by reasoning that 20 + 10 = 30, 7 + 3 = 10, and 30 + 10 = 40.

CONCLUSION

We started the work described in this volume with the distinction Piaget (1967/1971, 1945/1951) made among three kinds of knowledge based on their ultimate sources—physical, logico-mathematical, and social (conventional) knowledge. With 60 years of scientific research, he and others demonstrated that children all over the world construct logico-mathematical knowledge from within, in interaction with the environment, rather than acquiring it by direct internalization from the environment.

Piaget's constructivism led us to conceptualize educational goals and objectives differently from traditional instruction. For us, the basic goal is that children become able to reason logically, through the exchange of viewpoints with other children. For traditional instruction, by contrast, the goal is that children become able to produce correct answers, quickly. We deemphasize correct answers because if children can reason, they *will* get the correct answer.

Another difference from textbook instruction is that we conceptualize goals and objectives according to what is easy or hard *for children*, rather than through adult common sense and mathematical analysis. For example, subtraction is merely the inverse of addition for mathematicians and authors of textbooks, but 7 – 4 is much harder for first graders than 4 + 3. We therefore deemphasize subtraction in first grade but give many "multiplication" and "division" word problems that textbooks do not present at all in first grade. First graders and many kindergartners are perfectly capable of solving multiplication and division word problems with repeated addition.

If our goals and objectives are different from those of traditional instruction, it follows that our approach to evaluation is also different, especially from the achievement-test approach. In achievement tests, the only thing that matters is the number of correct answers produced quickly. By contrast, we evaluate children's ability to reason logically and numerically and their confidence in their own ability to figure things out. Children's knowledge of sums and differences is not worth much if they cannot logico-arithmetize reality, cannot reason numerically, and do not have confidence.

The Constructivist group was found to reason more logically than the Textbook group (refer to Table 14.1). Some of the children in the Textbook group successfully solved multiplication and division word problems, to which they had not been exposed. This ability demonstrated the logico-mathematical knowledge these children had constructed without any formal instruction. However, the proportions of success were significantly greater in the Constructivist group (e.g.,

Question 5, 86% vs. 22%; Question 6, 86% vs. 38%; Question 8, 76% vs. 32%; and Question 10, 86% vs. 43%). These differences show that constructivist teaching encourages children more than the textbook does to develop the potential they bring to school.

The Constructivist group's numerical reasoning and their knowledge of sums and differences were also found to be superior (refer to Tables 14.2 and 14.3). This superiority was especially noticeable with respect to children's use of doubles and combinations that make 10. For example, significantly more children in the Constructivist group produced correct answers within 3 seconds to problems such as 5 + 6 and 7 + 4.

"Tens and ones" were never taught explicitly in the Constructivist group, but 38% instantly produced the answer to 10 + 7, indicating that 10 and 7 were solid composite units for them. By contrast, only 5% of the Textbook group instantly produced the answer to 10 + 7. Furthermore, evidence of thinking about *tens* was found only in the Constructivist group. For example, 3 children (14%) solved 27 + 13 by reasoning that 20 + 10 = 30, 7 + 3 = 10, and 30 + 10 = 40.

By contrast, one of the Textbook teachers had taught the algorithm of aligning and adding each column, with the result that one-fifth to one-third of her class produced answers such as 22 + 7 = 11, 28 + 31 = 14, and 81 + 12 = 12. Textbook instruction not only failed to develop children's natural logico-mathematical knowledge but also began to harm their ability to reason numerically. No child who was free to do his or her own thinking produced such absurd answers.

The evaluation of children's confidence and their development of autonomy is difficult, and we ask the reader to make his or her judgment by viewing videotapes such as *Double-Column Addition* (Kamii, 1989b), *Multidigit Division* (Kamii, 1990), and *First Graders Dividing 62 by 5* (Kamii & Clark, 2000).

We pointed out in Chapter 1 that it took 150 years for the heliocentric theory to become universally accepted. The most powerful institution that retarded progress in the 16th and 17th centuries was the Church. The institutions now preventing progress in education are political and economic, which are selling, buying, and imposing textbooks and achievement tests. The number of educators who are autonomous enough to encourage children to do their own thinking has nevertheless been increasing steadily since the 1980s. Whether it will take 150 years for Piaget's constructivism to be universally accepted depends on how autonomous educators become, morally and intellectually.

Appendix: Resources

CATALOGS

Cuisenaire Dale Seymour Publications, P.O. Box 5026, White Plains, NY 10602-5026.
ETA, 620 Lakeview Parkway, Vernon Hills, IL 60061-1838.
Nasco, P.O. Box 901, Fort Atkinson, WI 53538-0901.

COMMERCIALLY MADE GAMES

Animal Olympics. Germany: Ravensburg, 1991.
Animal Rummy. Racine, WI: Western Publishing Co., n.d.
Candy Land. Springfield, MA: Milton Bradley, 1997.
Chutes and Ladders. Springfield, MA: Milton Bradley, 1997.
Fish. Racine, WI: Western Publishing Co., 1975.
FLINCH. Beverly, MA: Parker Brothers, 1988.
Huckleberry Hound. Commack, NY: ED-U-CARDS, 1961.
Jenga. Springfield, MA: Milton Bradley, 1986.
Parcheesi. Bay Shore, NY: Selchow & Righter, 1975.
Piggy Bank. Commack, NY: EDU-CARDS, 1965.
ROOK. Beverly, MA: Parker Brothers, 1972.
Snap. Racine, WI: Western Publishing Co., n.d.
TENS. Bramalea, Ontario, Canada: Waddington House of Games, 1975.
Tens and Twenties. Leicester, England: Taskmaster, 1981.
24 Game Primer, Add/Subtract. Easton, PA: Suntex International, 1993.
UNO. Joliet, IL: International Games, 1973.

References

Adjei, K. (1977). Influence of specific maternal occupation and behavior on Piagetian cognitive development. In P. R. Dasen (Ed.), *Piagetian psychology: Cross-cultural contributions* (pp. 227–256). New York: Gardner Press.

Ainley, J. (1990). Playing games and learning mathematics. In L. P. Steffe & T. Wood (Eds.), *Transforming children's mathematics education* (pp. 84–91). Hillsdale, NJ: Erlbaum.

Allardice, B. S. (1977). *The development of representational skills for some mathematical concepts* (Doctoral dissertation, Cornell University). Ann Arbor, MI: University Microfilms International.

Atkins, C., & Kuipers, J. (1990). *Cantaloupes, cantaloupes*. Birmingham, AL: Alabama Power Co.

Bovet, M. (1974). Cognitive processes among illiterate children and adults. In J. W. Berry & P. R. Dasen (Eds.), *Culture and cognition: Readings in cross-cultural psychology* (pp. 311–334). London: Methuen.

Burns, M. (1992). *Math and literature (K–3)*. Sausalito, CA: Marilyn Burns Education Associates.

Carpenter, T. P., Ansell, E., Franke, M. L., Fennema, E., & Weisbeck, L. (1993). Models of problem solving: A study of kindergarten children's problem-solving processes. *Journal for Research in Mathematics Education, 24*(5), 428–441.

Carpenter, T. P., Fennema, E., Peterson, P. L., Chiang, C. P., & Loef, M. (1989). Using knowledge of children's mathematics thinking in classroom teaching: An experimental study. *American Educational Research Journal, 26*, 499–531.

Carpenter, T. P., & Moser, J. M. (1979). *An investigation of the learning of addition and subtraction* (Theoretical Paper No. 79). Madison, WI: Wisconsin Research and Development Center for Individualized Schooling.

Carpenter, T. P., & Moser, J. M. (1982). The development of addition and subtraction problem-solving skills. In T. P. Carpenter, J. M. Moser, & T. A. Romberg (Eds.), *Addition and subtraction: A cognitive perspective* (pp. 9–24). Hillsdale, NJ: Erlbaum.

Clark, F., & Kamii, C. (1996). Identification of multiplicative thinking in children in grades 1–5. *Journal for Research in Mathematics Education, 27*, 41–51.

Dasen, P. R. (1974). The influence of ecology, culture and European contact on cognitive development in Australian Aborigines. In J. W. Berry & P. R. Dasen (Eds.), *Culture and cognition* (pp. 381–408). London: Methuen.

De Lemos, M. M. (1969). The development of conservation in aboriginal children. *International Journal of Psychology, 4*(4), 255–269.

DeVries, R. (1997). Piaget's social theory. *Educational Researcher, 26*(2), 4–17.

DeVries, R., & Zan, B. (1994). *Moral classrooms, moral children.* New York: Teachers College Press.

Doise, W., & Mugny, G. (1984). *The social development of the intellect.* New York: Pergamon. (Original work published 1981)

Empson, S. B. (1995). Using sharing situations to help children learn fractions. *Teaching Children Mathematics, 2,* 110–114.

Fisher, B. (1995). *Thinking and learning together.* Portsmouth, NH: Heinemann.

Furth, H. G. (1966). *Thinking without language.* New York: Free Press.

Furth, H. G. (1981). *Piaget and knowledge* (2nd ed.). Chicago: University of Chicago Press.

Gibb, E. G. (1956). Children's thinking in the process of subtraction. *Journal of Experimental Education, 25,* 71–80.

Ginsburg, H. P., & Opper, S. (1988). *Piaget's theory of intellectual development.* Englewood Cliffs, NJ: Prentice Hall.

Gréco, P. (1962). Une recherche sur la commutativité de l'addition. In P. Gréco & A. Morf, *Structures numériques élémentaires* (pp. 151–227). Paris: Presses Universitaires de France.

Greenes, C., Immerzeel, G., Schulman, L., & Spungin, R. (1980). *Techniques of problem solving (TOPS).* Palo Alto, CA: Dale Seymour Publications.

Hatwell, Y. (1966). *Privation sensorielle et intelligence.* Paris: Presses Universitaires de France.

Hoban, T. (1987). *26 letters and 99 cents.* New York: Greenwillow Books.

Hyde, D. M. G. (1959). *An investigation of Piaget's theories of the development of the concept of number.* Unpublished doctoral dissertation, University of London.

Ibarra, C. G., & Lindvall, C. M. (1982). Factors associated with the ability of kindergarten children to solve simple arithmetic story problems. *Journal of Educational Research, 75,* 149–155.

Inhelder, B. (1968). *The diagnosis of reasoning in the mentally retarded.* New York: John Day. (Original work published 1943)

Inhelder, B., & Piaget, J. (1963). De l'itération des actions à la récurrence élémentaire. In P. Gréco, B. Inhelder, B. Matalon, & J. Piaget, *La formation des raisonnements récurrentiels* (pp. 47–123). Paris: Presses Universitaires de France.

Inhelder, B., & Piaget, J. (1964). *The early growth of logic in the child.* New York: Harper & Row. (Original work published 1959)

Inhelder, B., Sinclair, H., & Bovet, M. (1974). *Learning and the development of cognition.* Cambridge, MA: Harvard University Press.

Johnson, D. W., Johnson, R. T., Holubec, E. J., & Roy, P. (1994). *Circles of learning: Cooperation in the classroom.* Alexandria, VA: Association for Supervision and Curriculum Development.

Kamii, C. (1982). *Number in preschool and kindergarten.* Washington, DC: National Association for the Education of Young Children.

Kamii, C. (1985). *Young children reinvent arithmetic.* New York: Teachers College Press.

Kamii, C. (1989a). *Young children continue to reinvent arithmetic, 2nd grade.* New York: Teachers College Press.

Kamii, C. (1989b). *Double-column addition: A teacher uses Piaget's theory* [videotape]. New York: Teachers College Press.

Kamii, C. (1990). *Multidigit division: Two teachers using Piaget's theory* [videotape]. New York: Teachers College Press.

Kamii, C. (1994). *Young children continue to reinvent arithmetic, 3rd grade*. New York: Teachers College Press.

Kamii, C., & Clark, F. B. (2000). *First graders dividing 62 by 5* [videotape]. New York: Teachers College Press.

Kamii, C., & DeVries, R. (1980). *Group games in early education*. Washington, DC: National Association for the Education of Young Children.

Kamii, C., & DeVries, R. (1993). *Physical knowledge in preschool education*. New York: Teachers College Press. (Original work published 1978)

Kamii, C., Lewis, B. A., & Booker, B. (1998). Instead of teaching missing addends. *Teaching Children Mathematics, 4*, 458–461.

Kamii, C., & Ozaki, K. (1999). Abstraction and representation in arithmetic: A Piagetian view. *Hiroshima Journal of Mathematics Education, 7*, 1–15.

Kamii, M. (1980). *Place value: Children's efforts to find a correspondence between digits and numbers of objects*. Paper presented at the Tenth Annual Symposium of the Jean Piaget Society, Philadelphia.

Kamii, M. (1981). Children's ideas about written number. *Topics in Learning & Learning Disabilities, 1*, 47–59.

Kamii, M. (1982). *Children's graphic representation of numerical concepts: A developmental study*. Unpublished doctoral dissertation, Harvard University, Cambridge, MA.

Kohlberg, L. (1968). Early education: A cognitive developmental view. *Child Development, 39*, 1013–1062.

Kuhn, T. S. (1970). *The structure of scientific revolutions* (2nd ed.). Chicago: University of Chicago Press.

Labinowicz, E. (1985). *Learning from children: New beginnings for teaching numerical thinking*. Menlo Park, CA: Addison-Wesley.

Laurendeau-Bendavid, M. (1977). Culture, schooling, and cognitive development: A comparative study of children in French Canada and Rwanda. In P. R. Dasen (Ed.), *Piagetian psychology: Cross-cultural contributions* (pp. 123–168). New York: Gardner Press.

Locke, J. (1947). *Essay concerning human understanding*. Oxford, UK: Oxford University Press. (Original work published 1690)

Lourenço, O., & Machado, A. (1996). In defense of Piaget's theory: A reply to 10 common criticisms. *Psychological Review, 103*(1), 143–164.

McMillan, B. (1996). *Jellybeans for sale*. New York: Scholastic.

Mohseni, N. (1966). *La comparaison des réactions aux épreuves d'intelligence en Iran et en Europe*. Unpublished thesis, University of Paris.

Morozumi, A. (1990). *One gorilla*. New York: Trumpet Club.

Nelsen, J. (1981). *Positive discipline*. New York: Ballantine Books.

Olivier, A., Murray, H., & Human, P. (1991). Children's solution strategies for division problems. In R. G. Underhill (Ed.), *Proceedings of the 13th annual meeting*, North American Chapter of the International Group for the Psychology of Mathematics Education (Vol. 2, pp. 15–21). Blacksburg: Virginia Polytechnic Institute.

Opie, I., & Opie, P. (1969). *Children's games in street and playground*. Oxford, UK:

Clarendon Press.

Opper, S. (1977). Concept development in Thai urban and rural children. In P. R. Dasen (Ed.), *Piagetian psychology: Cross-cultural contributions* (pp. 89–122). New York: Gardner Press.

Perret-Clermont, A.-N. (1980). *Social interaction and cognitive development in children.* New York: Academic Press.

Piaget, J. (1951). *Play, dreams, and imitation in childhood.* New York: Norton. (Original work published 1945)

Piaget, J. (1963). *The psychology of intelligence.* New York: Harcourt Brace. (Original work published 1947)

Piaget, J. (1965). *The moral judgment of the child.* New York: Fres Press. (Original work published 1932)

Piaget, J. (1966). Need and significance of cross-cultural studies in genetic psychology. *International Journal of Psychology, 1*(1), 3–13.

Piaget, J. (1971). *Biology and knowledge.* Chicago: University of Chicago Press. (Original work published 1967)

Piaget, J. (1973). *To understand is to invent.* New York: Viking Press. (Original work published 1948)

Piaget, J. (1977). *Piaget on Piaget* [videotape]. New Haven, CT: Yale University Media Design Studio.

Piaget, J. (1980). Experiments in contradiction. Chicago: University of Chicago Press. (Original work published 1974)

Piaget, J. (1987). *Possibility and necessity.* Minneapolis: University of Minnesota Press. (Original work published 1983)

Piaget, J. (1995). *Sociological studies.* London and New York: Routledge. (Original work published 1967)

Piaget, J., & Garcia, R. (1989). *Psychogenesis and the history of science.* New York: Columbia University Press. (Original work published 1983)

Piaget, J., & Inhelder, B. (1973). *Memory and intelligence.* New York: Basic Books. (Original work published 1968)

Piaget, J., Inhelder, B., & Szeminska, A. (1960). *The child's conception of geometry.* New York: Basic Books. (Original work published 1948)

Piaget, J., & Szeminska, A. (1952). *The child's conception of number.* London: Routledge and Kegan Paul. (Original work published 1941)

Piaget, J., & Szeminska, A. (1964). *La genèse du nombre chez l'enfant* (3rd ed.). Neuchâtel, Switzerland: Delachaux et Niestlé.

Price-Williams, D. R. (1961). A study concerning concepts of conservation of quantities among primitive children. *Acta Psychologica, 18,* 297–305.

Sheffield, S. (1995). *Math and literature (K–3), Book Two.* Sausalito, CA: Marilyn Burns Education Associates.

Sinclair, A., Siegrist, F., & Sinclair, H. (1983). Young children's ideas about the written number system. In D. Rogers & J. A. Sloboda (Eds.), *The acquisition of symbolic skills* (pp. 535–541). New York: Plenum.

Steffe, L. (1988). Children's construction of number sequences and multiplying schemes. In J. Hiebert & M. Behr (Eds.), *Number concepts and operations in the middle grades* (Vol. 2, pp. 119–140). Reston, VA: National Council of Teachers of Mathematics.

Steffe, L. (1992). Schemes of action and operation involving composite units. *Learning and Individual Differences, 4,* 259–309.

Suydam, M. N., & Weaver, J. F. (1975). Research on mathematics learning. In J. N. Payne (Ed.), *Mathematics learning in early childhood* (Thirty-seventh yearbook, pp. 43–67). Reston, VA: National Council of Teachers of Mathematics.

Taylor, F. S. (1949). *A short history of science and scientific thought.* New York: Norton.

Waddell, M. (1992). *Farmer duck.* Cambridge, MA: Candlewick Press.

Wakefield, A. P. (1998). *Early childhood number games.* Boston: Allyn and Bacon.

Index

About the Author

Constance Kamii is a professor of early childhood education in the School of Education at the University of Alabama at Birmingham. Following receipt of her Ph.D. from the University of Michigan, she was a postdoctoral research fellow under Jean Piaget at the University of Geneva and the International Center of Genetic Epistemology. She continued to study under Piaget with a joint appointment in the Faculty of Psychology and Sciences of Education at the University of Geneva, and the College of Education, University of Illinois at Chicago. Her interest since the 1960s has been in ways of improving classroom instruction based on a scientific theory explaining how children acquire knowledge and moral values. As she has studied Piaget's theory, therefore, she has worked closely with teachers in classrooms, first at the preschool level and subsequently in the primary grades.